This edition of my memoir contains not just my voice but the voices of other Elders and young people, sharing what the Stolen Generations and my song, 'Took The Children Away', means to them.

It's important that the voices of our young people are heard. Being a part of the Stolen Generations affected not just me, but my own children and grandchildren. The impact is intergenerational. Young people need to find a way to process the trauma as we have.

As a nation we need to talk about the Stolen Generations. We can't just pick out all the good things that have happened in our country's history. It's important that we tell the whole history and be truthful about it because it's the only way we can move forward as a country, as a nation.

When I started singing, 'Took The Children Away', and talking about it, there were adults that came up to me and said, 'We never knew this. We weren't taught this in school.'

It's time now that we *do* remember this and that it *is* taught in schools. The story's there, and we need to talk about it.

You young people can write a new story for this country, a good story, a positive story. And that's what I'm looking forward to, I tell ya.

ARCHIE

ACKNOWLEDGEMENTS

I would sincerely like to acknowledge the contributions from the Elders and young people in this book that were made possible by a unique and powerful partnership between Culture is Life, the Barpirdhila Foundation and the Archie Roach Foundation.

My deepest thanks to Aunty Lorraine Peeters, Aunty Iris Bysouth, Aunty Eva Jo Edwards, Uncle Sydney Jackson and Uncle Jack Charles and to the young people who have shared their reflections: Maya Hodge, Lauren Sheree, Deklan John Garcia, Seth Westhead and Neil Morris.

Thank you also to Belinda Duarte, Culture is Life's CEO, Thara Brown and Shelley Ware, project leads and curriculum writers dedicated to honouring all our stories and strengthening our connection with educators.

Strong women have always played an important and significant role in my life. Mum Dulcie taught me how to be a better person. My big sister Myrtle was the one who taught me who I am and who my family was. Ruby had that nurturing spirit and always looked out for me. My cousin Kath connected me to my father's people and country. And I was blessed to have had two dedicated music managers, Julie Hickson and Jill Shelton over my thirty-year career.

To the singer-songwriters and musicians I have worked with over the years, thank you for bringing my songs to the stage and beyond. To the people who have worked tirelessly and helped me to bring my story to life – thank you.

And to all my family who have looked after me since I've been back on country – you've been a big part of my healing.

FOR YOUNG ADULTS

TELL ME WHY

ARCHIE ROACH

SIMON & SCHUSTER

London · New York · Sydney · Toronto · New Delhi

Aboriginal and Torres Strait Islander readers are warned that this book contains images of and references to people who are deceased or who may now be deceased.

TELL ME WHY FOR YOUNG ADULTS
First published in Australia in 2021 by Simon & Schuster Australia

Simon & Schuster (Australia) Pty Limited
Suite 19A, Level 1, Building C, 450 Miller Street, Cammeray, NSW 2062

This edition has been edited and adapted for young adults from the original text, *Tell Me Why: The Story of My Life and My Music*, first published in 2019

10 9 8 7 6 5 4

Sydney New York London Toronto New Delhi
Visit our website at www.simonandschuster.com.au

NATIONAL LIBRARY OF AUSTRALIA

A catalogue record for this book is available from the National Library of Australia

ISBN: 9781760858865

Cover and text design: Joanna Hunt
Front cover artwork: Pierre Baroni, from the original *Charcoal Lane* album cover, courtesy Warner Music Australia
Back cover photographs: courtesy Archie Roach
Text artwork from the 2012 *Into the Bloodstream* album cover, featuring a painting of Framlingham Aboriginal Mission by Rob Lowe Senior
Archival photos courtesy of the Roach and Hunter families
Typesetting: Joanna Hunt
Publishing project management: Erica Wagner
Project management support: Jill Shelton
Printed and bound in Australia by Griffin Press

MIX
Paper | Supporting responsible forestry
FSC www.fsc.org FSC® C018684

The paper this book is printed on is certified against the Forest Stewardship Council® Standards. Griffin Press holds chain of custody certification SCS-COC-001185. FSC® promotes environmentally responsible, socially beneficial and economically viable management of the world's forests.

I dedicate this book to my mother Nellie Austin and my father Archie Roach, whom I never knew. To my sisters Alma, Myrtle, Gladys and Diana and my brothers Johnny and Lawrence.

And to Ruby and all those stolen and scattered who found their way home, and to those who never did.

To Mum Dulcie and Dad Alex, the Coxes, who showed me love.

Photo by Pierre Baroni.

CONTENTS

Me as the Form 2D class captain, taken outside our home in Mt Evelyn on my first day of school. This photo came from my ward file, courtesy of the Department of Human Services.

PROLOGUE

Lilydale, Melbourne 1970

Sometimes you can go years without really changing as a person. Maybe you get a little rounder, a little balder, but inside you're the same man. Same values, same hopes, pretty much the same bloke.

Sometimes, though, it can all change in a day. In the morning you have one life ahead of you and in the afternoon another.

That happened to me once, when I was a boy.

I was in Mrs Peters' English class, one of my favourites, minding my own business, which was something I used to be very good at. Then that moment came, through the rickety old speaker in the classroom.

'*PSSSSSHT*...Could Archibald William Roach come to the office, please? Archibald William Roach. Thank you.'

The message didn't mean much of anything to Mrs Peters or the other children – there was no Archibald William Roach at the school – but it had me squirming around in my seat like it was a stove. Archie Cox had been my name for as long as I could remember, or so I thought.

I tried to go back to my work after the message but couldn't. My eyes glazed over and all I could hear was that name – Archibald William Roach. Afterwards, something deep in me started to take over.

This something had tried to take over before…when I was alone in the bush, or when I was listening to certain sad and lovely music. It whispered in my ear, trying to tell me about another world and another life. I was usually good at ignoring those whispers, but on this day I couldn't.

I wanted to stay in my seat and finish my day, live Archie Cox's life.

'I think that message is for me,' I said, standing.

Mrs Peters was a lovely old lady. She loved my writing – especially my poetry – and would encourage me to share my work in front of the class, but I would stumble through it, embarrassed. She saw something in me, though, in my love of words. She still had her Canadian accent but had been living in Australia long enough to know something wasn't quite right.

'You'd better go then,' she said.

When I got to the office, the secretary asked if I was Archibald William Roach. I don't know why I knew that name was mine, but by then I knew it was. The secretary passed me a letter that seemed to vibrate in my hands.

Across from the counter was a wooden bench for students awaiting punishment, and there I sat, staring at the envelope. The front read:

Archibald William Roach
c/o Lilydale High School
25 Melba Avenue
Lilydale, Victoria

The boy I had started the day as would have handed the letter back and explained that he'd made a mistake. He would have said this letter wasn't for him and he would have gone back to his class, back to his schoolwork, back to his house where his guitar and supper and parents were waiting for him.

I took the letter out of the envelope and unfolded it.

Dear Brother,

Your dear old mum passed away a week ago. Her name was Nellie Austin and she had been living in Silvan. Your other brothers and sisters are Johnny, Alma, Lawrence, Gladys and Diana. Your dad already passed away, and his name was Archie too.

I thought it was time to get in touch with you.

Love,

Myrtle

The world started to spin with names and faces and thoughts and songs and feelings that were brand new and also old and familiar. I saw a dormitory packed with beds and black children. I saw two girls. Big girls, bigger than me, anyway. I saw their names, Gladys and Diana. These were my sisters. It was all so suddenly vivid.

I flipped the envelope over and saw a return address:

Myrtle Evans
1 Toxteth Road, Glebe
Sydney, NSW

I folded up the letter, tucked it into my school bag and dragged my feet to a classroom that was no longer mine. In Archie Cox's favourite class, I stared past his essay and thought of my dead mother. I thought about my father, too, also dead. I thought of the brothers and sisters I knew nothing of, and about my name.

I thought about Toxteth Road, Glebe, Sydney.

'Is everything all right, Archie?' Mrs Peters asked quietly.

It took me a little while to reply.

'I'm not sure.'

I reckon that was the last thing Archie Cox ever said.

My father, Archie Roach, outside our home on Framlingham Aboriginal Mission, south-west Victoria, with my big sister Myrtle peeking around him at the photographer, and an unknown man.

My mother and father, Nellie Austin and Archie Roach, with their first baby, Johnny Roach, later in life affectionately nicknamed Horse, in 1940. Nellie and Archie had been married in Lawrence, NSW, at the home of my grandmother Gladys Roach the previous December. This is the only photo we have of our mum and dad.

CHAPTER 1

TOOK THE CHILDREN AWAY

This story's right, this story's true
I would not tell lies to you
Like the promises they did not keep
And how they fenced us in like sheep
Said to us come take our hand
And set us up on mission land

Taught us to read, to write and pray
And they took the children away
Children away
Children away
Snatched from their mother's breast
Said this is for the best
Took them away

The welfare and the policeman
Said you've got to understand
We'll give to them what you can't give
Teach them how to really live
Teach them how to live they said
Humiliated them instead

They taught them that, and taught them this
And others taught them prejudice

They took the children away
The children away
Breaking their mother's heart
Tearing them all apart
Took them away

One dark day on Framlingham
They came and they did not give a damn
And my mother cried 'Go get their dad!'
He came running, fighting mad
Mother's tears were falling down
My dad shaped up and stood his ground
He said 'You touch my kids well you got to fight me'
Then they took us from our family.
Took us away
They took us away
Snatched from our mother's breast
Said this was for the best
Took us away.

Told us what to do and say
They taught us all the white man's ways
Then they split us up again
And gave us gifts to ease the pain
Sent us off to the foster homes
As we grew up we felt alone
We were acting white
Yet feeling black
One sweet day all the children came back

The children came back
The children came back

Back where their hearts grow strong
Back where they all belong
The children came back
Said the children came back
Oh the children came back
Back where they understand
Back to their mother's land
The children came back

Back to their mother
Back to their father
Back to their sister
Back to their brother
Back to their people
Back to their land
All the children came back
The children came back
All the children came back

Yes I came back

Melbourne, 1961–1970

A face came close; just as small as mine, just as black. This wasn't my first memory, but it was the first one that was vivid and happy.

He was looking me up and down.

I was in a place that seemed like a palace, all floors and walls of shiny white stone, and a big grand staircase that led up to walls groaning with framed pictures of men in suits and gowns. Now I know it was a courthouse, but then I saw it as a good place to run around. I did just that, weaving through a thicket of coppers and lawyers, until I found a small black face, like mine.

I wasn't sure I'd seen anyone who looked like me before. He was the same size and seemed the same age. I ran my eyes up and down him to make sure he was real. I think he was doing much the same. A couple of six-year-old black boys, wary and happy in equal measure.

'I'm sliding,' he said to me.

'That's real good,' I said.

'You tried sliding up here?' he said, taking me over to a big, fancy banister. 'It's good sliding here.'

This little fella climbed up the stairway and rocketed down, landing on the floor with a slight buckle at the knees. We both ran up the stairs and slid down, one after the other. Up and down we went until after one go

I landed at the feet of a proper woman, all done up with silver hair, brown stockings and a pressed frock, holding a clutch of papers.

'Archie, I see you've already met Noel.'

I didn't say anything.

'That's good, because you're coming with us. Come on,' she said, motioning to the sliding boy. They started towards the exit together.

'Come on, Archie,' the woman said, looking back. Noel motioned too. I followed – I was used to going along with different people.

The woman's name was Dulcie Cox. Soon she would be known to me as Mum.

Mum Dulcie, Noel and I caught a taxi through the working-class fringe of north-west Melbourne until we pulled up at a small house with a gate framed with well-kept vines. Waiting for me was a stocky, balding man with a big smile and an accent as thick as week-old custard.

'Aye, 'e's a proper wee lad!' he said.

To my ears this sounded like gibberish, but it seemed to be cheerful gibberish.

''E's a bonny wee lad!' the man said as he came at me for an embrace.

Mum Dulcie must have seen fear in me, or at least confusion, so she translated.

'He says you're a good young fellow, Archie.'

This man was Dulcie's husband, Alex, soon to be known to me as Dad. A storeman for an aviation company on the last stretch of his working life, Dad Alex was a proud Scot from Glasgow and someone I will always think fondly of till the day I die.

Alex and Dulcie Cox were in their late fifties when they took me in but were energetic for their age. Their motivation in taking me in seemed to be a surplus of love, even after having raised their sons, John and David, now grown and working down the road as used-car salesmen, and their daughters Jeanie, who had married and left home, and Mary, a teenager, who lived with us.

Mum and Dad Cox had chosen me the way they had chosen Noel and his older blood brother, Les – after seeing us in a government advertisement in a Melbourne newspaper. The ad asked for good Christians to open their hearts and homes to desolate Aboriginal children, whose faces peeked out of the page wearing their Sunday best and the broadest smiles they could muster.

I knew nothing of this at the time, nor that they chose me so I could be a companion to Noel, who was about to lose Les to a trade and early adulthood.

I started life at the Cox house quiet and wary, but soon I was just quiet. I quickly came to understand Dad Alex's brogue, and in his words I found humour and heart. He had no stomach for sharp words against children, so discipline was left to Mum Dulcie, but she wasn't much of an authoritarian either. There was an organ in the front room, which Mary played beautifully, extracting music of praise from the instrument with an impressive juggling act of key tinkling, valve pulling and pedal pressing. Mary also played the organ at the church we attended every Sunday. After I learnt the words to the songs, I'd fidget in my seat waiting to sing along to 'Onward Christian Soldiers' or 'The Old Rugged Cross'.

I started going to Strathmore North Primary, a school attended mostly by 'New Australians', the sons and daughters of Italian and Greek migrants, who would speak their native language at home to grandmothers who would never learn English.

I liked school, but I enjoyed weekends and holidays even more. Sometimes Jeanie would invite Noel and me to stay with her and her husband in Keilor. There we would ride horses, something Noel especially loved. Other times we'd all pile into David's or John's car and drive over to Mount Evelyn, which back then consisted of bush interrupted by a few shacks with no power. Dad

Alex owned one of those shacks, nestled among gum trees. There was a fish-filled creek nearby that I'd throw a line into.

I loved that Mount Evelyn place, but sometimes in the quiet night I would have waking dreams of another rural home where I now know I was previously fostered. In my dreams I would be back there, telling a large woman that I loved potatoes so much I could eat them raw, then getting nothing else but that to eat. I would be in a grain shed under a sack that worked as a blanket. I would be cold and hungry, staring at a locked barn door. I would hear a key turn in a lock. I would feel fear and then pain.

There were more reasons than love to take in a kid you'd seen in the newspaper.

After dinner, Mum and Dad Cox would reveal more of themselves than during the day. Mum Dulcie would take off her cat-eye glasses and let down her hair which she usually kept bound up on top of her head. The cascade of beautiful silver rushing down her back used to take my breath away. After the pop of a beer bottle-top Dad Alex would perch himself on a chair next to the organ or the record player and sing, with full throat, the songs of his youth.

Alongside him, I learnt all the lyrics of maudlin Scottish ballads like 'Drifting Down the Shalimar' and raucous ditties like 'Donald, Where's Your Troosers?' I took great joy in sharing those songs with Dad Alex, because I wanted to be close to him, and I also wanted to understand the power that the songs had over him.

Dad Alex used to take me and Noel to the Highland games where we would both stare at the things those huge men in kilts could do, like throwing the caber and hammer. Dad Alex would explain to us the significance of their tartan, and speak strange, guttural words. He explained that his had been a tribal people, and as pipes and drums filled our chests I thought I didn't just *know* what he was talking about, I *felt* it.

I was a happy child.

Mum and Dad Cox never treated me or Noel or Les any differently to their biological children, and at school there were healthy differences in the classroom too. Some kids were tall, some kids were Greek, some kids had red hair, others brown. One kid walked funny, a few were really smart, one had very dark skin. None of that meant much once we started playing games at recess and lunch.

I don't remember seeing myself as any different to the other kids until the day I took a friend named Chris home to meet my parents.

All had gone well, but as we walked back to Chris's place, I could tell he wanted to talk to me about something; something he had difficulty speaking about. Finally, I stopped and confronted him.

'Chris, is there something you want to ask?'

'Archie, I was just wanting to . . . wondering why . . . why are your parents white?'

I didn't really understand the question.

'It's just . . . because you're black,' he added quietly.

Chris had me stumped. There was a spectrum of skin colours at our school, and I knew I was a bit darker, but I'd never thought much about the fact that all the parents did largely have the same colouring as their children. I had no answer for him.

I went home in a minor state of confusion, and when I walked into the house I was happy to find Dad Alex sitting in his chair.

'Dad, am I black?'

He bolted upright, his face turning red with Glaswegian fury. 'Who tol ye that, son?'

'A mate from school.'

'The wee lad that were just 'ere?'

'No . . . no, another kid.' Dad Alex could get up a full head of steam if he wanted to, and I was scared for Chris.

'Who sayed it? I wannae have a chat tae him.'

'No, no, please, Dad. He's all right. He was just asking.'

I wished I'd never said anything. Dad Alex calmed down a bit and readied for a speech I think he'd been preparing for some time.

'Archie, ye nae black, what ye are is Ab'rig'nal. You and ye paepal are the first paepal on this land.'

He put his hand on my shoulder.

'E'rybody else here are bloon awee Pommies. Ye remember tha.'

I didn't understand what that meant for a long time. The way Dad Alex spoke frightened me, though. My skin felt a bit different after that, and sometimes I would look at my hands as though they were someone else's.

I thought maybe Noel might knew what it all meant.

'Has anybody ever called you black?' I asked him. He got very quiet and still. When he didn't say anything, I asked him again.

'Somebody did, but I chased him up the road.'

'Why would you do that, Noely?'

'I didn't like the way the kid said it.'

That night in bed I tried to remember if I had met any other black people, and then the faces of two girls, a bit bigger than me, appeared. I remembered sharing food with them, and I remembered them hugging me. I remember one of them standing with her fists up, ready to strike. More memories came, painful memories; this girl was protecting me.

I was sure it was a memory and not my imagination. The girls were real. They were special to me, I knew that. They made me feel good.

I was very confused.

I went into the lounge room where Mum and Dad Cox were listening to the radio. I asked if they knew anything about these girls, but they said they didn't. I could tell they were uncomfortable. I knew I'd had a life before Mum and Dad Cox, and I wanted to ask if these girls were my sisters but I felt ungrateful and ashamed – after all, Mum and Dad Cox had already given me two sisters, and good sisters at that. Jeanie lavished us with care whenever we visited her and Mary brought music into the house.

One time, Mary, Dad Alex and I went to the Essendon Town Hall, where Mary wanted to hear a man from Detroit talk about a new type of organ created by Laurens Hammond, an American engineer. His instrument was designed as an alternative to bulky church organs but had also become a favourite of keyboard players signed to Detroit's rock and rhythm-and- blues labels. My soul soared when I heard the American man playing, and I couldn't believe my luck when Dad Alex announced that he'd filed an order for one of these magic-sounding organs.

Having the sound of that organ fill our front room was like being able to see extra colours. It seemed Dad Alex saw those colours too. As he sang, I could hear in his voice a yearning for his childhood home. I could feel his longing in my bones too, and for years I thought I missed Scotland, a country I'd never been to. It didn't occur to me that the black faces of my memory and the pit of melancholy in my belly were related.

I was desperate to learn how to play music myself, and one day Dad Alex brought home a very small organ, with numbers on the keys. Mary tirelessly taught me and even when I could barely keep time or get my fingers on the right keys, Dad Alex was always there to offer encouragement.

For most of my primary-school years, I lived the life that was presented to me. I was the son of Alex and Dulcie Cox, I was a student at Strathmore North, I was a fan of Fats Domino and Elvis Presley, I prayed to the versions of God and Jesus Christ that our Protestant minister spoke about each Sunday. I often felt an ache in my heart that I didn't understand, and I was confused by the colour of my skin, but by and large I was happy. We all were.

Then, after a short illness, twenty-one-year-old Jeanie

Cox died. Our house suddenly became quiet. Noel, too, seemed to be affected deeply, and not only with grief.

By the time Jeanie passed, Noel knew of his other name and of siblings he'd previously known nothing about. He told me once he had asked Les about this other family, but Les had told him that the Coxes were all the family he would ever need.

Les never reverted to the surname of his birth parents, nor did he ever move far from the neighbourhood that he had been dropped into. The life he carved for himself in Melbourne was enough for Les.

Noel didn't like it, though. He was struggling with his own identity and started to hang out with kids who were drinking and smoking.

I remember when he came home late one night, three sheets to the wind. As I let him in, I pleaded with Noel to be quiet so our parents could sleep. That enraged him. He swayed around with balled fists and I thought he was going to punch me. I eventually got him to take some food and water before getting him into bed, but as he slept, I lay awake because I suspected he was going to stay angry with me.

I was right. We had been best friends, brothers, but now for some reason he saw me as an adversary. He often wanted to fight me, often after drinking.

He was still a child, but he had a man's rage.

When I started at Strathmore High School, I saw more rage.

With Noel at a technical college I was the only black boy in a school full of teenagers, and that's where the taunts of 'Abos' and 'golliwogs' and 'black bastards' started. Many of the kids who throughout primary school had known me only as Archie Cox now knew me as 'that black bastard'. Was it the new environment? Hormones? Was it what they were hearing from their parents? Had the times changed? I didn't understand why. I still don't.

In the beginning I'd never stand up for myself and would laugh everything off, sometimes even denigrating myself for the sake of an easy life. Maybe that made things worse. Maybe it wouldn't have made any difference.

When Dad Alex retired, he didn't take to his new life well and had what they called in the sixties a 'nervous breakdown'. As he suffered mentally, Mum Dulcie began to suffer physically with diabetes. Money got tight, our home was sold and we shifted into the bush shack in Mount Evelyn that used to be our holiday place. There, Mum and Dad Cox's health declined further. We were there for a year before moving to nearby Mooroolbark.

Although there were limits to the social standing of a 'black bastard' in high school, I had great friends at Lilydale High, my new school, people I really cared about. There was a Dutch kid named Hank, an independent soul who refused to compete in anything, a girl with cerebral palsy who had callipers on her legs, and another slight, very smart boy we called the Brain.

It was only with these friends that I would stand up for myself. I couldn't bear seeing these good kids disappear into themselves after a barrage of insults and cackles. I didn't care what people had to say to me, but if you picked on my friends I would fight. I was small, but wiry and athletic, and I had will. I guess I was a bit like Dad Alex in that way.

I remember one instance when an older kid cornered Hank, telling him that he was going to beat him black and blue. Then he looked me up and down and said, 'You, maybe just blue.'

You can laugh. I did. You have to laugh.

I fought that kid, but don't remember the outcome. I ended up fighting a bit at school, though I would always mind my own business any time I could. I wasn't there to fight; I was there to do sport and English and art.

In art I saw a vocation. I wanted to be the man who designed and painted the advertisements that you would see on the side of buildings. That job – part artist, part designer and part signwriter – doesn't really exist anymore, but in it I saw a way to a happy, normal life.

Mum and Dad Cox used to get on me about university, but each year they were less insistent about it. That wasn't just true about university, it was true about pretty much everything. It seemed in high school that for every year I aged, they aged five.

I started going to a huge Pentecostal ministry with some friends from school. An early precursor to the modern mega-churches like Hillsong, the ministry had little organised structure and instead was dedicated to letting the spirit of God flow through the parishioners. We would sing modern, soulful music and speak in tongues, a practice that was often maligned by other churchgoers and distrusted by Mum and Dad Cox, but I definitely got something out of it.

When I let go and started babbling what I thought was the word of God, my mind flowed without conscious effort, and long-latent memories would emerge, all the way back to a time before my foster family. Before any foster family. I'd go back to a place where there was bush, and black brothers and sisters, and black uncles and aunties, and a black mother and father. When I spoke in tongues, I felt a spirit in me.

It was also in that church that I first heard the music of Hank Williams.

One Sunday a woman got up with a guitar and played a song that took my breath away. There was little complexity to the chord progression but the tune, which was crushingly sad but also uplifting and beautiful, spoke completely to me about a feeling that I thought was mine and mine alone.

I'm a shy man and was an even shyer boy, but I had to approach this woman and ask about the song. She told me that the lyrics were a Bible verse and that the tune was a Hank Williams song called 'Your Cheatin' Heart'.

When I got home, I asked Dad Alex about Hank Williams and was overjoyed to find that not only did he know Williams but he had some of his records.

Eventually Dad Alex bought me my first guitar, and I'd spend hours and hours sitting in front of the record player trying to play along. Even though Mary liked different music, she would always help me find the chords that I needed. I'd play sad country songs and the blues for Dad Alex.

He was a lovely old bloke, Dad Alex. Good heart, good soul. Like many traditional Christians, he was wary of the Pentecostals at that time, but I think he figured if they were playing Hank Williams they couldn't be all bad.

Mum Dulcie was a tougher nut to crack. She didn't talk to me much about my Pentecostal church, but I could tell she didn't like me going. I was getting a lot from that church and didn't want to stop attending, but I loved her and tried to reach her however I could.

One way to do that was to help in the garden, weeding and cutting grass with a scythe. She decided that we needed to get an enormous stump out of the garden, and she was going to splurge on getting some men around to dig it out until I convinced her that I could do it.

The days became weeks as I attacked the stump with a crowbar and shovel. It was hot, strenuous work, but work I enjoyed. As I'd hack and dig, I'd see Mum Dulcie staring out the window at me with a look I could never quite figure out. One afternoon she called me in – I was all sweaty and stinky – and had me sit at a table. On the table was a bone-china tea set with a pot filled with hot brewed tea, along with a plate layered with scones and sandwiches.

A little ritual started between us; one we'd keep up for years. The talk at tea was usually very small, except for one instance that haunts me still.

Mum Dulcie had tried to talk to me about school and the weather, when her shoulders started shaking and her face bunched up, tears running down her cheeks. The old woman was crying about Noel; I knew that straight away.

Her concern about me and the church was small potatoes compared to her worries about Noel. He had distanced himself from life with the Cox family altogether. He still lived with us, but he had become withdrawn. Mum Dulcie and Noel had loved each other when we were younger, and I reckon they still did, but they just couldn't understand each other anymore. She was losing another child.

I sat there and felt deeply for her but couldn't say anything, and couldn't move because I was scared she'd be able to tell that what was haunting Noel had started haunting me.

When Mum Dulcie composed herself, she told me how worried she was about Noel. I told her I was worried about Noel, too. I put my arms around her and consoled her as best I could, without showing the restless heart that beat in my chest.

Mum Dulcie feared Noel was now a stranger headed for alcoholism and the streets. She never could have guessed that one day a letter would send me down that path, too.

This is me at five years old, in 1961.

Mum Dulcie and Dad Alex celebrating an occasion over cake. They were two people who showed me love and kindness when I needed it most. I'll never forget the wonderful memories I shared with them. Photo courtesy the Cox family.

CHAPTER 2

ONE FOR EACH PERSON AND ONE FOR THE POT

She called me in from my labour
As she smiled so soft and sweetly
I sat down at the table
Sandwiches and cake to greet me
Fetch a pack of tea
Is what she said to me
Take the kettle from the stove
When it is hot
Then one for each person and one for the pot

She set down our best china
Then a cheeky grin she gave me
There was nothing I found finer
Than sippin' tea with this sweet lady
Then she held my hand
And said ain't this grand
Just remember making tea
The rule is what?
One for each person and one for the pot
One for each person and one for the pot

The day I got Myrtle's letter, I sat staring at my schoolwork. I put pencil on paper but couldn't get any words out. Eventually Hank came over and asked if I was okay. I explained to him that a letter had come, from someone claiming to be my sister and telling me that my mother had just died.

'Are you sure it's for you?' he asked.

I told him I was. I didn't know why, but I was sure.

He didn't know what to say.

Mrs Peters must have seen a story on my face, because she asked if I wanted to go home.

Silvan. The letter said that was where my 'dear old mum' had been living. We'd driven though Silvan many times. I pushed my memory to produce a black woman. Just a glimpse would be a feast for me, but nothing came.

I had to know more. I walked home quickly from the train station, my curiosity more powerful than my reticence. Mum and Dad Cox asked me why I was back so early and I handed them the letter.

'Do you know anything about this?' I asked.

As they read, I could tell that they were deeply conflicted.

'We knae that was ye name – Roach,' Dad Alex said.

'I thought it was. I had it in my head. It sounded familiar.'

'Dad wanted you to use his name, even though we're just your foster parents,' Mum Dulcie said.

I told them that was okay. I had a mixed-up tangle of feelings, but none were anger directed against them. What had changed, though, was my sense of obligation. Suddenly I had no problems pressing them with questions. I asked about Myrtle, the sender of the letter, and they said they didn't know who she was.

'Do you know anything about any of these people? My mum, my dad? My brothers and sisters?'

They were really struggling with the answers now. Dad Alex said that the government had told him that my whole family had died in a house fire in Dandenong.

I was confused, frustrated. That couldn't be true! What was going on? Who was I? A sister, Myrtle, had written to me, telling me about my father, my mother, my brothers and sisters.

I asked how I could get more information and they said they didn't know how to help. I didn't know if they were lying, but I felt they knew more, or that they could do more. Even though I still loved them and appreciated everything they had done for me, after the letter came, I saw them differently.

At that point I started to understand Noel a little better, too.

I found Noel and showed him the letter. I told him it was from a woman claiming to be my sister, and before he took it, he said, 'Yeah, it probably is.'

As he read it, he showed little emotion.

'Pretty much the same as me,' he said, handing the letter back. He wasn't surprised I had another family just out of reach. He didn't show much enthusiasm or empathy. I'm guessing the window to connect with Noel about our shared journey of identity had closed some time back.

At school I tried to get my life back on track, but it was impossible. Questions of science and maths became insignificantly small when set against the question of what my dad had been like, and my mum, and how they'd lived and died.

I had brothers and sisters, blood of my blood. What were they like? Were they tall, were they short? Were those two girls from my distant memory the sisters mentioned in the letter? I wasn't sure.

My grades started to slip, as did my tolerance. Before I got the letter, you'd have to physically attack me or my mates for me to put my fists up, but afterwards, if you called me a black bastard, I was going after you. I became a bit isolated at school. Hank, the Brain, my friends – they stayed beside me, but others started to avoid me.

At home I tried not to show that I was changing, but old Mum Dulcie and Dad Alex could tell. It seemed the government knew I was changing, too, because one day, a few weeks after the letter, they sent a funny little bloke with a moustache, not that much older than me, to our house.

The bloke asked Mum and Dad Cox if it was okay for he and I to go for a walk. They said it was up to me. I was happy to go with him because I thought he might have some answers to my questions. Turns out he did, but none that were useful.

I asked if the information in the letter I got was right; he didn't deny it. I asked if he knew where my brothers and sisters were, and he said he didn't know. I asked if I would ever get to see them, and he said maybe I would one day.

I reckoned that someone in the government knew about my family and he was the only person I could ask.

'Why was I taken away?'

'It wasn't just you, Archie. Most of your family were moved to other places.'

'Why, though? Why would you do that?'

'We decided to move you and your brothers and sisters to new homes where we thought you'd be better off. We didn't think things were very good at home.'

I had no idea what that might've meant.

'Why didn't anyone ever speak to me about it before?' I asked. 'I have brothers and sisters, but no one ever told me.'

I said it all quietly. I wasn't angry; I was confused. I really wanted to know why the government had done this to me.

'We thought it would be best if you were with the Cox family. You like them, don't you, Archie?'

Of course, I liked them. I loved them. I didn't tell this fella that, though. I told him I wanted to see my real family, and he said that maybe one day I could.

My perspective changed with that letter, and it changed again after his visit.

I stopped asking questions of Mum and Dad Cox. I knew it was just as confusing for them as it was for me. While I still trusted that they did what they did because they thought it was the best thing for me, I was hurt.

I thought a lot about the government. The Government of the Commonwealth of Australia. I'd never really thought about my relationship with the government before, but knowing that they'd taken me away from my mother, father, brothers and sisters a bit more than a decade ago, and now got to decide whether or not I could see my family, I thought about them quite a lot.

I thought about Toxteth Road, Glebe, Sydney. For a kid like me in Melbourne in 1970, that address might as well have been on the moon. Most people I knew had never even been to Sydney.

I saw the teachers at school very differently after the man from the government came. I had been a respectful kid – well mannered, attentive, with a love of learning and words. Now I no longer wanted to learn the things they were teaching; I had problems seeing the need for deference. This came to a head one afternoon while I was smoking at the train station and a male teacher approached me, telling me to put out my cigarette. I told him the school day was over and the school was streets away, but he said he didn't care – he was still in charge of me. I didn't take well to his choice of words.

I told the teacher to fuck off.

I feel bad now thinking about it. This man, whose name I can't remember, wasn't out of line. In fact, he was trying to do me a favour and help me kick smoking before it became an addiction. I didn't listen. I wish now that I had.

I went home and thought about what the next morning might look like. I'd have detention for sure, and would certainly be forced to apologise, something I had no interest in doing. It occurred to me, that night, that maybe I was done with school. I was only fifteen, but it wasn't unusual to leave school at that age back then.

Dad Alex didn't say anything but Mum Dulcie tried to change my mind. The way she did it hit me right in my heart, telling me that the favourite part of her day was reading the stories and poems I wrote for English class. I was steadfast, though. School was no longer a place I could bear. I told her that I'd still write poems for her.

I never did, though.

I got a job at a farm near us where I picked flowers and put floral arrangements together for sale all around Melbourne. It wasn't bad work, and I enjoyed the company of the people I was with, most of whom were older and some itinerant. Pay started to come in, and I gave the bulk to Mum and Dad Cox; the rest I squirrelled away, with smokes my main outgoings.

Life settled down with a new routine established until one day Noel came to me with something to say.

'I've got to go, Archie,' he said, shaking my hand.

He had a bag packed.

'Where are you going to go?' I asked.

'I don't know yet. I just have to leave. I might try to get some work… I might try to find my family.'

I told him to take care and he said the same. I wished there had been more warmth there in that moment, but for Noel, I think I represented a part of a life he wanted to leave behind.

Noel walked out of my room and out of our house, and I never saw him again.

While I worked at the farm, I often thought of what Noely might be up to. I saw him in the back of a truck, and I saw him picking fruit, and I saw him meeting brothers and sisters and sharing stories. I was still only fifteen, but the road started to call me, too.

It called me at work, and it called me at church. After a service, with my thoughts and feelings loose, I told the brother of our pastor, a friend of mine named Hamish, that I was thinking about leaving the Cox family home and setting out on my own.

He thought it was a good idea, and he was happy to help me out any way that he could. I asked if I could stay with him for a bit and plan my second step. He said that wasn't a worry.

Hamish probably thought that Mum, Dad Cox and me were clashing a lot because of the church, and that there was no reconciling those differences – the

Pentecostal church was often a wedge between idealistic and excitable teens and their more conservative parents.

I told Mum and Dad Cox one night over dinner. I remember the silence before I spoke, and how unsure I was of my tongue as it started to move. When the words came out, they didn't even sound like they were mine.

'I reckon I have to go away for a little while, like Noely,' I said. 'I have to figure out what's going on.'

I know they were heartbroken. Mum Dulcie was disappointed at first, and then she was angry.

'This is stupid, Archie. Stupid. You have a good life here, a good job,' she said.

I told her I was sorry, but it was something I had to do.

Dad Alex didn't say anything. He just stared at his dinner, shaking his head slowly. I apologised to him too, but it was Mum Dulcie who replied.

'Haven't we been good to you?' she asked, tears in her eyes.

I told them they had been, and then I got up and started packing. They were wonderful, caring people, and I think of them often and fondly, but I knew they'd never completely understand what I was going through. To tell them was to break their hearts and mine, but it was something I had to do. I dreaded having to do it twice, so I resolved to leave immediately and never come back. I called Hamish and asked if he could pick me up the next night after work and take me to his house in Canterbury.

Mum and Dad Cox cherished me. They had given me all the opportunities they could, but there was always a restlessness in me, like a fault line waiting to rupture.

They never understood that, but how could they?

My spirit was stirring. I needed to find out who I was, who my family was.

As I was leaving the house, bag in hand and guitar over my shoulder, Mum and Dad Cox stopped me at the door. Dad Alex grabbed me and said, 'Bifay ye leave me and Ma, I jes wanted tae say... Well, we hope ye fin what ye lookin for, Archie.'

I never saw them again. It hurts me now to even write the words.

Hamish and his family were very good to me, letting me stay for a few weeks while I figured out what to do next. I found a new job close to his place, working nine to five on the production line of a factory, turning out paper products. On the weekends I'd go to services at the Emmanuel Temple, one of the biggest Pentecostal churches in the state at the time, nearby Hamish's house.

There I'd sing and pray and look for mental clarity and guidance, and one day it came, of a sort. Out there, in the congregation, I saw two Aboriginal faces – a couple in their thirties.

After the service I sought them out. The only Aboriginal lives I really knew about were mine and my foster brothers Noel and Les's, and I was hungry to know anything they could tell me about my mum and dad, brothers and sisters.

Al and Shirley were gracious and patient as they explained that they were just in town for a little while. They lived in Shepparton, almost two hundred kilometres north of Melbourne, with their three little ones in a house next to a gully, across the field from another Pentecostal church. They said I should come and visit them sometime, and I thought that was a good idea.

After Al and Shirley left Melbourne, I thought about them often during the long, dull hours on the production line. I also thought of them in the euphoric, spirit-raising hours I spent in church. I wondered how they lived their lives and whether they could give me an idea of how I might live mine.

Sydney still seemed like another world, but the way Al and Shirley described it, I could get to Shepparton in a day, perhaps even in a morning. Shepparton was on the way to Sydney – I would be one step closer to Toxteth Road, Glebe.

Curiosity became resolve, and one afternoon I told my boss I was finished. Then I told Hamish I was moving on, to spend some time with Al and Shirley. He understood and wished me well.

I packed a bag with my clothes, slung my guitar over my back and headed to the Hume Highway, where I stuck out my thumb while I walked north. I'd never hitchhiked before, but I'd seen a lot of people do it. My first ride came along after a short while, and I can't describe the exhilaration I felt, heading closer to Sydney.

By the time I was dropped off in the middle of Shepparton the sun was on the wane, so I hunted down a toilet block, laid my clothes out under me like a bed, spread my jacket over me like a blanket and slept the sleep of the dead.

I woke just after dawn, with a man standing over me.

'You'd better get out of here, fella. I'll call the police.'

I'm guessing he was a cleaner. I mumbled an apology, packed my things and wandered out into an unfamiliar town. The working day was yet to start so there were few people around, but as luck would have it, I saw a group of Aboriginal men walking down the street. I approached them and asked if they knew Al, and sure enough they did. They pointed me down a road and there I found the gully, and the church, and the house.

Al opened the door with a surprised but welcoming grin.

'Archie, what are you doing here?'

'I just wanted to visit. Is that okay?'

'Of course, of course. Come on in.'

Al and Shirley told me I could stay as long as I liked. Later that night I told Al why I wanted to go to Sydney and about the letter and my foster family and my parents, the little I knew about them, and about the fella from the government who came to the Coxes' house.

'I've heard about this,' he said. 'I've heard about children being taken away from their parents by the government.'

I asked if anything like that had happened in his family. He said it hadn't, but he thought that was because it usually happened to the blackfellas on the missions. I had no idea what the missions were, and Al only knew a bit more than me. He said the missions had something to do with the church, and that it was a place where Aboriginal people were forced to live out in the countryside.

I wondered if I'd lived on one of these missions out in the countryside.

I stayed with Al and his family for a while. I liked them a lot, and I liked learning what he knew about the history of our people. I got a job fruit picking and packing at the nearby SPC factory so I could contribute to the rent and the cost of food, and I had no problems sticking around Shepparton when Al asked me to look after the place while he and his family went to visit his relatives.

I lived in Al and Shirley's house alone for a week or two. Then, one day, a family member, Jim, turned up. I liked him instantly. He had a maverick spirit and wasn't like anyone I'd met before. He was also someone I was slightly apprehensive of.

Jim had some mates with him, and after a few days we were all but out of food and cigarettes. One night, Jim asked me to help him and his friends get more, and while I walked with him through the dark, slowly but surely, I became aware that we were on our way to do a burglary.

The target was a closed petrol station nearby, which we got into by way of a small window round the back that had been left ajar. As we snuck around the shop, grabbing armfuls of bread, cold meats and cigarettes, I could feel the wrongness of what we were doing, but also a rebelliousness that felt good. Back at Al's place, we smoked and ate our fill, and I felt like a rebel. I didn't mind the feeling at all.

A week later we were hungry again and did exactly the same thing – we broke into the same shop and stole almost exactly the same stuff as last time.

While we were pilfering, I thought a lot about Mum and Dad Cox. I could see Mum Dulcie crying and Dad Alex shaking his head but saying nothing, and I felt really sad. When we got home, I felt none of the rebellious lift. I gained nothing from that burglary, except some smokes and food that I could have got anyway from the money I'd earned from work that I actually quite enjoyed.

I resolved not to steal again. It wasn't who I wanted to be. It wasn't how I was raised.

The cops came to the house a few days later. The first I knew about it was when they were shining torches in my face. I realised that I was alone in the house. I'm not sure where all the others were. They must have seen the cop cars coming.

They told me they knew what me and my mates had done, but I denied it. They searched the house and found cartons of cigarettes in a roof cavity. After that I changed my tune, saying I'd acted alone. It was a story I managed to keep up throughout.

I spent ten days in the lock-up in Shepparton because

the cops didn't exactly know what to do with me. I was a minor but had no real guardians. My parents were dead, the Coxes were in my past, and Al and Shirley were away.

I was left in the charge of a policeman named Detective Cameron, and he treated me pretty well. I got cereal in the morning, and unsold counter meals from the Goulburn Valley Hotel for my dinner. He gave me cigarettes and cups of tea when I asked for them, and we'd share them over a chat. One day Detective Cameron turned up with a magistrate who told me what he figured he would do. They were going to put me on a two-year good behaviour bond, which meant for that period I'd have to stay out of trouble and regularly check in with a court-appointed mentor. If I failed to do either, I'd be off to juvenile detention.

When I got back home Al had returned, and he was disappointed.

'Why'd you go off with Jim and do that, Archie?' he asked. 'I thought you had more sense.'

I think Al felt guilty, too, because I'd been led astray by an adult. We didn't really talk about the incident after that, but he said I could stay while I fulfilled the term of my bond.

My court-appointed mentor was Max, a well-known

and liked former boxer who ran a menswear shop in town, and a man I ended up having a great relationship with. Max got me a job helping out a roofer, introduced me to some other young fellas and took me to a boxing gym, where he hoped I'd start training.

As he showed me the basics of throwing a proper punch into a bag, we talked about Lionel Rose, one of the few Aboriginal men I'd ever seen on television. He linked Lionel, a legendary boxer, whom I hugely admired, to the pride of being able to hold your ground against another man trained in the pugilistic arts. Max told me about the greatness of other Aboriginal fighters, describing sturdy men with fast hands. I loved hearing about it, but when he said he'd be interested in training me, I told him I didn't think it was for me – I was smoking too much and wasn't fit enough. That was true, but it probably wasn't the only reason. I just didn't want to fight at that time.

With my feet stuck in the mud of a good-behaviour bond and a steady job arranged by Max, a comfortable life emerged in Shepparton. Things were great with Al and his family, my roofing job was strenuous and hot, but as a young fella it was nothing I couldn't handle, and I even started to build up a good gang of mates, who I'd hang out with each night at the bowling alley.

We'd eat hamburgers, drink milkshakes, play music

from the jukebox and try to kiss the local girls. Once I even managed it, kissing someone you could describe as my first steady girlfriend.

These were all white people, my friends and my girl, but they didn't treat me any differently from anyone else. Routine set in; weeks became months. I was happy, but somehow a little hollow. Whenever I heard people talking about Sydney, I'd think about my sister Myrtle Evans and Toxteth Road.

I'd count down the months left on my bond before I could even try to go up north... twenty-two, twenty-one, twenty, nineteen. The numbers made me anxious. Each morning I spent in Shepparton was another day my sister might move, or worse.

One day a panic built up that was so unbearable I found myself packing my bag. When I was done, I slung my guitar over my shoulder once again, walked out of my room and told Al I was leaving. He understood and after a shake of hands I was on the road, my thumb pointing north. I didn't think of my friends at the bowling alley, or the people at work, and obviously I couldn't tell Max. I'd saved almost no money, but I wasn't concerned. I'd been picking the brains of some older Aboriginal men who'd come into town for a bit of work. They'd given me tips about where and how to get a meal, and a ride, and a roof.

That's all you need, really.

When I got on the Hume Highway and saw a sign for Sydney, I had hope in my heart and fire in my veins. My head spun when I saw how many kilometres there were between me and my destination, but every step was a step closer.

I did a lot of a walking and got a lot of lifts. Sometimes I was picked up by truck drivers, who'd buy me a meal. Sometimes I was picked up by salesmen who just wanted to listen to the radio. Sometimes families asked me to play music while we drove, and I'd strum my favourite old country songs.

Sometimes I got dropped off in a town in the afternoon and I'd hang around the bakery, waiting for them to close. I'd knock on the door, ask what they were about to throw out and then have a hobo's feast of cake, pies, pasties and milk. I slept in toilet blocks when it rained and in parks when it didn't, and every night I'd go out like a light as soon as my head hit my jumper and wake just before dawn.

I walked through Albury and Wodonga and Wagga Wagga and Yass, getting a lift just outside of each town. It took me a week, maybe two, to get to Goulburn, and there I got my last lift, pushing myself into a Kingswood full of country boys.

'Where are you lads heading?' I asked.

'Sydney,' they said in unison.

That was music to my ears. I asked them what they were doing in Sydney, and they said they weren't doing anything specific – they were just going to go.

'Is it that good then, Sydney?'

'Best place in the world,' one said.

'There's heaps of stuff you can do there that you can't round here,' another said.

'Make sure you check out Kings Cross,' said another, the car filling with laughter.

I had no idea what he was talking about, but I started to get excited. I got my guitar out and played happy songs and funny songs and we all sang together.

I found kindness and charity out on the road, a place that would become a second home. I found kindness and charity in Sydney as well, but also depravity, disappointment and sin.

That was okay, I suppose, because after the depravity, disappointment and sin, I did find what I'd come to Sydney for.

I didn't find Myrtle, but I eventually found family. Or perhaps it'd be truer to say, it found me.

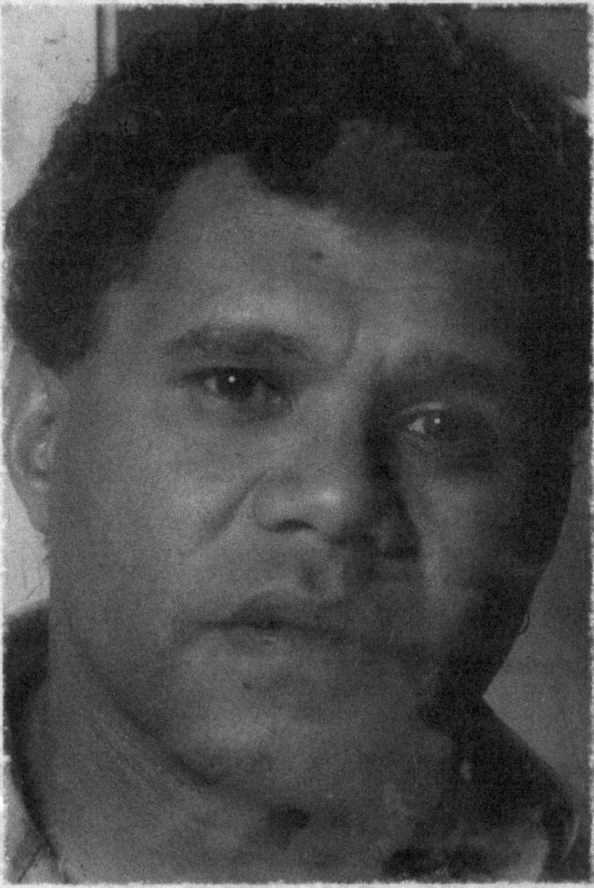

This is an old photo of me, date and photographer unknown.

CHAPTER 3

BEGGAR MAN

Biting on the street one day, I saw a policeman
He come up to me and he did say, what are you doing son?
I said I didn't think that I was doing any harm
Then he went and moved me on, said I was taking alms

Have you got alms for the beggar man?
Have you got alms for the beggar man?
Ah, they call me the beggar man
The beggar man, beggar man
Whoa the beggar man, the beggar man
I am the beggar man

So I went to another street, yes to another place
Then I started biting, I thought that I was safe
Then someone came up to me and grabbed me by the arm
Ah, it was a police man and I was taking alms

Have you got alms for the beggar man?
Have you got alms for the beggar man?
Ah they call me the beggar man,
The beggar man, beggar man
Whoa the beggar man, the beggar man
I am the beggar man

Have you got two bob, can you give me a job?
Have you got ten in silver or gold?
I don't want to steal, for my next meal
Ah, won't you keep me from the cold

Have you got alms for the beggar man?
Have you got alms for the beggar man?
Ah, they call me the beggar man
The beggar man, beggar man
Whoa the beggar man, the beggar man
I am the beggarman

I had a wife, I had a home, I had a family
Then I went and did them wrong and I am so lonely
Now I walk around all day with tired and aching feet
And I am just surviving, go biting on the street

Have you got alms for the beggar man?
Have you got alms for the beggar man?
Ah, they call me the beggar man
The beggar man, beggar man
Whoa the beggar man, the beggar man
Yeah the beggar man, the beggar man
I am a beggar man

The young lads dropped me off somewhere that looked a lot like the middle of the city. They gave me a few smokes and wished me well. I wished them luck in Kings Cross, and off they went.

I walked down the biggest street I could find, which was George Street, and through a suburb called Haymarket, all hustle and bustle. While I was looking at the shops, and up at the tops of the tall buildings, I wondered how I might get to Glebe until I was stopped by a man who had probably picked me as fresh in the big city.

'Where are you going, young fella?' he said.

He spoke with a European accent I wasn't familiar with. Not Italian or Greek, that's for sure. Maybe it had a bit of Russian in it. He looked a little over forty, was well dressed and smelled like he had a bit of cash.

'I'm not really going anywhere,' I replied. I thought about asking him about Glebe, but I was a bit wary from the moment I clocked him.

'Where are you staying tonight?' he asked.

'I don't know,' I answered.

He pointed to a pub across the street and told me that's where he was staying. I could stay with him, if it suited me – the rooms were big and comfy, and there was a couch I could sleep on. I wanted to take his offer, but something didn't seem quite right. I think he could tell I was uncertain.

'Have you eaten something today?' he asked. I hadn't and was starving. 'Let's go and get something to eat.'

He suggested we get hamburgers. I can't go past a

good hamburger, so we went into the pub. He wanted me to have a beer as well, but I wasn't interested. I told him I didn't drink.

We ate, he drank, and the alarm bells in my head were silenced by my fatigue. I told him I was tired and he pointed me to the stairs. His room was up there. He told me the room number and gave me the key. I was asleep as soon as I lay on the couch.

I woke with his hands down my pants.

'What are you doing, you dirty bastard?' I sprang up, now very much awake.

'No, no, just let me. I'll make you feel good,' he said, coming towards me again.

I gave him a right cross that Max taught me, catching him on the end of his chin. I was out the door as he was still stumbling.

I sprinted down the dark street. Soon I couldn't see the pub or anyone else, so I slowed to a walk and then stopped. I felt sick to my stomach and my hands wouldn't stop shaking.

I should have stayed in Shepparton. I had no money, and no place to stay. I didn't know anyone and didn't understand this place. I had an address in my mind, but I had no idea what kind of greeting I would get, or if I'd get one at all.

Suddenly I felt very alone.

I even thought about going to a phone booth and ringing Mum and Dad Cox. I didn't, though. I knew how badly I'd hurt them, and I thought calling them would probably end up hurting them more. I slouched into a doorway, leant my head on the cold concrete, and soon I was just another fella in the big city, sleeping on hard ground, dreaming of a soft bed.

The morning came with someone standing over me, already talking as I rose.

'You'd better get out of here. The police'll come soon.'

It was a woman with keys in her hand. I could tell this was a familiar routine for her. She didn't even look at me as she unlocked the door to her shop.

I rubbed my eyes, apologised, grabbed my stuff and was off walking through the city again. I hoped to find some Aboriginal people – they were always a help – but I must've been in the wrong part of town because all I saw were well-dressed white people on their way to work.

I asked a few people where Glebe was.

'Toxteth Road, specifically,' I sometimes added.

I reckon perhaps a dozen people ignored me, their heads down, walking fast, until one woman stopped and pointed back past the pub I'd been at the night before.

'Up that way,' she said. 'There'll be a park on your left

and to the right, up the hill, is Glebe Point Road. Walk up a little bit and Toxteth is on your left.'

It wasn't a long walk, maybe not much more than half an hour through the city, then through a leafy suburb.

Number one Toxteth Road was a big old boarding house. I wasn't the type to go knocking on strangers' doors, so I just hung around, waiting to see if an Aboriginal woman emerged. When none did, I swallowed hard and knocked on the first door I found, then the second and third and so on.

No one knew any woman named Myrtle Evans, except for a man claiming to be her closest friend in the building.

My heart raced until he said that she'd moved a few months ago with no mention of where she was going or why. One day she was there, the next she wasn't. The man had no idea where I might try to find her.

I thanked him and walked my way out of Glebe. I was at a loss. I didn't know what to do for that moment, for that day, for my life. I wondered if there was any point in this fool's errand that the letter had sent me on. I was at an address that had got me nowhere, chasing a sister who was no longer there, in a city full of strangers.

I thought about Shepparton and Melbourne. I had left those places and thought it would be shameful to go back. I had to go forward, but what did that mean? Maybe

I could try to get work in Sydney? I was thinking about the lads I was in the car with the day before, wondering if I should go to Kings Cross and try to find them.

I was walking to the city, heading towards Central Station through Belmore Park, when I realised a voice was calling out to me: 'Bud, bud, bud. *Hey, bud.*'

I looked over and I saw it was an old Aboriginal man with long hair and a beard, wearing a long coat, sitting on a park bench. He beckoned to me.

'Young fella, come here. Come over, bud.'

I did what he said and asked what he wanted.

'I don't want anything. I just wanted to ask ya how ya goin'.'

'I'm going good.'

'That's good. It's just, ya seem a little lost.'

'I'm not lost. I've just been up to Glebe to meet someone, but they weren't there.'

'Who were you going to meet?'

I was a bit wary after the previous night's incident, so I didn't reply.

'I go to Glebe sometimes, go to the pub up there,' he said. 'There are a few blackfellas who I hang out with. Maybe it's one of them you were looking for?'

I told him my sister's name, but it wasn't one he'd heard before.

'Sorry, young fella.'

It looked like he meant it, too. He seemed like a good old bloke. He put his hand out and offered his name, which was Albert. After shaking my hand, he reached into his coat and pulled out a bottle of brown muscat. It was then I noticed that the only arm he had was the one holding the bottle.

'Have a charge, bud,' he said. 'Helps after being disappointed.' I wanted something, and maybe that was having a drink with this old blackfella. I had nothing else to do. As I slugged from the bottle my throat burned like a bushfire.

'Keep it down, keep it down, young fella. First one's the hardest.'

I wondered how he knew I'd never touched a drop before, and then I realised he was talking about the first drink of the day.

That muscat was nice in my guts once it was down. It was a crisp morning, and the drink made me warm from the stomach out. I had another slug and found the booze made it easy to talk. I told Albert a bit about myself, and about Shepparton and Melbourne. He told me that he was from South Australia but had been captivated by Sydney.

'This city can do that to blackfellas,' he said. I got the

impression that it wasn't a bad or a good thing, just a fact. We were yarning and drinking, and before I knew it, we'd finished the bottle.

'That's okay,' he said. 'I've got enough money for one more bottle.' Albert asked if I could go, pointing to a pub in the distance. He put money in my hand and off I went.

It felt odd to have a stranger's cash in my pocket. It felt odd to ask for liquor from a bottle-shop attendant since I'd never bought alcohol before on my own. It felt odd to have a paper-bagged bottle in my hand.

It was odd, but it was also fine. The booze seemed to be flattening everything – loss and fear, sound and light, time and space.

I liked it.

I handed the bottle to Albert, and before he took a slug he poured a little of the liquor into the bottle's cap and tipped it onto the ground.

'That's for the old fellas,' he said. 'For the old drinking mates who aren't here anymore.'

It made me sad to hear that.

Albert slapped me on the shoulder with his one and only hand. 'I'm still here, bud. Most of me.'

In the middle of that second bottle Albert took it from me and said I should take a break. There are only a few things I remember after that. I remember asking for a cigarette, and Albert giving me papers and a pouch of tobacco. I remember making a mess of my first-ever attempt at a roll-up cigarette. I remember Albert laughing as he made up a cigarette for me expertly with one hand.

'You don't know much about anything do you, young fella?' he said.

I remember him telling me not to worry because he was going to look after me.

I remember dozing in the park and waking and feeling sick, and I remember more Aboriginal people coming and going. I remember wanting to ask them questions, but not being able to get the words right. I remember drinking more and feeling better, and I remember dusk falling fast.

'I'm guessing you got no place to stay,' Albert said as the park got dark and chilly.

I shook my head. Albert told me to grab my things and follow him. We walked through Haymarket and the city. We walked through Hyde Park and to a long street that ended with a giant, illuminated sign telling people to drink Coca-Cola. We walked towards the sign, then turned off on a street, into an alleyway, and through a door.

We walked into a lobby that looked a bit like a hospital and a bit like a motel. Albert was greeted by a large man, who warned that they only had one bed. We were in a homeless shelter called the Matthew Talbot Hostel, which is still run by the St Vincent de Paul Society to this day.

'That's okay,' Albert said. 'Just look after my mate here.'

'Where are you going to go, Albert?' I asked.

'I always find a place, bud,' he said. 'Get your head down and I'll come see ya tomorrow.'

I would have gone with him if I wasn't so drunk and sick. But the word 'bed' had put a spell on me.

After Albert left, they took me to a dormitory, where there was a bed and pyjamas waiting. I slept the sleep of the dead and woke to find hot showers and a hot breakfast. I couldn't keep much down, but I ate what I could.

A few cups of tea later, I started to feel better. I sat out the front of the hostel for a few hours, smoking and listening to the men who'd slept around me the night before. In their presence I reverted to the shy young fella I'd been without booze.

I was relieved when I saw Albert shambling down the alleyway.

'Come on, bud, let's head off. We got places to go and people to meet.'

We walked down the big street with the Coca-Cola sign, and I asked what places and which people.

'I think we'll go to the Burlington first. I've got entrance fees for both of us.'

I wondered what the Burlington might be, having an entry fee and all. Was it a zoo? A theatre? Of course, when we got there it was a pub, but not just any old pub – it was the one I'd been touched up in two nights ago.

I told Albert that I didn't want to go in – there was someone I didn't want to bump into – but he told me not to worry. He said we'd be with friends; it would all be fine.

Albert took me to the bar and paid the entry fee, which was the price of a couple of schooners. I didn't like beer as much as the sweet, sticky port we'd been drinking the day before, but I worked through it nonetheless. Minute by minute, Albert welcomed more Aboriginal people. Although I'm sure I had met some the day before, this is where I remember first meeting the group of men who would become the friends I would spend most of every day with for months to come.

There was Jasper, a very tall, very funny Queenslander, and Russell, a former boxer who we then thought of as 'punchy' but was likely suffering from what we now know as chronic traumatic encephalopathy, or CTE. There was Paulie, an older man closer to Albert's age, who told long, epic stories, and then there was Albert himself, a resilient man with a huge capacity for kindness.

Albert cared for my every need in those first few weeks in Sydney. He'd make sure I always had a drink when

I needed one, and a smoke when I craved one. When I was hungry, he got me a feed, and when I was tired, he showed me where I could lay my head.

In a city that gave nothing up cheaply, there was a way for us to live without means, and Albert was a master in that way. Albert taught me how to turn tossed cigarette butts into reconstituted full smokes, and showed me the locations of all the hostels, like the one I'd slept in on my second night, and the 'empties' or disused houses, where I could take shelter if the hostels were full or if the weather came in. He took me to church halls where you could get a meal after a sermon and told me which ones offered the best cakes and the best pies.

I thought of my church in Melbourne and how, not long ago, it had been the centre of my life. Now the church was nothing to me but a place to get a free feed. And my congregation was the blackfellas I drank with.

It only took a couple of days to figure out where we got food, smokes and shelter, but after more than a week I couldn't figure out where the entry fees and bottle-shop cash came from. I asked Albert one afternoon and he looked at me for a spell and said it probably was time for me to start biting people.

I stared at him, shocked.

'You want me to bite people?' I asked.

‘I reckon it’s time,’ he said.

‘Who do you want me to bite?’

‘Anyone, really. It doesn’t matter.’

‘I don’t think I could do that.’

‘I reckon you can. It doesn’t mean much to them, bud.’

I thought Albert had lost his mind. I thought people would care quite a lot if I went up and bit them. I also couldn’t for the life of me figure out what we would get out of it.

As I stood there looking like a country mouse, Albert put two and two together and doubled over in laughter.

‘Bud, we’re not actually biting people! We’re asking for money – that’s just what we call it. We call it “biting”.’

I can tell you this was an instant load off my shoulders. I felt like an idiot, but a relieved idiot.

Albert took me out to George Street for my first session of biting, only it wasn’t as easy as it sounded. Albert had told me what to do – I needed to come up with a sob story, a short one, and it’d be best if that story involved displacement and hunger.

‘Just go up to someone, maybe a woman, and say, “Excuse me, miss. I just got here to Sydney and I don’t have any work yet. I’m very hungry and was wondering if you have fifty cents or a dollar you could give me so I can get a pie." Look hungry, look sad and you'll be right.'

Albert perched himself in a doorway and pushed me out into the lunchtime crowd. And there I stood, trying to pick the perfect punter to bite. Not this bloke, he looks too busy; and not this woman, she looks too mean. This one is too young, that one doesn't look like they have any money. No, no, no, no...

I glanced over at Albert and he looked frustrated. He picked a woman coming down the street some twenty or thirty metres away and followed her with his finger, then pointed at me. That was an order, I guessed.

'Excuse me,' I said quietly.

She didn't stop. I followed her.

'*Excuse me, miss.*'

'Yes? What do you want?'

I didn't really know what to say.

'My name's Archie...' That was all I got out before I burst into laughter. It was all too absurd.

As she walked off, I turned to Albert, who was coming towards me, shaking his head.

'Two things, bud. One, you never give anyone your real name. Always have a name in the back pocket that you don't want to keep. And two...watch this.'

Albert stopped the next man who walked past and wove a perfect web of bullshit about being a country man who was trying to find his wife in the big city and was ashamed to admit that he could no longer even provide for his son.

When he motioned to me, I tried to look hungry. It wasn't hard – I was a little peckish. The man gave Albert two dollars. I was stunned; that was a lot of money.

'I want to help, Albert, but I just don't think I can do it,' I told him. It felt shameful, begging, no matter what you called it.

'Do you think you'd be able to do it after a bit of a charge?' he asked.

That's what we called drinking, getting a charge. I nodded and from his coat Albert produced a bottle that he was saving for later. After a drink I managed to pick up a few bucks that day, usually when I was at my most wretched looking. But the truth is, I never really got used to biting.

When Albert was biting, Jasper and Paulie and sometimes even Russell were usually off doing the same thing. When we'd all finished we'd meet up in Belmore Park and we'd pool the money. After we'd counted how much we had, we'd figure out what we could buy. Sometimes smokes, sometimes food. A lot went into the cash registers of the pubs and licensed grocers nearby.

Back then the pubs closed at ten, and closing time

meant it was time to find a bed, but some days we'd head back to the park with a bottle, or to one of the late-licence pubs, like the Civic Hotel in the CBD.

One Thursday at the Civic, I went upstairs and there was an Aboriginal fella dressed like he had money, on stage singing, backed by a band. He was singing like he had a deep well of soul. When he finished the song, the room erupted. He was followed by a whitefella who didn't have a tenth of this blackfella's skill. After that there was a woman, and then another man. Neither were much chop and when they were done the crowd called the name 'Ivan', and the Aboriginal fella got back up on stage. Everyone cheered and someone came up and gave him fifty bucks cash.

Fifty!

This scene was repeated whenever we went to the Civic on a Thursday. Lots of different people came and sang, but everyone lost to this well-dressed Aboriginal fella with a deadly voice named Ivan.

I'd think about that fifty bucks every time I walked past the hock shop on George Street. It had a nice-looking guitar in the window with a price tag of fifteen bucks. If I won that singing contest, not only could I get that guitar, I'd have thirty-five to stick into the kitty. That was a lot of biting we wouldn't have to do.

I started going up on stage at the Civic. I had to get a good charge going before I did, but I got up there and sang the sad Hank Williams songs me and Dad Alex used to share. I was a little unsteady and a little slurry, but I felt the music and think I did all right. People clapped and cheered, and pretty much every week I came second to Ivan.

One week after Ivan had won again, the organiser told me he was going to give me a special second prize. I hoped for a moment it might be fifteen bucks. It wasn't; it was a bottle of wine that I was allowed to drink on the premises. That was still pretty good, I thought.

I became a little more obsessed with the guitar in the hock shop and thought about the day when I might have the money to buy it. When I heard there was cash-in-hand work available unloading trains down at Central Station, I was there in the morning, trying to look healthy and sober.

After a few days' work I had enough money for the guitar, and some left over. When I got that guitar, I stopped going to the station and had a few glorious days in the park, playing and singing with Albert, Jasper, Russell and Paulie, drinking our fill.

Carefree and happy. That's where we all wanted to be. The charge got us there.

I look back now and see the darkness that would have touched every moment unless we numbed it with beer and port and sherry. We were part of an obliterated culture, just intact enough to know it existed, but so broken we didn't think we could ever be put together again. We'd lost mates and family young, and we would again. We had lineages we knew so little about. There was death in our past, and death in our future. We wanted to forget, and to retell the stories of our lives as triumphs and comedies, not tragedies.

In our Belmore Park drinking school we looked out for each other, but that wasn't the case for everyone we drank with. There were thieves in the pubs where we used to drink; some who stole clothes off backyard lines, selling them in bulk to vendors from places like Paddy's Markets. Some stole valuables from houses in Sydney's east, selling them to gangsters.

There were also girls at the pub who would doll themselves up and get blokes to pay for their drinks. Sometimes these girls would work with the thieves.

One day an Aboriginal girl came to me for help.

'Can you do something for me, Phil?' Almost everyone knew me as Phillip Brown, a name I'd assumed after my biting lesson with Albert.

'What do you need?'

'I can't get to this bloke's wallet so I'm going to take him down the alley, where he reckons he's getting a bit. While we're kissing or whatever, can you come and smack him over the head with a bottle or something? We'll see what we can get.'

I told her there was no way I was doing that, but she begged me to give her a hand.

'Usually there are other brothers who help out, but they're not here. Could you help please, my brother?'

'Brother?' I asked.

I told her I barely knew her, but she said all Aboriginal men were her brothers and all Aboriginal women were her sisters. I hadn't heard that before, and quite liked it, but it didn't change my mind about robbing this poor fella.

'Well, if I'm your brother then as your brother I reckon you should leave the poor fella alone.'

I had my own moral code at sixteen, and one I shared with the rest of my drinking school, and that code didn't extend to hurting strangers. But that didn't mean I didn't have my own run-ins with the demons, though.

That's what we called the coppers – demons. I first got that demon hand one afternoon when I was confident enough to bite on my own.

I was down the road from the Burlington, having picked up a few coins from the passers-by. I had a smoke in my mouth and my mind on very little when a car pulled up and two big demons got out. They were plainclothes detectives, not the uniformed coppers who used to chase us out of the park and the empties.

'What are you doing, son?' one said.

'Just having a smoke.'

'No, you were asking for money – asking good people for money,' the other one said.

'So?'

'So? That's "begging alms" and that's an offence. You'd better come with us.'

Before I knew it I was in the car, then up the stairs of the Sydney Central Police Station, then in an interview room.

'Name?'

'Phillip Brown.'

'Age?'

'Nineteen.'

'Place of residence?'

'I don't have a place of residence.'

Albert would tell me later that Phillip Brown didn't just need a name but an address, too.

'Where do you sleep?'

'I sleep where I can. Sometimes at the hostels, sometimes elsewhere.'

'You have no fixed address?'

'No, not right now.'

'I guess you don't have a job, if you were begging alms.'

'I wasn't begging alms, I was biting.'

'It'll do you no good to be cheeky,' one of them said.

'You have no money, and nowhere to live. That's another offence. That one's called "vagrancy".'

'Not having a place to live is a crime? That doesn't make sense to me,' I said.

'It doesn't matter what makes sense to you, son. I'm a policeman and you're a criminal, so who do you think knows the law?'

I didn't say anything after that. If they said I was a criminal, then I guess I was a criminal.

'You're a nineteen-year-old named Phillip Brown?' one asked.

'Yep.'

'Where are you originally from, Phil?'

'Essendon.'

'Where exactly?'

I racked my brains and all I could think of was the town hall, and I knew that wasn't going to fly.

'Just round about there,' I said.

The coppers looked at each other. They weren't buying it.

'This all sounds like malarkey to me,' one of them said. 'If you don't have another name and another story, then I reckon we might send you off to jail.'

I didn't say anything. There wasn't anything else to say. I was never going to bother the Coxes with this shameful business, and there wasn't really anyone else I could contact.

The demons stared at me, I stared at them, and then a moment later I was back in the lock-up. After a little I was in front of a magistrate who narrowed his gaze at me after the charges were read out.

'It's been recommended to me that you go to jail for two weeks. What do you have to say about that?'

What do I have to say about that? Leave me alone is what. Who was I hurting?

I didn't think any of that would have helped, though, so I didn't say anything.

The hammer dropped and I was off to Long Bay Prison, in the south-eastern Sydney suburb of Malabar.

A guard barked a number at me that I had to memorise for the next fortnight. My old name may have been Phillip, he said, but now it had been replaced. Then I was taken straight down to the yard so I could be washed.

They found nits in my wild matted hair, so I was shorn and covered in cream that stung to the touch.

After I was clean and clothed, I was dropped into the general population and was quickly found by some older Aboriginal fellas.

'You don't look nineteen, you look about sixteen,' one of them said. 'Don't worry, brother, we'll look after you.'

And like Albert, they did. I never went hungry during that stint, and never got bashed or touched up.

I was assigned a job on my second day, and it was literally the shittiest job in the joint. In the section of the prison we were in there was no plumbing; instead, each prisoner was given a shit tin that we deposited our expulsions into, solid or liquid. My job was to go around the cells, collect the tins and pass them on to another fella who would empty and clean them and pass them back.

The only good part about that job was that the contents of the tins had to be taken to a building close to the prison bakery, so after my nose was filled with the most unimaginable pong, it was cleared with the delicious smell of rolls and loaves.

Some of the brothers knew a fella who worked at the bakery, and after our rounds we could swap some of the freshest bread with the dank prison tobacco that every prisoner was issued. We'd smuggle jam and butter into our pockets at breakfast time and in the afternoon, we'd melt them against the piping-hot bread. I'm not sure I've ever eaten anything so fine.

Prison was an awful waste of time. I learnt a couple of useful tricks, like splitting matches into two and sometimes four so that they could still catch enough flame to light a cigarette, and I finally learnt how to properly roll a smoke, although our prison smokes were so thin we'd call them 'racehorses'. I was ready to leave as soon as I arrived. That fortnight felt like a year.

When I was released we were bussed to Taylor Square and there, at the Courthouse Hotel, I had a few morning starters before heading over to find my drinking school at Belmore Park. They asked where I'd been, and my answer brought no surprise to their faces. I realise now that prison was a part of our drinking story, like sickness, fights, laughter and song, and our drinking story happened all at once.

I was too young, too inexperienced, too unwise or too unwilling to understand it then, but we were part of a journey that was unlike most. In most journeys there are two directions – 'past' and 'present' – but in ours the directions were 'now' and 'death'.

For the first time since my sister Myrtle's letter came, I had found a bearable way to live – as a drinker – so that's what I did, to the detriment of everything else.

I came out of prison and stayed a drinker, in the same parks and the same pubs. When Russell died of pneumonia on Christmas Eve just shy of his fortieth birthday, I stayed a drinker. When Albert got sad one day and told us he had to leave, and then disappeared with no trace, I stayed a drinker. As a birthday went by without me even noticing, I stayed a drinker.

For anything to change, something drastic would have to happen. And then, one day, something did.

It was on a day when I couldn't find anybody. I started at the Burlington but only saw strangers or people who knew me as Phillip Brown. I decided to get a charge on my own. I went to the grocer in Chinatown, then down an alley, and got smashed. I walked back to the pub drenched in a melancholy I planned to numb with a few extra schooners. More than a few later, I was the drunkest I'd been in a long time; it felt as if I were watching myself slumped in my chair.

I watched as a group of Aboriginal women eyed the wretched figure that sat in my seat. I wondered what they would want of him.

I heard one call out, 'Hey boy, who are you?'

It didn't feel as though I answered, but I heard the words, 'I'm not anybody. Leave me alone,' come out of my mouth.

The woman didn't take no for an answer. She asked again, this time specifically what my name was. They'd seen me around, she said, but didn't know my name. I wanted her to go away.

'Archie Roach,' I heard. The name tumbled out before I could give it any thought.

One of the other Aboriginal women bolted upright and her chair tumbled to the ground. Next minute she was in front of me.

'What did you say your name was?'

'I'm Archie Roach. My name's Archie Roach.'

She was shaking when she asked about my brothers and sisters and, scared of her intensity, I told her that a man named Johnny was my oldest brother, and that my other brother was called Lawrence. I had sisters too, Myrtle and Alma and Gladys, and my youngest sister, Diana.

Not satisfied with that, she then asked me who my mother and father were.

'My mother's name is Nellie Austin, and if you know my name then you'll know my father's name – I was named after him.'

She hit me hard, right on the chin.

I fell to the ground and there I stayed, yelling. 'Leave me alone, ya mad woman! I didn't do nothing to you.'

She stood over me and sternly asked again what my name was. I was almost crying now, angry and sad at the same time. I yelled at her that I was Archie Roach, like my dad before me, and now could she please go.

The woman reached down; I was scared she was going to hit me again. Instead, she picked me up and hugged me close. She started sobbing, and through the sobs she said something over and over and over.

'It's me, it's me, it's me, it's me, it's me…'

'It's who?' I asked.

'It's me. Your sister Diana.'

She broke the embrace for just a moment, looked me up and down, then pulled me back close, whispering, 'You're my baby brother – Butter Boy.'

Front cover of my 1997 album, *Looking for Butter Boy*.
Photo and album design by Pierre Baroni.

My dad, Archie 'Snowball' Roach.

My mum, Nellie Austin.

CHAPTER 4

TELL ME WHY

There's many great loves in history
That we know about
But a tale of two lovers that was told to me
Makes me want to scream and shout
Like Romeo and Juliet
A love story you won't forget
Tell me why, tell me why did they destroy a love like that?
Tell me why, tell me why, tell me why did they do that?

Snowball Roach and Nellie Austin loved each other well
Oh and I don't think that they argued often
Somebody broke the spell
Yeah they broke the spell and broke their hearts
And they drifted far apart
But tell me why, tell me why did they destroy a love like that?
Tell me why, tell me why, tell me why did they do that?

Well they tore two hearts apart
Left them bleeding all alone
And they threw them in a river made of stone
Oh they're dead now
He was from the Bundjalung clan and she was
Kirrae Whurrong
He was a big strong fighting man

She was proud and strong
Their love was great
Their love was free
But what happened to them was a tragedy
So tell me why, tell me why did they destroy a love like that?
Tell me why, tell me why, tell me why did they do that?

Well they tore two hearts apart
Left them bleeding all alone
And they threw them in the river made of stone
Made of stone
Made of stone
Made of stone
Yeah, they threw them in the river
Made of stone
Made of stone
Made of stone
Made of stone

I had so many questions. Drunk as I was then, and old as I am now, it's hard to remember which questions Diana answered that night and which ones she answered the next day, but I remember there was one thing I asked her over and over, that day and the next; a question she could never explain.

'Why did they take us away from Mum and Dad?'

'I'm not really sure,' she replied.

I asked if Myrtle was our sister, and Diana said she was. I asked what had happened to her; Diana said she'd gone to Melbourne to be near Alma. She said those two were like peas in a pod.

That accounted for three sisters, but what about the fourth, the other girl I could remember alongside Diana in the dormitories?

'What about Gladys?' I asked.

That question flushed my sister's face with sadness.

'Dead,' she said. 'Killed.'

That didn't seem right at all. Gladys couldn't have been much older than Diana, who was still a teenager herself. Diana was reluctant to talk about it, and I didn't want to have to ask. She did me a favour and went first.

'It was a car accident. She died with her husband.'

My brain overloaded when I found Diana, and my heart overloaded, too. I had found a sister and, moments later, had lost another, forever. The fury and confusion that had simmered inside me when the letter arrived at school now started to bubble and boil again. I began to remember things about Gladys but was too sad to ask any more questions. And didn't want to hurt Diana with them.

I asked her if she remembered the day we were taken away, and she did.

'We were there at the mish. Then a big black car

arrived full of white people, showing some papers,' she said. 'They grabbed you and me and Gladys. I looked out the car window and saw Dad coming towards us. He was screaming like a madman. They grabbed him and tried to hold him down on the ground, and he was fighting and throwing them demons around.'

Diana's words echoed in my brain. I saw a tall man, with long limbs and curly hair, reaching towards me as policemen took hold of him. He was screaming. That was Archie Roach, my dad. I remembered Gladys, too. She had her arms around me as I cried and cried.

'Don't worry, Butter Boy,' she'd said. 'We'll come back. It's okay.'

Butter Boy. More memories of Gladys came with that name. She used to say it all the time in the Homes, when I was scared or hungry or when I was crying.

'It's going to be okay, Butter Boy.'

I asked Diana where we went after we'd been taken from the mish. She told me about a big place that looked a bit like a mansion, but also a bit like a prison, with enormous gates and bars on all the windows. There were a lot of other Aboriginal kids there, and a lot of white men wearing uniforms with shiny buttons and belts.

I remembered they gave us cordial and sandwiches. I remembered one of the men picking me up and putting me on his shoulders, walking around, joking with his mates. I was trembling and crying. I remembered looking over at Diana and Gladys, who were yelling at the man, telling him to put me down because I was scared. I now know this happened at a rest and refreshment stop at the old Geelong Prison after we travelled from the mish via the Warrnambool Magistrates' Court.

Next stop was Baltara, at the Turana Juvenile Youth Detention Centre, where we stayed a while for processing before Gladys, Diana and I were taken to an orphanage in Canterbury and to the dormitories that were to become my home for the next couple of years.

'Salvation Army Home for Girls, but it was also called William Booth Orphanage,' Diana said. 'After a while I ended up with some Dutch people. They were all right.'

'I was with a family and the father was a Scotsman. They were all right, too,' I told her. I decided not to mention the other family and the hunger and pain and fear and shame I experienced at the hands of the foster mother.

Diana said our brother Lawrence was also in Melbourne, but she didn't know where Johnny, known by everyone as Horse, was. He'd been in Melbourne as well but had got in some kind of fight and had to leave. I asked her why, after Gladys died and Myrtle had moved back to Melbourne, why she didn't go as well.

'They know Melbourne. I don't. I like it here.'

I asked what had happened to our mum and dad, but all she knew was that they were dead. But we still had aunties and uncles who were alive.

'There's one old uncle, Stan, who's been trying to get me back in the Homes. He said that would get me off the streets and out of the pubs. But I like the streets and the pubs.'

I understood what she was saying.

When I met Diana, she wasn't on the street; she was living with her boyfriend, Peter, on the way to Newtown. He had a nice room with a balcony that he was happy to share with Diana, but not with me. I told her that was fine – I'd been shown where to stay and where to eat. I was good where I was.

Soon Diana started hanging out with me more than with Peter. She'd stay in the empties with me, and we'd drink together and bite together. Once there was this fella, who was also sleeping rough, who came over to me and asked, 'Is your girlfriend warm enough? Does she need a blanket?'

'Archie's not my boyfriend; he's my brother,' Diana snapped.

My brother. It felt great to hear that.

One day Peter turned up at the Burlington, telling Diana that she had to come home with him and clean herself up. She told him she had no interest in doing that. She'd rather be in the pub and in the empties with me than in a house with him. This enraged Peter, and when he strode towards my sister, full of bad intent, I told him to leave her alone. It's no surprise that this angered him further. He started throwing punches at me, and for a while I managed to duck and weave away from him until one punch caught me flush behind the ear.

I was done; my head was ringing, my brain sparked, and my ear was red and hot. Diana started wailing on Peter, swinging at him like a maniac. Peter retreated and left the fight, left the pub and both our lives. We never saw him again.

Diana and I were very happy in each other's company. So happy, in fact, it seemed we needed nothing else. There were only two types of events that would break our routine of drinking and biting and empties and charity soup – one good, one bad. The good was when we caught up with family, be they uncles or aunties or sometimes cousins like 'Tiny', Uncle Stan's baby sister, Alma's daughter.

Tiny, like a few members of our family, had a life of church and work and children, away from the pubs and parks. Every so often, though, we'd catch up, singing songs and telling yarns about the mish and about our dad and our uncles and the old people.

It was always good to see Tiny.

The bad events were getting pinched by demons. There were two policemen who had come to know me. If I saw them on the street, I'd disappear but, if they saw me first, quite often they'd disappear me with a heavy hand on the shoulder, a trip in the car and then a stint in the lock-up.

Sometimes I'd be there for a few hours, other times for a night behind bars. I'd occasionally get a kicking, or a punch or two in the back of the neck. Sometimes I'd end up in front of the magistrate, which always meant fourteen days in Long Bay. It was always fourteen days – never more, never less.

One morning I hadn't yet had a drink, and I hadn't even got my hand out for a bite. I was walking down the street in Haymarket, and next moment I was being forced into the back of an unmarked police car.

'What's wrong with you bastards?' I yelled at them. 'What did I do?'

'Swearing at a policeman. That's an offence you,

know,' the cop said as he pushed me into the car.

'Why are you always picking on me?' I asked.

To this demon's credit, he did think about my question. 'I don't know. I just don't like you.'

Fair enough. The feeling was mutual.

When we got to the station, he told me I was going to be charged with a number of offences, including loitering, loitering with the intent to commit a crime, being drunk in a public place, vagrancy, and swearing at a policeman. We went through the normal procedure of my name, age, residence and I lied, lied and lied.

'You know what? I don't think your name is Phillip Brown,' he said. 'It doesn't come out your mouth quite right. I know what you people are like. You lie and use aliases.'

I didn't even know what aliases were.

I spent a night and a day in a cell, and in the afternoon I was marched into court. When I got to the dock, there was the magistrate who'd sent me to Long Bay a handful of times, and Diana, who'd heard that I'd been taken off the streets.

'Mr Brown, I've discussed your case with the detective, and we've decided that we're a little bit sick of the sight of you,' said the magistrate. 'You've been telling officers that you're from Essendon in Melbourne, so we think it would be better if you were there instead of here. As you've been charged with vagrancy, it's safe to assume you have no personal effects, so I'm going to ask officers to facilitate your passage to Melbourne post haste.'

Two uniformed policemen took me straight out of the dock and down to Central Station. They picked up a train ticket and frogmarched me to one of the interstate platforms, holding me as they waited for the train.

Diana arrived before the train did, out of breath from running and crying. She asked the policemen to leave me alone, then begged for the same. They ignored her. As the train pulled into the platform, she tried to get on with me, but one policeman pushed her aside while the other pushed me into the carriage.

'Go find Alma and Myrtle!' she said.

'Where are they?' I asked.

She had no idea. I yelled to Diana, telling her I'd find them and that she should come to Melbourne so that we could all be together again.

As the train left the station, I allowed myself a moment of hope and joy, thinking about the possibility of being with all my brothers and sisters. Then, just as quickly, came the crushing realisation that it could never happen. One of my sisters was already dead, one would soon be a thousand kilometres away, and the others and my brothers were just strangers in the crowd.

Unfamiliar country rushed past the windows of the train.

I was all alone again.

Me and my sisters (From left): Alma, Diana and big sister Myrtle.

The Roach Brothers, somewhere in Fitzroy, late 70s. (From left): Johnny 'Horse', me, our friend Darren and Lawrence. This is the only photo I have of me with my brothers.

CHAPTER 5

F TROOP

I was only sixteen years, when I met my brother
He looked at me, and his face lit up with joy
After the tears, he talked about our mother
Held me close and whispered 'Butter Boy'

I remember drinking wine, and talking with my brother
Had a drink, then he didn't think I should
I told him I could handle it, and I said 'let's get another'
Sitting in the kitchen, in Dight Street Collingwood

We'd take a walk to Fitzroy, early in the morning
When sometimes family life became a strain
We'd stand outside the cellars
Greeting friends we knew were coming
Grabbed a quart, and walked to Charcoal Lane

I remember sitting in the laneway with my brother
Sharing cigarettes and company
Drinking with some friends we knew
Who said they knew our father
Sitting in the laneway, my brother and me
Now the lanes were not forgotten
But the parks became our haven
And everybody knew the parkies law

And I see my brother standing
On that hill side, and he's saying
F Troop doesn't ride here anymore

I remember dancing 'round the jukebox with my brother
Dancing to, and singing 'I Can Help'
Acting just like children in the joy we gave each other
Dancing 'round the jukebox, in the Champion Hotel
Dancing 'round the jukebox, in the Champion Hotel

It felt like a neverending journey. My mouth was dry no matter how much I drank from the bathroom tap, my stomach rumbled and there was no food to eat. My hands trembled as the train rolled on, through night and day. Hour after hour, I was stinging for a drink and a smoke.

Finally we stopped at Spencer Street Station. Everyone else alighted with purpose, but I did so reluctantly.

I had no idea where I was or where I was going.

I walked out of the station and wandered for a bit, hoping to run into some Aboriginal people, but after an hour or so I'd had no luck. I figured I was in the middle of the city, which is where the Aboriginal people were in Sydney, but perhaps that wasn't the case in Melbourne.

I stopped someone on the street and asked where

I could find the city centre. They pointed down a long street, adding that I could get there on the tram that was coming. I jumped on the tram and eventually a conductor asked me if I had a ticket. When I told him I didn't have one, or money to pay for one, I had to get off. So it took me three or four trips and three or four apologetic conversations with conductors before I got where I wanted to. I'd figured out that that was the trick of getting around on a tram.

Bourke Street was all hustle and bustle, and I felt pretty confident I was in the right place. I sat down on a bench and waited for a black face to emerge from the crowd, but as the hours ticked by, none did. After a while, I did see someone who I thought I could talk to – an older whitefella with a straggly beard wearing a tattered suit. While everyone else was looking up or at each other, he was scanning the pavement. I knew what that meant.

I walked up to him and asked how he was going. He looked shocked, maybe even scared.

'What do ya want?' he asked abruptly.

'Nothing, nothing. You looking for bumpers, right?'

He was. I asked if he wanted a hand, then the two of us scrounged around looking for enough butts to make a smoke we could share. He smiled as I puffed and told me he didn't think he'd ever seen anyone enjoying a smoke so much. I said I'd been a couple of days without.

'Where are you from, young fella? I don't reckon I've seen you round here before.'

'I've just come from Sydney. I'm used to the streets there, but I don't really know anything about Melbourne. I don't know where I'd get a bed or a feed.'

The thought of seeking out Hamish or the church people was a thousand miles from my thoughts, let alone Mum and Dad Cox. I considered myself to be a ward of the streets now.

This old fella told me he was going to get a feed soon and that he'd take me along to get one, too. I hadn't eaten for at least a couple of days and my guts were rumbling.

We walked together past the Royal Women's Hospital, through Carlton, to a building with big, open bay windows where women were handing out sandwiches and hot cups of tea.

If the old bloke thought I'd enjoyed my smoke, he hadn't seen anything yet. I sat there full and happy for quite a while, until he asked me if there was anything I needed. I asked if he knew where I'd be able to get a bed for the night. He gave me directions for a place called Ozanam House, which ended up being only a short walk away, and there I found fresh sheets, a hot shower and a few moments to stop yearning and start thinking.

In the way that there had been a community of Aboriginal people in Sydney, I figured there had to be a group of brothers and sisters in Melbourne. I just needed to find them. And I thought the best way to do that would be to look for the parkies and the drinkers.

The next morning, I went over to some fellas in the park next to the Ozanam.

'You fellas right?' I said.

They were.

I asked if I could get a smoke off any of them, and not only did they give me one, they offered up a tailormade – not hand-rolled – the height of luxury. They didn't just give me that, either; they gave me a patch of grass to sit down on and offered a swig from the wine bottle they were sharing. These whitefellas introduced themselves, except for a young fella who couldn't have been much older than me.

'Haven't met too many other young fellas like me,' I said.

He just shrugged and didn't say anything.

I asked if there were any blackfellas around, and they said there were some who turned up from time to time. I thought I could try to pick up some work while waiting it out. They suggested the markets nearby, warning me that I'd have to get there early.

That night I slept at the Ozanam again, discovering that if I was happy to make beds and clean, I'd always have a place to lay my head. I woke well before the sun and headed for the door, but was stopped by a staff member, who said the gate for the facility was closed until dawn. I told him I was trying to get some work at the market, and he said he could let me out, but only this one time.

I did get a bit of work that day, helping set up the fruit and veggie stalls. I was paid in cash, which got me and the fellas in the park nice and drunk. From there I fell into a bit of a new routine, sometimes sleeping at the Ozanam and drinking with the fellas, and sometimes setting myself up in an alley off Elizabeth Street, in a lean-to made of old bits of tin and cardboard.

There was a bit of biting going on then, too, but I was pretty nervous doing it as the fellas had talked about how bad life could get at the local Pentridge Prison.

I'd been in Melbourne for a month and hadn't seen any blackfellas until one day, in the park next to the hospital, I saw a fella with dark skin and a bottle in his hand approaching us. As he came closer I started to clock him as Aboriginal. When he asked if he could join us, I was quick to welcome him.

'I've got a bit of money and wanted to get away from all the other brothers,' he said to me. 'Go into the city for a bit, you know?'

I nodded. 'It's good to see another blackfella,' I said. 'Don't see many around here.'

'No, not many around here,' he said. 'That's why it's good to come here every now and then. The cops tend to ignore you more and you can be more, I don't know...anonymous.'

I thought it was an unusual word to use here in the park: anonymous. 'You an educated fella?' I asked.

By way of an answer he shrugged. 'I use them jawbreakers sometimes, even though some countrymen don't like me to.'

I knew what he was saying. Back in Sydney, when I started drinking, I told an Aboriginal woman that it made me feel 'euphoric' when I first got drunk, and she told me that I'd do well to keep those jawbreakers out of my mouth. 'People will think you're up yourself,' she'd said. I remember thinking that I couldn't help how I was brought up.

I asked where this man had come from and he told me Fitzroy. I asked if there were countrymen there, and he said there was a whole mob. The reason I hadn't seen many black people in the city was because Fitzroy was our place and that's where we all ended up.

I started to get excited that maybe my family was there. I asked him how far Fitzroy was and he said I could easily walk there. I bounced up and he pointed down a street he said would take me to a park where there was a building with a big dome on it and lots of Moreton Bay fig trees. If I kept going I'd come to Nicholson Street, which intersects with Gertrude Street. Around there I'd find our people. I thanked him and told him I'd see him again soon.

I followed his instructions, and only twenty minutes or so later I was on a street full of blackfellas. They sent a nod my way as I walked past, or a 'Hey, brus', except for one fella out the front of the pub who squared up when he saw me, raising his hands in a fighting stance.

I kept an eye on him as I continued to walk past, and when I got closer he dropped his hands and called out to me.

'Hey brother, sorry about that. You look a lot like a friend of mine and I thought you were him.'

'You were going to fight your friend?'

'No, no, that's just how me and Horse used to say hello to each other. We used to box together.'

There was a spark in my mind and my heart. Diana had told me that our brother Johnny Roach used to box, and that most people called him Horse. Could this fella be talking about my eldest brother?

'What's his real name, your mate, Horse?' I asked.

'Roach. Johnny Roach.'

'That's my older brother! I'm Archie Roach,' I said, nearly leaping out of my skin. He shook my hand with a huge grin. He told me not to go anywhere and disappeared into the pub called the Champion Hotel.

This fella, Chris, known to everyone as 'the Perse' or 'Mr Personality', was my cousin, but that was a fact I'd find out a little while later. When the Perse came out of the pub, my focus wasn't on him but on the person with him.

She was a big, beautiful black woman with a smile to match. The woman caught her breath when she saw me.

'That's my baby brother, Archie!' she said, hugging me.

'Myrtle?' I asked.

'Alma. I'm Alma. Let me look at you, Archie.' She stepped back. 'How old are you?'

'About sixteen, I think.' I wasn't quite sure. It had been a while since I paid much attention to the date of my birthday.

'You old enough for a beer?' she asked. If only she knew.

We went into the pub and she ordered pots for both of us, but before I'd even taken a sip, she told me we should move on to the Builders Arms. She reckoned we'd be able to find our brother Lawrence there. My head spun and I downed the beer as quickly as I could.

When we got to the Builders we found a white woman sitting with a group of blackfellas. They were all listening intently to a song on the jukebox, and when Alma called out 'Lawrence', a tall, handsome fella turned around, annoyed.

'What d'you want, Alma?'

I'd learn that Lawrence was doing what he loved best – getting charged up with his wife and enjoying the songs playing on the jukebox.

'You know who this is, Lawrence?' Alma pointed at me. Lawrence looked at me blankly, until it started to dawn on him. Before Alma had a chance to explain, he was knocking over chairs to get to me.

A third sibling wrapped their arms around me. A third sibling called me 'Butter Boy', which I misheard as 'brother boy' for a long time.

Tears welled up in his eyes, and in mine, too. I'd feared that my family might have forgotten me, that the tyranny of time had muted the memory of their baby brother. Now I'd met three siblings, and their responses told me they'd kept me in their hearts over the years.

Lawrence introduced me to his wife Sally, the white woman he was drinking with. Alma suggested we all have a drink and Lawrence told her that I wasn't old enough. It took a little bit to convince him I was.

I figured Lawrence was about ten years older than me. Alma, the eldest of the girls, was a few years older than him. If I was sixteen, Lawrence would have been in his mid-twenties, and Alma and Myrtle would have been pushing thirty. As the eldest, Horse would have been in his early thirties. They wanted to know where I'd been, and when I told them I'd come from Sydney and that I'd been with Diana, they only had more questions. I said Diana was fine, and then they had questions about Dad's family and the Ferguson side of our family. I told them what I could, but it wasn't much more than they already knew.

I wanted to know where I was from, and Lawrence said our family came from a place called Framlingham Mission in south-western Victoria, near Warrnambool. I asked why it was called a mission, but he didn't know why.

'There used to be lots of Aboriginal families living there. No one goes there much anymore,' he said. 'With our parents dead... Did you know that Mum and Dad are both gone?'

I told him I did know, and that I'd gone to Sydney after getting a letter from Myrtle telling me about our mother. Talking about Mum saddened Lawrence, and he grew quiet. He said he didn't know much about her – he'd only seen her once after he'd been taken, by chance.

'It was in Silvan. I was up there picking beans and carrots. I didn't really know what to say,' he said.

I didn't know what to say, either. After a few long moments, Lawrence suggested we go back to Alma's flat and see who else was there. On the way we stopped by a bottle shop to pick up a flagon of wine, which Lawrence called his 'piggy'.

We got to Alma's place on Dight Street, in Collingwood, and as soon as we walked in Lawrence went into the lounge room, where Myrtle lived with her husband and two daughters.

'Myrtle, come out. I've got someone for you to meet,' said Lawrence.

When Myrtle saw me, and the look on Alma's face, her lungs seemed to fail. She couldn't cry – she didn't have the air for it.

I told Myrtle I'd been looking for her for more than a year. Then I told her a little bit about Shepparton and Sydney, and my time in Melbourne.

She was shocked. 'I didn't mean to do anything wrong

with that letter. I didn't mean to break up your family.'

'*You're* my family,' I said, and we all sat together for the first time. It was a moment that was a lifetime in the making.

Lawrence offered sips from his piggy, but Myrtle wouldn't have a bar of it, getting beer from the fridge and offering it to me.

'Don't drink that rubbish, Butter Boy.'

I did what my big sister told me and drank her beer.

There we were, all together in one room – all except for Diana, who was in Sydney; Gladys, who sadly would never join us again; and big Horse, Johnny Roach, the eldest of us. I asked where Johnny was and they told me he was off with the wind.

'Perth, we last heard,' Alma said.

'It's been years, though, since we've seen him.' Myrtle said that Horse had always had itchy feet.

'He'll be right, Horse. He knows how to look after himself,' Lawrence said. 'He always has.'

They told me that Horse was never taken off the mish like we were. He was a big fella, and when the government came and took us they assumed Horse was an adult and left him alone.

Alma, Myrtle and Lawrence all rushed in to describe Horse's pugilistic skills, and to say that boxing talent seem to grow out of the ground in and around the Framlingham Mission. There were uncles and cousins who were great boxers, and apparently Dad was a fine fighter in his day, boxing in the touring tents for the legendary Jimmy Sharman.

I asked about Mum. I knew she was gone, but I knew nothing of the circumstances of her life.

'Mum was living in Silvan with a Dutchman at the end,' said Myrtle. 'They were living in a friend's house. When she got sick, he didn't look after her well and she got sicker and sicker...' Myrtle became too upset to continue.

A long pause hung in the air before Alma spoke.

'See, after we were taken from the mish, we were taught how to be domestics,' she started. Both she and Myrtle hated it and would often run away, trying to find Mum and Dad and us. They would always end up back at the school, hungry and chastised.

The pair split and worked for a number of people, cooking and cleaning, getting back together regularly for a charge and to catch up with family. Sometimes they'd see Dad in Fitzroy. He'd tell them that he had things to do and places to stay, but he'd never be specific. He was their father, but he was estranged, a man who struggled with the trauma of losing his children. Alma ended up working in Frankston for a famous fashion model, who was kind to her. One day, when Alma came home, visibly distraught, the model asked her what was wrong.

Dad had died, suddenly, if not unexpectedly. He'd been in the Fitzroy lock-up. He was usually in there until he sobered up and got right, but one night they pulled him out of the cell dead.

No one knew why then, and no one knows why to this day.

When Alma finished telling her story she sobbed, and then she wailed, uncontrollably and completely. We all crowded around her and hugged, comforting her and each other. I'd never felt such bitterness, nor such sweetness.

'Fuck 'em all!' Lawrence shouted. 'We never gave anyone anything but respect, and all they've done is treat us like dogs and kill us one way or another. This all happened for no reason. Why did they do all this to us? Why? Tell me why?'

Alma and Myrtle joined, too, and it became a chorus: 'Why? Why? Why?'

'Why, my brother?' Lawrence asked me.

I racked my brains. Was there a reason? Why was I taken away? Why were we all taken? Why would they leave Dad on the floor of a prison cell? Why was Mum left to become so sick? Why did we have to spend our lives searching? I had no answers.

'There's no reason, brother,' I said. 'No reason.'

We cried ourselves to exhaustion in each other's embrace. We were quiet when the door opened, and there stood a smiling man who surveyed the scene. Then his eyes rested on me.

'Who's this?' he said with a thick accent.

'I'm Archie... Who are you?'

Arnold was Alma's partner and the father of her children, a German fella with a passion for cooking. He decided he would do what he knew best – he would cook us all a meal.

We ate delicious sauerkraut and pork knuckle and spätzle made by an expert. We drank more, too, and even if that didn't lift our moods, it muted them as it always did.

That Dight Street flat became the centre of my life.

We'd spend most days away from the flat, drinking in the park or the pubs, hearing stories about Aboriginal life and history and experience from the many men and women who came in and out of our group and in and out of Fitzroy. When the sun waned we'd return to the flat in Collingwood to eat and drink and talk. We'd sing together, too, and often I would play Lawrence's battered old guitar, which I tuned as best I could, and got a nice, unique sound from. It turned out almost all of the family liked the old, sad country songs that I loved. Hank Williams was a particular favourite.

We decided to name our Fitzroy 'drinking school' F Troop, because we used to love the show on television by the same name. It was an American Wild West satire about these bumbling cavalrymen, and we had a good laugh every time it was on.

One day, we went over to where Lawrence was staying to watch *F Troop*, and *Countdown* was on, hosted by Ian Molly Meldrum. We were sitting there, having a charge, when Molly introduced this band. The lead singer was a young whitefella. I'd seen a few university students and he looked like one.

We didn't pay much attention to him when he started playing, but the song eventually caught our attention. He kept on talking about 'standing on solid rock' and 'sacred ground'. I was thinking to myself, *This is Aboriginal. He's talking about Aboriginal land.* It got us all interested, and when the band finished we looked at each other and someone said, 'Ah, young white kid, what would he know about it?'

Old Pop Daley, the elder of the F Troop, turned to us and said, 'Hang on, when was the last time you heard a whitefella sticking up for Aboriginal people and land rights, telling it like it is?'

We all shook our heads. 'Never.'

'Well, you just heard it now. Give him a break.'

That whitefella was Shane Howard and his band Goanna. Little did I know that Shane would become a big part of my music life later on up the track, and a good friend.

Most of these days were spent at our meeting places in Fitzroy, which doubled as drinking spots where the demons were unlikely to find us. We named these places the Hole in the Wall, a secluded spot just off Smith Street, which could be accessed via a tumbledown wall, and Charcoal Lane, an alleyway off Smith Street, adjacent to a now-demolished briquette factory. They were our watering holes, our places to feel safe, our havens.

Charcoal Lane is where I met Jock.

I first saw him on one of those early days, under a blistering summer sun. He had a huge afro and moustache, and was wearing reflective shades, matching blue flares and singlet. He was a big fella, too, someone whose eyes you would catch. As soon as I saw him, I wondered who he was.

'I heard there's an Archie Roach down here,' he bellowed as he came into the lane. 'Where's Archie? Where's Archie Roach?'

Lawrence and the others shifted uneasily and turned away. I was left as the only one staring. He caught my gaze and strode towards me. I started to get more than a little worried. What did this man want from me?

'Lawrence, who's this...?' I began to ask, but the others were standing up and walking away.

The strange man doubled his pace and was on me, with a stern look on his face.

'I heard you were in Fitzroy,' he said in a steady, terrifying tone.

I didn't know what to say. He balled his fist, drew back his shoulder and swung. It was a two-action combination – the first was a punch that landed on my chest, and the second was a hug that came with a huge hairy smile.

'I've heard so much about you, Archie!'

Lawrence and the others came back and burst into laughter. They were all in on it! Lawrence explained that this man, Jock Austin, was my cousin, which was a huge relief.

Over the months I'd get to know Jock very well as a thoughtful and powerful man who loved his community, both down around Framlingham and in Fitzroy. His generation were pioneers, men like Johnny McGuinness and Bootsie Thorpe. They had lived hard lives that taught them the importance of community and family, but also self-control and self-determination. Before there was any government support for us mob, before the Aboriginal Health Service, these men took it upon themselves to help community in the ways they saw fit.

I remember one morning when Jock surprised me at the pub and told me he needed my help with something. He piled me into a van and said we were going to go round the boxing gyms and see if they'd give us any equipment they were about to throw out. He'd found a room on Gertrude Street that he planned to set up as a gym for young blackfellas coming into town, so they wouldn't simply gravitate to the pubs and parks.

Jock told me about his drinking days, which were now past him, and his boxing days, which were too but he remembered more fondly. I was amazed and heartened to find that most boxing gyms we visited contributed something to Jock, be it pads or gloves or a bag or two.

It didn't take long for Jock to get people into his little gym, which eventually became the Fitzroy All Stars gym, known today as the Melbourne Aboriginal Youth Sport and Recreation (MAYSAR) headquarters.

I reckoned one of the people Jock wanted to get out of the pubs and parks and into the gym was me, but I wasn't particularly interested in that. Dight Street was the centre of my life, and the Builders Arms and the Champion

Hotel. That's where my brothers and sisters were; that's where my life was. That's where the stories were.

I never lost interest in boxing, though, and I even fought for a short spell.

That all started at the Builders, where I was drinking with Lawrence.

'Ah, shit, it's Leachy,' he said.

I turned and looked, and saw a gnarled little white bloke scanning the pub. When he saw Lawrence, a salesman's smile crept across his face.

'Piss off, Leachy, we're not interested,' Lawrence yelled out before the man had even got to us.

'Let me get a jug and we'll have a chat,' he said.

Lawrence explained that the man was Billy Leach, a tent-boxing promoter who worked the shows around Victoria, but mainly in Gippsland. People like Leachy were showmen – like Jimmy Sharman, who toured our father. I wanted to learn everything Lawrence knew about our old man's experiences in the tents, but he didn't know much. He knew Dad was a good fighter, smart and rangy, and that he fought under the name 'Snowball', due to his wild, prematurely grey hair.

'He'll want us to go with him,' Lawrence said. 'He's all right, Leachy, but I can't be arsed. I'm not fit enough.'

Billy came back with a jug and after the introductions

and a few inquiries into Lawrence's health and circumstances, Billy went into his sell. Show season was starting. The truck was outside. He'd pay Lawrence five bucks a house and he could go home anytime. But Lawrence wasn't interested, and seemed adamant about it, too. So Leachy turned his interest to me.

'How about it, young fella? See a bit of the state and get a bit of money in your pocket?'

That didn't sound too bad to me.

'You've got to be careful, Archie,' Lawrence said, when Billy went to the bar again. 'They feed you some pretty big, strong farm boys. You can get hurt.'

'It was good enough for Dad. It's good enough for us,' I said.

'Yeah, but Dad was good,' Lawrence said.

Billy returned with more beer, and then more beer, and I think some wine, too. The next thing I remember after that was waking up in the back of Billy's truck.

Lawrence was annoyed too when he woke up but resigned.

'We'll do a house or two and piss off, right?' Lawrence said.

I nodded.

'What's in Gippsland?' I asked.

'Not much. Go to sleep, you'll need your rest.'

After a few moments Lawrence piped up again. 'We have family in Gippsland. Who knows, maybe we'll run into them.'

I tried to sleep, but a spark of excitement and curiosity kept me awake. Dad may never be able to tell me his stories, but now I was going to live through one of his experiences. I had no idea what was going to happen next, but I knew it would be an adventure.

Archie Roach Snr leading a boxing tutorial. The *Daily Examiner* in 1939 described 'Snowball' Roach as 'an experienced fighter of higher than ordinary ability . . . [He] has a good record in the fighting game, having appeared at Sydney and Melbourne stadiums, and he has also toured with Harry Johns and Jimmy Sharman.'

CHAPTER 6

RALLY ROUND THE DRUM (A. ROACH AND P. KELLY)

Like my brother before me
I'm a tent boxing man
Like our daddy before us
Travelling all around Gippsland
I woke up one cold morning
Many miles from Fitzroy
And slowly it came dawning
By Billy Leach I was employed
Rally round the drum boys
Rally round the drum
Every day, and every night boys
Rally round the drum

Hoisting tent poles and tarpaulin
Billy says 'now beat the drum'
Rings out across the show grounds
And all the people come
Then Billy starts a-calling
Step right up, step right up, step right up one and all
Is there anybody game here?
To take on Kid Snowball
Rally round the drum boys
Rally round the drum

Is there anybody game here?
Rally round the drum

Sometimes I'd fight a gee-man
Yeah, we'd put on a show
Sometimes I'd fight a hard man
Who wants to lay me low

Sometimes I get tired
But I don't ever grouse
I've got to keep on fighting
Five dollars every house

Rally round the drum boys
Rally round the drum
Every day, every night boys
Rally round the drum

Like my daddy before me
I set 'em up and knock 'em down

Like my brother before me
I'm weaving in your town

Rally round the drum boys
Rally round the drum
Rally round the drum boys
Rally round the drum
Rally round the drum boys
Rally round the drum

I woke to a big Aboriginal fella shaking my shoulder.

'Come on, time to get up.'

'Righto, Tundah,' Lawrence said, slowly rousing himself from sleep in the back of the truck.

Tundah was someone who Lawrence evidently knew. We were at Logan Park in Warragul, a small town a few hours east of Melbourne, where a wafting smell of fresh dung and bubbling fat was filling my nose. Show folk, vendors and farmers were in the early stages of setting up.

'First house is just after lunch,' Tundah said. 'Get something in your belly, then we'll get set up.'

There was no sign of Leachy as the three of us got the big tent up and lugged around hay bales that would serve as a ring and seats. Later he appeared with a group of young local fellas, fit and full of fight, who were going to box alongside Lawrence and me.

As the showground filled, Billy pushed all of us lads up on the boards next to the tent and handed one of the fellas a drum. To a steady drumbeat, Leachy called in a crowd like a siren.

'Step right up, step right up, ladies and gentlemen. What d'ya reckon! Is there anyone game here to take on one of these blokes? Step right up, step right up, and have a go if you think you're good enough. But be warned, you have to be good because these killers will lay you out!'

Billy Leach was a deadly showman. He walked his way down the line of fighters, selling the pugilistic virtues of each. He started with a fella he called the Brown Bomber. Next, was a gaunt and rugged local whitefella called Cowboy, who had the ears and nose of a brawler. He moved on to Lawrence, who he called Lachie Boy and claimed was dangerous, despite his impish grin. And then he got to me, the only fella on the boards who hadn't fought for Billy before. He fixed his face with a curious look and leant in close.

'What was your old man's name again?' he whispered.

'Hey?'

'Didn't your old man used to fight? What was his name?'

'He was Archie, too.'

'Snowball,' Lawrence jumped in. 'They used to call him Snowball.'

'*And here's Kid Snowball!*' Leachy hollered. 'More fights than feeds, this fella. He's as deadly as he is young.'

After my introduction, a young bloke was pushed forward by the gathering crowd, who cheered loudly as Billy Leach caught the newcomer's eye.

'You wanna fight, young fella?'

This kid, a farm boy with choppy ginger hair and splotches of freckles, nodded unconvincingly.

'Who do you want to fight?' Billy asked as he waved his arm at the fighters behind him.

The farm boy raised an uncertain finger that fell in my general direction. There was another cheer from the crowd.

'Gloves on, then!' Billy hollered.

With a full and baying tent, this kid and I faced off. As soon as Billy rang the bell, I could tell my opponent had no heart for the fight. I stepped into his range, inviting him to engage, but he did nothing. I gave him a light jab on the nose, but that didn't rouse him, either. I clinched with him and asked if he was all right. He nodded. I told him to have a go, that I wasn't going to hurt him.

I broke the clinch and threw a few little punches to the ribs, nothing too vicious. That did get him going a bit, and he did get to my head a couple of times, but he wasn't much of an athlete and couldn't get any weight behind his punches.

He started to look exhausted, and in the next clinch I told him I was going to give him one on the chin. It wouldn't be too hard, but he should go down. And he did just that after not much more than a love tap, and the crowd yelled their approval.

I didn't get called up in the next house; instead, I got to watch Lawrence fight from his corner. He was a natural, with a fast tongue and quick fists that landed on a local man easily.

In the third house I was chosen by another farm boy with few boxing skills, but unlike my first opponent this kid was game, fast and fit. He moved around me, left and right, tiring me out as I threw punches to his head. I tried to keep up with him but found it impossible. Eventually, with my hands down and my chest heaving, he clattered a big right into my forehead and I dropped on the floor.

His mates rushed in to congratulate him, and when one of them peeled me off the floor he consoled me, saying there was no shame in losing since this guy was a good athlete.

I asked what his sport was and they told me it was tennis.

Tennis! I vowed never to play the game of fists with a good athlete whose sport was not boxing.

The next morning, as we were packing up the tent in preparation for the move to the next town, Leachy came over and told me he was going to give me a 'plant' in the first house of the day. Maybe he'd seen I was still a bit rocked from the evening before. Lawrence explained that a plant was someone in the crowd who was with us, a Gee Man, someone who was there to gee up the crowd and wasn't going to hurt me. I asked what I had to do, and he told me to go out there and put on a show, as if I was fighting for real.

'Throw most of your punch but leave that last little bit, then keep going with the follow-through.'

He also told me to give an oversized reaction from anything the other fella landed.

We moved on to Nar Nar Goon, closer to Melbourne. In the first show, the plant was a strong whitefella who levelled a big finger in my direction to the roars and hoots of the crowd. As he stood, he revealed himself to be quite a considerable unit, and as I raised my gloves I hoped he wasn't going to get caught up in the moment.

I danced and he slugged as we flew around the makeshift ring. The crowd cheered and I marvelled at how easy it was to fake a fight. I had no experience at all pulling punches, but the crowd loved it when a half-speed punch harmlessly bounced off this big man's gloves and sent him flying to the dirt.

You could only have so many plants, though, and so many fixed fights. My next fight was a real one, and one that was also real memorable.

I saw my opponent while I was up on the boards, with the drum thrumming and Leachy's routine in my ears.

'He's had more fights than feeds this one. Who'll take on Kid Snowball?'

It was my opponent's hair that first caught my eye. It was long, dark and straight.

'I'll take him on,' he said with a scowl.

'Good man!' Leachy exclaimed. 'Kid Snowball will be taking on…'

'People call me Geronimo,' he said. With his dark complexion and hair, I figured this was a Native American fella, but found out later that this was just a name given to him because of his appearance.

As Tundah helped me pull on my gloves, I looked for Lawrence, who had cornered me in all my fights but now was nowhere to be seen. Soon, I was face to face with Geronimo, fighting.

He had the best of the opening exchange, starting with a gambit I'm not sure I've ever seen since in a boxing match. He swung two simultaneous hooks, thoroughly confusing my defence. Both landed.

My temples rang, my mind raced, and my mouth formed five words: 'What the hell was that?'

Geronimo was giggling and dancing around, and it was then that I decided I very much wanted to win this fight. I put my gloves next to my eyes, tucked my elbows by my side and went in, bobbing, feinting and weaving, until a gap opened up just below this fella's ribs. I ripped in as hard as I could and could feel his bone against my knuckles.

I moved away feeling satisfied, but when I looked at Geronimo he was smiling and shaking his head, as though to say, *You'll have to do a little bit better than that.* The crowd loved it, and hoots and hollers started raining down on us.

I really wanted to land one of my punches on his chin and moved forward again, but as I did, I saw Lawrence in the corner of my eye. He was waving and trying to tell me something. A long, strong right-hand sailed towards me, and I only managed to miss it with microseconds to spare.

I threw the last of my energy into a combination that clattered into Geronimo's guard until my arms fell limp and the bell for the round ended. I trudged to my corner where I thought I'd find Lawrence, but he was nowhere to be seen. I turned to look for him and found him in Geronimo's corner, laughing and having all kinds of fun.

The bell sounded for the new round and Geronimo danced forward just as he had for the first. He drew his arms back as though he was once again going to throw double hooks, and I brought my arms up in defence. This time, however, he didn't aim for my head but instead around my body, holding me close for a hug.

'Lawrence told me you're his brother,' he said. 'Bud, I'm Arthur, your cousin, your mum is my mum's sister.' He broke the embrace. 'I can't believe I gave my own cousin the Tomahawk.'

I guess he was referring to that double-handed punch.

The crowd grew more confused when Lawrence jumped into the ring and hugged the both of us. Then Leachy jumped in and declared the fight a draw. The crowd seemed happy enough.

After that house, Lawrence told Leachy that he and I were done. We took our pay of five dollars per house, went to Arthur's place and got nice and drunk. We hung out with Arthur for the next week and parted ways when the money ran dry. Lawrence and I thanked him for his hospitality and jumped on a train heading back to Melbourne.

I never boxed again, but I reckon Max was right – it did mean something to be able to raise your hands in the ring with another man. I was no boxer, but I learnt just a little of that boxing wisdom. There was art and science in pugilism, and also equality. Once you're in the ring, the colour of your skin is no impediment; boxing is a great equaliser.

I'm glad I had a run with Billy Leach and felt a bit of what Dad had felt a few decades earlier, and so many of the men in our family. It was great to meet cousin Arthur and have had this adventure with Lawrence, too.

Back in Fitzroy I quickly fell into the old routine. Drinking was what we did.

I got myself a job, though, working for the Collingwood Council, ripping up pathways so they could be replaced. It was hard, sweaty work but I liked it, especially the satisfaction I felt at the end of the day, seeing all that had been achieved since the morning.

Work was never a priority; family and drinking went first, and in that period those two things were inseparable. I got paid every Thursday after work and, without fail, when I'd come out of the gate of the council facility at the end of the day, Lawrence was there with a collection of cousins.

He'd always give me that cheeky grin.

'What, I can't come and say hello to my little brother after he finishes work?' he'd deadpan, and then it would be off to the Builders or the Champion. We always got good and drunk on Thursdays, and then it was hard to get to work on Friday morning sober.

'Archie, I reckon you're pissed,' my boss told me one morning as I was finding it difficult to walk steady and get my words in a straight line.

'I…I'm sorry.' There was no point in lying.

He sent me home with a warning. No days were easy, keeping up my drinking and work, but Fridays were always the most difficult, so I asked the boss if he could hold on to my pay every Thursday for twenty-four hours. That way I could get my money for the weekend instead and have that become the start of my drinking week.

That helped a bit, but I was still a pretty unreliable employee, and after a few weeks I quit.

Soon, an Aboriginal employment office opened in Fitzroy, and I picked up a few jobs from the posting board there. I never kept any of them for long. I was a drinker who worked, not the other way round. My life in Fitzroy and Collingwood was sharing wine and beer, and singing songs and telling stories, and that life was sometimes rudely interrupted by work, or hospital visits, or maybe even a run-in with the demons.

I always thought work could be a bit of a gateway to something a little bit different, though. *Maybe.* Maybe if the right job ever turned up at the right time. Then one day it did.

Seasonal fruit pickers needed. Mildura, Victoria.

This I could do. I'd break out of the orbit of drinking; far enough away that I wouldn't always want to drink and have fun, but close enough that I could come back to family if the yearning got too much. It was short-term work so I'd be back soon, but I'd have a bit of cash in my pocket and a clear head. From there, I could figure out what I wanted to do next.

I called the number for the job and told them I reckoned I could be there in a week or so. The farmer on the phone said that would be great; they were about to start the sultana pick and they needed as many hands as they could get.

I came home and told everyone what I was going to do and was relieved to find that they knew exactly what I was talking about. It seemed most of my family had done at least a season or two of picking. Lawrence had even picked in Mildura before, and when he told me I lit up.

'Come with me, brother!' I had a vision of the two of us with sweat on our brows, smiles on our faces and money in our pockets.

'Nah, it's shit work. Too hot, too hard. You don't want to do that,' Lawrence said.

His words didn't dampen my enthusiasm. I told Lawrence I wanted to go anyway and he just shrugged.

'I'll see ya soon.'

He wouldn't, though. My trip wasn't going to be at all what I'd expected.

I packed a bag and headed for the highway. I started walking vaguely in the direction of Echuca, which I hoped would be my first stop, with my thumb out. A few Fitzroy people told me that there was a good community of blackfellas there, and that it was on the way to Mildura. They said it was a nice spot to break the journey up.

It took me less than a day and only a handful of rides to get there.

When I first got to Echuca, I went to the American Hotel, where I was told I'd likely find other Aboriginal people. I did, and a couple of beers later I was invited to spend some time at a camp down the river.

It was great down there. They had a few tents set up, and had thrown some fishing lines in the water, but apart from that, I reckoned the bush was the way it had been for thousands of years. I hadn't thought much about how we'd lived before the Europeans came, but I thought about it then, and I couldn't help but think a bit about who I was, and who we were.

I knew very little about the old ways. But I tell you, it always felt good to meet a group of blackfellas.

That evening we pulled fish from the river, got them straight onto a fire and then ate them fresh, hot and delicious. With the white flesh in my mouth, I thought about how life would have been for my people living safely in the bush, where they belonged, in the years prior to 1788.

For a moment I imagined a life where booze didn't exist. That wasn't the world we lived in, though, and down at the camp we had beer bottles cooling in the river, which I happily drank when offered.

I don't remember the names of any of the people at that camp, except for a woman named Gladys, to whom I said 'Beautiful name' without telling her why, and Brian, a fella who I'll never forget.

A little further away was another camp where an older Aboriginal fella lived. He drew incredible pencil sketches of local people and places, and sometimes sold them in town to buy supplies.

'Bit of flour for damper, to go with the fish I catch, some salt, pepper and tea. I don't need much,' he told me when we got to talking about what his life was like. 'I'm happier here on the river than in town. You can get in a bit of trouble in town.'

He was right.

A few days after arriving I was ready to leave Echuca and planned to end my time in the town the way I'd started it – drinking at the American Hotel. I was going to drink my fill with my new friends, wake up with the sun and start the hitch, hoping to get to Mildura before dusk.

I don't know exactly when Brian arrived at the pub, but I know it was dark outside and I was very drunk inside. I remember him telling me he had to go to Mildura himself, to pick up his cousin and bring him back home. I remember Brian saying he was leaving soon, in his car. I remember wondering out loud where he'd got a car from, and I remember being told it was his uncle's.

I remember getting in the car, in the back seat, and lying down. The next thing I remember is a bright light shining in my face.

I didn't know what was going on, or where we were, except that it was still night-time, and we were stopped. Then I heard a voice coming from behind the light.

'Come on, get out of the car.'

I got out of the car and saw cops and flashing lights... but no sign of Brian.

I knew instantly what was going on. I have no idea why, but every policeman in the country seems to have the same cadence, the same character in their voice when talking to us.

'Come on,' the policeman with the torch said, leading me to his car. 'Let's go.'

'Go where?'

'We're going to Echuca.'

'No, I'm on my way to Mildura to pick fruit.'

But I wasn't on my way to Mildura to pick fruit; I was on my way to a police station to be charged with car theft. I told them what I knew – that Brian had got this car from his uncle, and that he'd picked me up from the pub, and we were going to Mildura; me to work and him to pick up a cousin. I asked them to speak to Brian; he'd tell them that regardless of where we got the car from, I had nothing to do with it. I didn't know anything about it at all. But it fell on deaf ears. They didn't seem to care.

I didn't get any legal representation in those couple of days in the cells in Echuca, where I spent time pleading my case to a number of disinterested policemen and cursing out Brian and my dumb luck.

Eventually one of the cops came to tell me I was going in front of a magistrate to face a charge of being an accessory to car theft. I told him I was going to tell the judge I had nothing to do with it. The policeman advised me, in what I still believe he thinks was good faith, to plead guilty.

'Look, mate, you've been caught red-handed. It will be easier on you if you plead guilty, you'll probably get a lesser sentence.'

I got to the courthouse and my blood was boiling.

I couldn't believe I was going to be sent down again. Everything happened very quickly after that. The charge was read, I pled guilty, and I was convicted. I stared straight ahead throughout, except when the magistrate told me I was going to jail for a year, with the possibility of parole after seven months. I still didn't say anything, because there was no point in saying anything, but I shook my head.

It was bullshit. I had done nothing wrong. It was bullshit then and it's bullshit now.

The next day I was ferried from my cell in Echuca to Her Majesty's Prison Pentridge, a more than a century old slab of bluestone in the Melbourne suburb of Coburg. I was taken immediately to J-Block, where most of the younger prisoners were, and the first thing I looked out for was plumbing, which I found to my immense relief. Whatever was in store for the next who-knew-how-long, at least I wasn't going to be lugging around pails of other men's shit.

I got to Pentridge perhaps three or four days after I'd been peeled out of the back of what I thought was Brian's uncle's car, so it had been at least seventy-two hours since I'd had a drink. Maybe adrenaline and nerves had kept me together in Echuca, but now in Pentridge, with my circumstances set, I started to get crook.

The sickness took me real bad. I was vomiting anything I ate or drank, sweating through my sheets when I lay down and barely able to move out of my cell when ordered to do so. There were some other Aboriginal fellas in my block who'd experienced what I was going through, and they told me good news and bad news. The bad news was that there was no way of feeling better except by gritting my teeth and getting days behind me, but the good news was that, in a week or so, I'd find a day that felt just a little bit better than the day before. Then the day after that would be even better.

They were right. First, I felt okay, then I felt good, and eventually I felt incredible. I'd gone through some very long days and nights, but when I got to the other side, I found a place I'd completely forgotten. I felt strong, I felt awake. I felt young again.

I *was* young, but I'd forgotten what it felt like to *be* young. I went to the gym, and I ran. I started to enjoy sweating, and that buzz as I took a shower after exercise. My body began to work properly again, as well as my mind. The first was a good thing, but I'm not sure the second was.

With a clear mind I looked around the prison and I saw all the wasted days, months and years.

I started thinking about my life and the path

I'd chosen. There were a lot of us blackfellas here at 'Bluestone College'. We were criminals, our bodies and minds controlled within the prison walls, but we were also treated as criminals outside.

You don't start out as a criminal. I started to think, *Who makes the rules? Who decides and who benefits? Why are we treated the way we have been?* I'd been asleep when I was grabbed and forced in there without any legal representation. The screws told us 'yoggies', as the young fellas of J-Block were collectively known, not to get too friendly with the older blokes, but we couldn't help but spend time with them in the exercise yard.

In the yard I became friends with an older Aboriginal fella called Bobby, who was one of the long-termers. He'd done his cell up like a little apartment, with pictures and knick-knacks, and also a guitar. I spent long hours in Bobby's cell, strumming away with him, singing country music songs. Bobby liked Hank Williams and Charley Pride, whose simple songs with honest lyrics said everything we could never say to each other. These songs were places we could meet. Even though we were imprisoned, singing would take us away somewhere else.

People didn't talk much about what they'd done to be in Pentridge, but Bobby told me he'd killed a man. He didn't mean to, but he did mean to hurt. He was sorry.

I felt for Bobby, but I felt for the man he'd killed, too.

My mind clogged up in prison, trying to make sense of it all. I had to try to keep my thoughts from going sour, so I boxed in the gym, and ran and read anything I could get my hands on, becoming especially fond of a cowboy series about a couple of whitefellas called Larry and Stretch, who had endless battles against black hats and corrupt lawmen in the wilds of 1800s Texas and Arizona.

With the right amount of running and reading I'd shrink my head, focusing into one, singular thought:

I'm never going back to prison again.

I'm never going back to prison again.

I'm never going back to prison again.

I repeated that mantra over and over as I was granted my early release, and again as I pulled on my own clothes, and again as I took my gate money, and again as I walked out the gates of Pentridge.

Just outside the prison was Sydney Road, where trams rattled north to Craigieburn and south to Carlton and home. I was so close to family, I could even go back to Fitzroy if I really wanted to, but I'd left home for a reason. The seven intervening months hadn't changed that. In fact, when I walked out of Pentridge it was like unpausing a song that had been halted when I was driven in; I once again became that person who had crashed out in the back of the car on my way to Mildura with Brian.

After only a few steps from the gate, another thought emerged:

I could use a drink.

There was a reason behind the madness of this thought. I felt good, and I wanted to stay feeling good, but I was a young fella who'd been locked up for more than half a year. I hated the control they'd had on me, and having a beer now would be seizing back control of what I wanted to do. *I'll have just one*, I thought, on my own at the nearest pub. *One beer and then I'll walk out.*

And that's exactly what I did.

I felt pretty good about myself after that and decided the rest of my gate money was going on a bus fare. I had set off for Mildura seven months earlier, and Mildura I would reach.

I caught a bus to Seymour, and then another to Echuca. When I was dropped off, I went down to the river to see if I could find Brian. Several months of my life were gone. I had no retribution in mind; I just wanted to ask Brian why.

Why?

I could only find the old fella who sold his drawings in town. He said no one had seen Brian for months. No one knew where he was. I didn't tell him what had happened.

The telling was Brian's business.

With my gate money getting low I stuck my thumb out on the highway leading to Mildura. I got as far as Swan Hill on my first ride, and while walking down the road looking for a second, I met an Aboriginal bloke with a flagon of port under his arm.

'You want a charge, brother?' he asked when he saw me.

I didn't, but I didn't want to offend him either.

'Ah, you got the good stuff there, brother. I used to drink that in Melbourne,' I said.

'I used to drink in Melbourne. What's your name, bud?'

I told him my name, and he asked me if knew a Roach lad by the name of Lawrence. Shortly afterwards I was as drunk as I'd ever been.

When I woke up the next day, I was back to square one. I was sick and trembling and couldn't wait to scratch the itch. That triumphant moment of being able to have one beer in a pub and walk out may as well have been a lifetime ago. I was stinging for another drink, but I also knew I had to keep moving. I could still taste that prison food and felt danger in my blood.

I hitched all the way to Mildura and turned up at the address I'd seen on that jobs board back in Fitzroy. I was greeted by a friendly bloke who told me that I'd missed the sultana season, but they were about to pick the shiraz grapes. He asked me if I'd be keen on doing that, and I told him there was no difference between a sultana grape and shiraz grape as far as I was concerned.

That evening I slept in my own little hut, with a radio and a fridge stacked with food, a day's work ahead of me.

On the advice of the farmer, I was up very early the next day, picking grapes off those bushes before the sun could get too high and too hot. We were paid by volume and could work the hours that we wanted, so I kept a routine up of early to bed and early to rise.

When the first payday came, I asked the boss to hold on to my money for me, most of it anyway. They were covering my food and board, so I told him I just wanted enough to get some cigarettes and wine and books. He was happy to do that, and it worked for me.

I went into town sometimes, to buy books at the second-hand bookstore there on the main street, and met some fellas who would drink in town, but I was careful not to spend too much time with them in the pubs or parks. I was wary, seeing the cop cars roll around town, slowing when they saw us blackfellas. I saw the demons, saw the booze, and saw Pentridge again.

I was done with prison.

I kept up my drinking, but I did so in my hut, listening to music and thinking my own thoughts. I liked the other pickers and was happy to have a chat to them here and there, but I wanted to keep to myself as much as I could. I had my own place, the first I'd ever had, kept my own hours, and came and went as I chose. It was a good time for me after those long months in prison.

The season seemed to end quickly and abruptly, which isn't to say I wasn't sick of pulling grapes off a branch under the hot sun. I thanked the farmer and was out the door, with a bit of money in my pocket and a broad horizon of possibilities.

I walked out to the highway with thoughts only of the places I'd been before. I thought about going back to Echuca, to see if Brian was there so I could ask him the questions that still bounced around my head. Or should I go to Shepparton for a bit and see who was still there? Should I go back to Melbourne and see the family? I did wonder what everyone was up to.

I had a few dollars in my pocket, and I reckoned if I went back to Fitzroy, it would only go to booze. I had no obligations, so maybe I should just throw myself to the wind and see where I would land. If I didn't like it, I could always go back home, where I was pretty sure nothing would have changed.

I walked along the highway, my bag on my shoulder and a smoke in my mouth. A decision had to be made, and all options seemed equally good. Melbourne and home? It would be deadly to see Lawrence and my sisters, but who knew what treasures another destination might bring?

I kept walking until I saw a sign that said 'Adelaide'. I knew nothing about Adelaide or South Australia, and all of a sudden that hit me as a pretty good reason to go. What would the blackfellas there be like?

I was struck by indecision, so I stuck my hand in my pocket and pulled out a twenty-cent coin. I decided that heads would mean Adelaide and tails, Melbourne.

The spin sent me west, and I reckon few men have ever gained more from a simple coin-flip. See, there was a girl waiting for me in Adelaide, one who would change my life forever.

I stuck my thumb out and made my way across the border, with every hour I spent in the back of charitable people's trucks and cars taking me closer to the city, to her.

These would be the last hours before finding Ruby Hunter.

Photo of Ruby Hunter by Maree Clarke.

Me and Ruby from a 1993 *Age* article about Aboriginal identity. Photo by Mike Bowers.

CHAPTER 7

NOPUN KURONGK (GO TO THE RIVER)

Don't say goodbye
My child
And always look behind you
To that beautiful wild
And all the things that remind you
Of being free
That remind you of being free
Nopun kurongk, Nukun kurongk

Oh I sang my song
To some children in Meningie
And a feeling so strong
Started coming over me
Like I was free
Yeah it felt like I was free
Nopun kurongk, Nukun kurongk

My grandmother I can see
Wrapped around her taraki
Standing safely on the shore
Underneath the dress she wore

We were hidden secretly from the welfare 'cause you see
Granny knew they'd taken children

Many times before
Nopun kurongk, Nukun kurongk
Nopun kurongk, Nukun kurongk

Say goodbye to my pain
These city shadows chill me to the bone
Oh I'm going back again
To that place where they took me from
To my home
Lord, oh I feel like going home
Nopun kurongk, Nukun kurongk

Go to the river
Look to the river

After a couple of hours walking, a truck stopped and the driver asked, 'Adelaide?'

I couldn't believe my luck.

It only took an afternoon to get there, and they were fast hours, too. The truck driver dropped me off within distant sight of the CBD skyline.

'I'm going to the port, but if you get off here and go back that way you'll be close to the city,' he said. 'You right? Got everything you need?'

I told him I did, thanked him and walked on. I could see the city so I chose not to hitch, but it took a few hours to hit the shade of those big buildings.

I had a pretty good feeling when I got to the middle of the city. I made my way to the Torrens River because that seemed like a nice spot to sit and contemplate what to do next.

I saw some black swans on the river and sat there on the bank, with a couple of bottles of port, watching the birds and wondering what I'd find in the city. Blackfellas hopefully, but what would they be like? I felt free, and ready again for opportunity to take me. When night fell, I crawled into some shrubs on a hill just behind me and crashed.

When I woke, I had a charge. I wandered around the river, and then up King William Street, but there were no blackfellas to be seen. It started to get really hot. The heat was prickling my skin, creating tiny beads of sweat all over my body. The grog was oozing out of me.

I took refuge on the steps of the post office nearby, waiting for the bottle shops to open, when I heard a voice saying hello. Once my eyes had adjusted to the light, I saw this little grey-haired gentleman.

'Hey,' I replied, wondering what this old whitefella wanted.

'Are you so and so?' he asked.

'No, old fella, I'm not – I'm not even from here. I got in last night.' It was then that I noticed some Aboriginal people gathering in the park opposite the post office.

'Oh, where did you stay?' he persisted

I was getting annoyed so I snapped. 'I slept in the park near the river, all right!'

'Calm down,' he said. 'I can help you with accommodation till you're on your feet, if you like?'

That dear fella got me two weeks' free accommodation at the People's Palace, a grand old hotel run by the Salvation Army.

It was built as a club for German immigrants in the mid-nineteenth century, but now it had served for almost a hundred years as a place where those who don't have anywhere else to stay can sleep. There was kindness on the road, and apparently there was kindness in the city too.

My room was on the fourth floor. There was a lift but it was like a cage where you could see the gears, cogs, cables, everything. A little scary, I thought, so I used the stairs.

I bought a flagon of port and a packet of smokes and spent the whole day and night in my room, drinking, smoking and reading a book I'd found downstairs. Before I crashed, I thought about meeting the local blackfellas tomorrow.

I woke up the next day with a light in my face and panic filled my veins.

'No! I didn't do nothing wrong!' I said, sitting bolt upright.

When my eyes and mind straightened out, I saw that it wasn't a torch aimed at me but the morning sun from the window. My eyes began to focus on the room and I could see a sink with a small mirror on the wall above it, and the medium-sized bed I was sitting on. Outside, I could hear the awakening city and wondered where the hell I was. I reached for my wallet, reassured that most of the money I'd earned in Mildura was still there, then retraced my footsteps.

It slowly came together – the truck driver, the river, the old whitefella, the People's Palace.

I was in Adelaide, and I reckon I'd been here about two days already. It had been a long time since I'd tried to get close to strangers. I worried about where I'd start here in this city.

I calmed down a bit, had a slug from the bottle and felt the excitement of being in a new place. I resolved that, by the end of the day, I would have met some local blackfellas.

It took me quite a few more slugs from the bottle before I managed to find the courage to head out. I was coming down the last flight of stairs to the foyer when suddenly the lift door opened. I was there at exactly the right time.

I can still see her in my mind today. I can see the look on her face: intense, intelligent and kind. I can see her eyes: wide, deep and dark brown, and I can see the most beautiful, round checks I reckon I've ever seen, all framed by waves of dark hair. I can see her blue dress cut just below her knees, and a white cardigan, and matching white socks disappearing into black shoes.

She looked about my age. Our eyes met and then averted. She was with an older couple, so I approached the man and asked, 'Where do all the blackfellas drink?'

Before he could speak, though, this girl jumped in.

'So you want to know where all the blackfellas hang out? This is Mick, and her name is Missy. And I'm Ruby. Follow me.'

So I joined them, and on our way Ruby asked me about myself. I told her my name, and where I'd been over the last few months, and where I was from. Ruby was particularly interested in hearing about my time in Fitzroy, and the community there.

We arrived at a place called Victoria Square, diagonally across from the post office where I'd been sitting the day before. It was familiar; it could have been Fitzroy. Uncles and aunties, young men and women having a charge, sitting around yarning, telling jokes and just being together.

The yarn that day was about the coppers who had come to the park the day before, grabbed a couple of the fellas and chucked them in the divvy van but left the door open.

These fellas had run away, going to the office of Don Dunstan, then treasurer of South Australia and soon to be premier.

'If the cops give you a hard time, Mr Dunstan is the fella to talk to,' one of the uncles told me. 'That's his office over there.' He pointed to a building nearby.

'He's a good one,' another said.

From then on I realised that there were influential people like Mr Dunstan, who cared about us mob drinking in the park.

Later in the day, we went from the Square to the Carrington Hotel, and just before the pub closed we went looking for a pie-floater van. That's where I had my first pie-floater – a meat pie in a bed of mushy peas and tomato sauce. Absolutely delicious. I scoffed it down. Oh yeah!

All the while I found myself gravitating towards Ruby, the girl in the blue dress.

Eventually I crashed, trashed, at the People's Palace. That day was repeated again and again. I became good friends with Mick and Missy and the others in the Square and Carrington Hotel. But the rapport I built up with

Ruby was something else altogether.

I wanted to be close to her wherever we went.

I was fascinated by Ruby and felt comfortable around her, and even though I was a quiet person and didn't talk much, I could talk to her. She never seemed to tire of my company.

Our stories felt like they overlapped in uncanny ways. One time I shared with her that I'd gone on *The Happy Hammond Show* when I was in primary school. A school friend had been given tickets for his birthday and invited me to go along with him and his family to the Channel 7 studios to sit in the audience. Happy Hammond – in his tartan jacket, matching hat and thin moustache – hosted a popular children's variety show that featured personalities like Princess Panda, Lovely Anne and Sylvester the Talking Sock. Towards the end of the show, they'd pan the camera around the audience and we were asked to smile. There was a special circular framing effect on the lens, with the aim being that the circle would stop on the child with the best smile.

I could see the camera moving, panning through the audience, until it fell on me. Then it continued to move until it returned to my beaming face.

'I used to watch *The Happy Hammond Show!*' Ruby said. 'I saw that one! I even turned to my foster mum and said, "I'm going to marry that boy."'

I said, 'Nah, stop it, Ruby, that's crazy mad,' but she swore it was true.

In those early days Ruby looked after me; she'd ask how I was going. She'd come up with some money and go buy a roast chook and some bread and put it in front of me, making sure I had something to eat, often before she did. It was that same nurturing spirit I remember from my time with the Coxes and when I met my sisters.

I started playing music again in Adelaide. One day a fella called Billy came by the Square with a guitar. He asked everyone if they could play, and when it came to me I was charged up enough to say that I could. I tuned the guitar a bit and strummed away. The guitar was quite old but had a really nice sound. Billy liked that, but what he really wanted was a song.

'Maybe later,' I said, trying to hand the guitar back.

'No, keep it until you're ready,' he said.

When I had a few more sips I sang an old country song called 'Crystal Chandeliers', made popular by Charlie Pride. It told the story of a heartbroken man whose one-time girlfriend became a social butterfly and left him.

When I finished the song everyone asked for another,

including Ruby, so I sang 'Today I Started Loving You Again' by Merle Haggard.

While I played that second song a crowd started to build, and I could feel one of the old fellas hanging over my shoulder. I started to get a little nervous and sped the song up a bit too much at the end, but it didn't seem that anyone cared.

'More, bud, more! Let's have another song now.'

'Leave him alone!' Ruby said, grabbing the guitar and handing it back to Billy. 'He'll sing when he wants to.'

It felt good having Ruby look out for me like that. I liked it then, and I'd like it for decades to come.

'That was deadly, brus,' Billy said.

'The guitar has a nice sound. Got a bit of soul to it,' I said.

Billy tried to hand the guitar back to me but I refused. 'I don't really feel like playing any more, Billy.'

'No, no, I want you to have the guitar.'

'I can't take that.'

'It only cost me twenty bucks, and I can't make it sound that good. You should have it... please. If you tell me you'll play some more songs on another day, you'll be doing me a favour.'

I looked at Ruby and she nodded. So I took Billy's guitar and thanked him. The truth was it was good to have a guitar in my hands again so I could play it when I felt like it.

I'd play music for Ruby from then on, and for the others. I wasn't the only person who could play guitar – there was one young fella who was a far superior player than me, able to pick his way through nearly any song you cared to name – but it seemed I was the fella who could give you a song.

My two weeks at the People's Palace flew by. I realised I had to find some other accommodation. So I asked Mick. He got me a room at a boarding house and helped me get a job at a foundry just outside the city.

That job was real work – all molten metal, blistering heat and endless noise – but it felt good to be working again. I knew the job wouldn't last, so I hoarded as much of my pay as I could, knowing that my drinking would again become my priority. I lasted at the foundry for six weeks or so. It didn't take long until my coffers were low and I had to decide whether to pay for my room or pay for a train ticket back to Melbourne.

But I wasn't ready to go. I wanted to get to know Ruby more. I didn't relish the idea of sleeping rough again, so was very relieved when a man came by the Square one day, looking for able-bodied men to work on a construction site just outside the city in the Adelaide Hills.

They were building a camp for young offenders, a place where they could get some fresh air away from the city and get their heads straight.

With the dark thoughts of Pentridge still fresh in my memory, that sounded like a great idea. I felt good that we were building a place in the Hills for young offenders, some of whom would be young local Nunga fellas. They would be among the trees and animals in a quiet place. I hoped that I was helping them find peace and that gave me some peace.

I gave my guitar to the publican of the Carrington Hotel and asked him to hold onto it until I got paid.

I began work in Stirling in the Adelaide Hills and stayed out that way. I made friends with one of the other workers, an older Italian man named Sam. He must have figured out my circumstances and started bringing enough lunch for the two of us.

Lunchtime became heaven for me, and I'd count down the hours until I'd get to tuck into fresh crusty bread, cheese, olives and cold meat. To this day, it's one of my favourite meals. Sometimes Sam would bring me homemade wine, too, fermented from apricots.

After work, I'd pretend to all the fellas that I was going back to the city like they were. But I'd head to the little camp I'd set up under a bridge nearby, eating a dinner of crisp, sour apples from a nearby tree washed down with Sam's wine.

I was happy there. Don't get me wrong, I was looking forward to getting paid and sleeping with a roof over my head, but I appreciated those quiet nights, my only company being my own thoughts.

I tell you, though, I missed Ruby, especially when I started drifting off. Her face would emerge with those big brown eyes, her cheeks bunching up on either side of a broad smile, and with that image I'd go to sleep.

As soon as I got my first pay, I came back to the city and went straight to the Carrington Hotel, where they were happy to cash my cheque. It was where Ruby was as well.

'Where have you been, Archie Roach?' she asked.

'You know, I'm working in the Hills, Ruby.'

I told her about the bridge and the apples, Sam and his wine – everything. But maybe not how I felt about her, not just yet.

'Well, I'm glad you're back. I wanted to introduce you to some people.'

And in the next days and weeks she did just that, introducing me to uncles, aunties, cousins and friends, all connected in a giant web of family that Ruby untangled for me as best she could.

Then one day there was some shouting in the park, with my name ringing out.

'*Archie Roach!* I heard there's an Archie Roach round here. Where's Archie Roach?'

A tiny little woman with wild, woolly hair was stomping through the park with purpose.

'Who's this mad woman?' I asked Ruby.

'Don't say that, Archie. That's Aunty Sissy – she's one of our Elders.'

'Archie Roach! Are you Archie Roach?' Aunty Sissy said after someone had pointed me out.

I reluctantly told her I was.

She looked at me with a grin. 'I used to wipe your shitty arse and blow your snotty nose, Archie Roach!'

I had no idea what she was talking about until we sat down and she told me her story.

See, a long time ago, Aunty Sissy used to live in Victoria. She was in Mooroopna for a spell, and so too were Mum and Dad, who were picking fruit in Shepparton while living in a camp on the Broken River. When I was a little fella, Mum and Dad used to send the others off to school and then go to work, leaving me to be looked after by Aunty Sissy who, apparently, used to wipe my shitty arse and blow my snotty nose.

This was all news to me.

'Mooroopna, close to Shepparton?' I asked.

'That's the one.'

I'd been to very few places in my life, but the riverbanks in Mooroopna were one of them. I couldn't believe that my travels had taken me to the place where I was born. It seems Aunty Sissy had known Mum and Dad very well, and when I asked her to tell me something about them, the one memory that stood out for her was that Dad never wore shoes.

'Even on Sunday, he'd be dressed up in a suit going to church, but with nothing on ankles down.' She shrieked with laughter. 'Never did get the hang of wearing anything on his feet.'

This was exactly what I was looking for, pieces for the jigsaw puzzle of my life, my history, in the hope that if I got enough of them a picture would form.

'How do you know Aunty Sissy?' I asked Ruby later.

'She used to look after me, too, back in the Riverland. She's Ngarrindjeri, like me.'

'What does that mean – Ngarrindjeri?'

'That's us. That's our clan, our people, the people from the Murray River and the Coorong. That's our mob.'

I asked about the Coorong, as I'd not heard of it before.

'It's the place where the Murray River meets the sea,'

she said. She told me about the giant sand dunes there, and the wetlands and different types of animals, like freshwater turtles, sand dragons and sea eagles.

'That's our place,' she said. 'The place where us Ngarrindjeri are from. Maybe I'll take you one day.'

The idea of Ruby taking me to her place made me blush, but it also made me wonder if I had a mob.

'Are you all Ngarrindjeri? Mick and Missy and everyone?'

Pretty much everyone was. As I'd meet people round the Square I'd ask about their mob, and most were Ngarrindjeri. It occurred to me that this was a Ngarrindjeri meeting place, where Ngarrindjeri people could piece together what it meant to be Ngarrindjeri.

I couldn't say anything about my mob because I didn't know, so I kept my mouth shut. But I reckoned Ruby could sense the awkwardness I felt about it.

Ruby remembered the Coorong well, back when she was a little girl. She told me that her brothers, Wally, Jeffrey and Robert, sister Iris and herself used to live with their grandmother, Nan Tingie, and grandfather Old Man Richards, at the reserve near Point McLeay on Lake Alexandrina in the Coorong.

Life was good on the Coorong, Ruby told me. I loved hearing her descriptions of life with her grandparents, living on the water, learning to hunt and fish. Every so often, she said old men would arrive for important tribal business with Old Man Richards. Then, one day, her older brother Wally went to a town called Meningie with his uncle to get oil and flour for the camp.

The government grabbed him, right there, off the street, and took him away – no one knew where.

After that, government people started coming to Nan Tingie and Old Man Richards' home on the water. Ruby said that when Nan Tingie saw them coming, she'd gather the children and hide them under her huge billowing dress, telling the government people she didn't know where they were.

'One day, though, Nan Tingie didn't see the government people coming,' Ruby said. 'There was no time to hide us children. The government people asked Nan Tingie if they could take us to a circus nearby.

'They were already grabbing us before Nan Tingie could protest. She pleaded with one fella to bring us back before sundown. He said he would, but he lied. They weren't taking us to the circus at all, they was taking us to the Homes, where we were all split up.'

Ruby lived in the Homes and spent time with a foster family in Woomera, a town set up for testing rockets out in the bush. She ended up in Vaughan House in Adelaide.

By now, she was older and had got work at the Levi Strauss factory.

It was during this time that Ruby met other Aboriginal people and told them about her family. She asked where she might find them, and they said to try Victoria Square – that's where they usually find each other. And that's where she found out more.

I couldn't believe how close Ruby's story was to mine. I thought it was only us in Victoria who were taken away from our families. But that wasn't the case.

'I was taken away from my parents too when I was a little boy,' I told her. 'I don't remember it much, but the police came to our mission and took me away. I was brought up in the Homes and with white families.'

She looked at me, her eyes widening.

'You too?' I told her what I could remember. 'So you thought you were from Melbourne?'

'No, I knew I wasn't from Melbourne. I've just been living there, since I met my brothers and sisters.'

'That's where you met your brothers and sisters?'

I told her a little about the Cox family, but didn't want to say too much, fearing it could lead to questions about the other family, who were less kind.

There were parts of my story I wasn't ready to tell anyone.

When Ruby looked at me, I could tell she was excited to learn of our shared experiences but confused as to why I hadn't told her earlier that I had also been taken.

'We're different, you and me,' I told her. 'I'm quiet, reserved.'

She smiled a smile that said she understood.

There was a push and pull going on inside of me again. I was happy where I was and who I was with, but I suddenly felt an urge to go back to Melbourne. I'd felt the same urge when Myrtle had first written to me: who are my people?

I thought about Johnny, Alma, Myrtle, Lawrence and Diana and wondered about our mob, and about the animals that belonged to our story.

I'd heard new stories of my mum and my dad, but I still had no idea who they were, who their people were, and their people before them. Their people were my people, and I didn't even know anything about them. I didn't know what I was.

'I reckon I've got to go home,' I whispered to Ruby one day in the Square. She nodded and grew very quiet. She understood. In Adelaide she'd found culture and family, and in Adelaide I'd found it too, but she knew it wasn't mine. I had to find my people.

I needed to be with them, to learn more about them,

and there was no question of Ruby not staying with hers.

When I booked a ticket on the Overland train, I knew I was going to miss Ruby Hunter. I'd never had a relationship with anyone like this. We weren't physical or anything – we'd never even kissed – but she and I spoke about things that I hadn't shared with anyone. I felt better and stronger when she was nearby. Her presence seemed to make things a bit more hopeful.

When the train pulled away, though, I wasn't ready for exactly how much I'd miss Ruby. By sheer accident we had found each other. This was to be the happiest moment of luck I'd know in my life, but it was to be happiness delayed.

The long journey back to Melbourne and family was laced with hope – hope that I would find out more about myself, and that I would see the girl with the brown eyes and the blue dress again some day.

The Salvation Army People's Palace, Adelaide, South Australia, where I first met Ruby, the girl in the blue dress, in the early 70s.

Front page of the *Age* in 1996 under the headline 'Back home, where the spirit belongs'. The image is of me returning to my mother's country – Gunditjmara country – from where I was taken. The caption reads, 'Aboriginal singer Archie Roach rediscovers his roots in the peace of the Framlingham bush. "I feel great. I woke up this morning and looked around and thought, *I'm home*."' Photo by Angela Wylie.

CHAPTER 8

WEEPING IN THE FOREST

Uncle Banjo told me
Before the children went away
Life was good and life was free
Not like it is today

Children running everywhere
And the trees were looking after
Little spirits dancing there
Amongst the sweet, sweet laughter

Oh but there's weeping in the forest
Now that the children have gone
And the trees at night get no rest
But they were there
When the children were born

Uncle let me fly away with you
And let me see the things you see
When children laugh, as children do
When they played among the trees

Oh but there's weeping in the forest
Now that the children have gone

And the trees at night get no rest
For they were there
When the children were born

As soon as I got back to Fitzroy I fell straight into the rhythms of my former life. My first stop after getting off the tram from Spencer Street Station was the Champion Hotel, where I was happy to find some old-timers – Pop Daley and Uncle Edgar Murray 'Cod', and my cousin Bundi – all there drinking.

They regarded me as though I'd never left, until Lawrence walked in, put a song on the jukebox as he always did, and then spotted me.

'Archie! Archie, Archie, Archie! Where the hell have you been?' he said, wrapping me in an embrace.

My stint in prison had been broadcast across the bush telegraph but also my release, and Lawrence asked why I hadn't come home straight away. I couldn't explain, really, but I told him I'd set out to pick in Mildura, and wanted to make sure I did just that, and afterwards I felt like wandering.

He told me he understood, saying he used to be a wanderer too, but not anymore. He liked to stay still now.

'You got any money? Let's get a flagon,' Lawrence said.

I had a little bit so we retired to the park.

It felt great to greet all and sundry as people came by and were surprised to see me. An Aboriginal Health Service had popped up nearby, and a Legal Aid office, too, so the area drew in the workers, students and families. It seemed the Aboriginal community had grown and grown. People would walk by and then stop and tell me how their lives had changed, talking about children being born and parents, uncles and aunties passing on. Hearing about all that made me realise just how long I'd been away, I thought about a year. I wondered how things may have changed for Alma and Myrtle.

I asked Lawrence what they were up to, and he said that Myrtle had had another little one, a boy named Shane. That was wonderful news. I asked about Alma, but Lawrence said Alma's story was her own to tell. That made me wonder what he meant. We found Alma at the Royal, which was a pub between the Builders and the Champion that we didn't go into much. I could tell as soon as I saw Alma that she wasn't in a good place.

'Archie! Come here.' She pulled me close. 'Come here, Butter Boy, come and have a drink. Let's have a dance and a drink. Let me look at you. Where have you been? Where are you staying?' she asked.

'Archie's gonna stay with me,' Lawrence said.

'What happened to the Dight Street flat?' I asked.

'I'm not in that place anymore, not with Arnold anymore,' said Alma. As she spoke, her voice changed.

'Things have changed a bit, Archie,' Lawrence added.

'Where are you now?' I asked. 'Where are the children? Are they with Arnold?'

'Irmgard and Lionel are with me,' Lawrence said.

'And what about Nola?'

Nola was Alma's new baby. Alma couldn't tell me; she was struck sad and mute.

'She's with a foster family. They're good people, and Alma can see Nola when she wants,' Lawrence said.

Lawrence told me later that Alma had been doing a fine job with Nola – with all her children – but people started putting pressure on her to give up the children for a while, while she got on her feet. Lawrence said that when Nola left, Alma was never the same.

I couldn't reconcile myself with how things were now. I thought about us, and the deep yearning for family I'd felt with the Coxes. The rupture I felt when Myrtle first contacted me. It all pained me deeply.

'It's not right. We should get Nola back. Myrtle can help, and I can help,' I told Lawrence later.

'Yeah, okay,' he said.

'We have to do this. We have to help.'

We did nothing but drink. We drank that day and we drank the next. We drank the day after, and we kept drinking. We drank and drank and forgot and forgot until, a few days later at the Builders, the light came.

It started as a dot as bright as the sun, then it grew to a spot, and then a ball, and finally a flood of blistering light. I felt myself spinning and falling, and then all around me turning into shadow. I didn't feel myself hitting the floor.

I remember cold metal being crammed into my mouth. When I got it out, I spat out blood and stared at the circle of drinkers standing around me.

'What?' I asked.

Lawrence took me to the newly opened medical centre and the doctor did some tests. He concluded that I didn't have epilepsy but had suffered an acute seizure caused by alcohol abuse. After hours at the clinic, my blood pressure was still dangerously high and the doctor wanted to admit me into hospital. I wasn't interested in that.

'Please, lay off on the grog for a while,' he said as I left.

I told him I would, but he must have heard the lack of conviction in my voice.

'Just know you can't keep this up, okay?'

While I didn't stop drinking, his words rang in my head. I think that's one of the reasons I resolved to find work, and both Lawrence and I took jobs at another foundry close to his place.

It was hot, exhausting work, as I knew it would be, but it did help me with my drinking because some days I'd be so tired at the end of a shift that I'd only have energy for food and bed, not a charge. I'd only ever string a few of those sober days together, though.

In those moments I thought about Adelaide, and Ruby, and her mob and mine. I tried to talk to my family, but they didn't know much about it or didn't want to talk about it. Either way, it didn't seem right to keep bringing it up.

A cousin, I can't remember who, told me to talk to Lloydy and his partner, Darkie, if I had any questions about culture. They were an older couple in the Fitzroy community who regularly visited Framlingham Mission, coming back with big bags of eels caught at the Hopkins River, happy to share them with anyone who wanted them.

They were good eating, those fresh eels, especially fried up with butter and garlic.

I did ask Lloydy and Darkie about where I came from, about who I was, and they told me I was from the Framlingham Mission. All the Roses, the Austins and the Clarkes – surnames of many of the Aboriginal people around me in Fitzroy – were Fram people, they said.

I wasn't one to press, but I felt compelled to understand. They told me we were all family, we were all mob. One of them said we were Gunditjmara. That word means a lot to me now, but it meant very little to me then.

I decided to go down to visit the mish and see what it was all about. I found it a nice, tranquil place, but I had no memories of being there, and had no direct family left, so it didn't really clock with me. That's where I first met Uncle Banjo, who lived on the mish. Whenever a young fella came with a questioning soul, he was there with a quiet word of wisdom.

Uncle Banjo said that we were the keepers of the forest, protectors of the river. I didn't understand why he'd chosen to use the word 'we'. I wasn't the keeper or protector of anything.

From time to time I went back to the mission, but not for any spiritual reasons, just to get away from Fitzroy when things got a bit too hectic. I always came back to Fitzroy, where my family was, and where my drinking was, too.

My seizures soon became a semi-regular occurrence. It was just another price to pay for my drinking, as far as I was concerned.

I started dating a bit in Fitzroy round then. We

needed the approval of our aunties and uncles, who'd do a bit of research first to make sure we were not related. Another consequence of being stolen from our family and communities.

I'd never been in anything approaching love before. I enjoyed the company of girls my age round Fitzroy, but they weren't anything like Ruby Hunter. I thought maybe it just needed a bit more investment, so I started seeing a lovely young girl named Anne.

We had a good time together, but I never felt about her the way I had about that girl in Adelaide. Then, one day at Lawrence's place, Alma handed me a note.

'I met this girl at the Champion today who was looking for you. When I told her I was your sister she gave me this,' Alma said.

I unfolded the note and it read:

Archie,
You may not remember me, but I remember you. If you do remember me, meet me at the pub tomorrow.
Ruby

How could I forget her?

The next day Lawrence, Alma and I went to the Champion at opening. There we sat and drank and waited.

'Bit special this one, is she?' Lawrence asked. I was too shy to say anything, but I nodded.

Ruby turned up at lunchtime and my heart nearly pounded out of my chest when I saw her. She looked very different to the girl I'd left a few months earlier, and I could tell it was from the effects of drinking, but she was still Ruby: heaven in a blue dress, who was now wearing jeans.

I kissed her as soon as I saw her. That was the first time I ever had.

The people in the bar and my cousins looked on, wondering who this girl was. They wondered why I, a shy bloke who never liked to bring attention to myself, was kissing some girl in the middle of the day. No doubt they also wondered what had happened to Anne.

None of that mattered. Ruby and I were together now.

Anne turned up at the Champion later that day and asked me if I wanted her or Ruby. I told her I was sorry, but that I wanted Ruby. I'd never been more sure of anything. Anne walked over to Ruby, looked her up and down, and then left with some of the other girls.

After that, Ruby didn't get the welcome in Fitzroy that I'd enjoyed in Adelaide. Quite a few people saw her as an outsider.

I was happy to hear that Ruby was going to be in

Fitzroy for some time. Ruby's sister Iris, who lived elsewhere in Melbourne, had heard that Ruby had gone 'to the pack'. That was a commonly used term that meant someone had let themselves go.

Iris had gone to Adelaide to pick up Ruby and bring her back to Melbourne to live with her and her partner, Nicky.

We were together after that, Ruby and I. No awkward friendship, no unspoken bond, no hoping for the brush of hands – just together.

Ruby stayed with her sister for a while, but she was staying with me so often it just made sense for her to move in with me. Lawrence and I would work during the day and at night we all drank, and happily. Many were the joyful nights when Lawrence, Ruby and I danced about the living room, singing at the tops of our voices while I bashed away at my guitar.

That was real happiness. Nothing existed but us and our song. That was true in those drunken moments, anyway. That kind of giddy feeling is fleeting, though, and blows away like embers.

We drank months away together in Fitzroy, and months more, blissful and carefree, but after a year or so together the damaging rot of addiction came to reveal itself.

Things might have been out of control, but what came next would change our lives forever.

Ruby had been feeling sick for a while and had seemed a little bloated. It didn't seem anything to be too concerned about. We all felt sick, a lot of us were bloated. But Ruby could tell something else was going on and asked Iris to take her to the medical centre. There the doctor sent Ruby straight to hospital.

When I arrived, a doctor got to me before I could see Ruby.

'Are you the father?' he asked.

I didn't know what he was talking about. My head was spinning. He explained that they couldn't save the baby, the one Ruby had no idea was growing inside of her. The pregnancy had failed.

As soon as I saw Ruby I broke down. We cried and cried and cried. Ruby had to stay in hospital, and I stayed with her, but we didn't really talk much. We couldn't. We shared silence.

The death of this child could have sent us away from each other, maybe forever. It didn't. At least we had each other. This could have stopped us drinking, but it didn't. We were addicts.

I lost my job at the foundry and I can't even remember why.

Drinking with Ruby in the months after, I'd often think about what our little baby might have looked like. I knew Ruby was thinking the same. We never talked about it, though. Maybe she spoke about it with her sister, but I couldn't talk to her about it. Perhaps I should have, but I couldn't.

I'd hold Ruby a little bit closer. Sometimes we'd cry. We'd moved into a boarding house room on Nicholson Street, Fitzroy. I got a few jobs here and there; a couple of months here and there. None lasted. There would always be a day when I couldn't get up, a night when I'd had just a few too many. I started to really beat myself up. It seemed things only ever got worse – our drinking, our circumstances.

Some mornings I'd resolve to make changes. But nothing ever did change, not really.

Why can't you keep a job like a normal person? I'd ask myself. *Why can't you drink a little, like normal people? Why can't you even get the first few steps right? Why can't you just have one or two beers and go on with your life?*

Then Ruby fell pregnant again.

I drank heavily through the pregnancy, despite giving Ruby advice about how she should stop drinking.

I recognised how hypocritical that was. I think I truly started to hate myself, because I wanted to be a better man. With Ruby pregnant, I needed to change.

I always thought I could.

I stumbled through week after week of Ruby's second pregnancy, and then one afternoon, when drinking at the Builders, I started yarning to a whitefella from Geelong named Ronnie. He had come to Melbourne to find an Aboriginal girl he'd been living with – one day she'd up and left him.

'I thought she might be here,' Ronnie said. 'If she doesn't want to come back, that's okay. I just miss her, that's all.'

I had no luck in helping find her, but Ronnie appreciated the effort, and we quickly became friends. When he heard a bit of my story about Ruby being pregnant, he asked if we wanted to stay with him for a little while. I was sceptical at first, but when Ruby met him she said he was just a nice fella with a broken heart looking for some company.

Ruby ended up being right. We moved in with Ronnie in Geelong and got to know him very well. He was on a disability pension with a big house and a bit of money. There wasn't much going on in his life, except the search for this girl.

The distance from Fitzroy was good for us. I got another foundry job close to Ronnie's place, and Ruby and I lived almost like a normal couple.

I took mostly afternoon shifts, so my day started late in the morning. I'd hang out with Ruby and Ronnie for a while, make my lunch, go to work, eat my tea at midnight and head off to sleep a couple hours later. That didn't mean I didn't drink at all, but I managed to stop drinking port, which was usually my undoing, and mostly drank beer. That helped.

I couldn't get that negative voice out of my head, though: Go back to what you know. I couldn't get away from the fear I felt constantly. I had a job, things felt relatively normal. I was giving Ronnie board money. But I felt loneliness, too, being away from my brother and sisters. Fitzroy might as well have been Perth. Even though I was with Ruby, I missed the pubs and the park, and I always felt there was a sword hanging over my head. I always felt that I was going to stuff it all up. Eventually, I guess I did.

I have a strong memory of making my lunch and walking out the door, fully intending to go to work, but somehow along the way I found myself hitching back to Melbourne. I was feeling the pull of home.

I was about to walk into the Builders, but blocking

my entry was a mountain of a man with curly white hair and a look that I recognised from the faces of some of the fellas in Pentridge, the ones who'd been there long enough to develop hardened souls. I reckoned I knew this fella. I couldn't for the life of me place him, though.

As soon as I got into the bar, my cousin Buddy saw me and called me over.

'Archie, did you see your brother?'

At that moment, Lawrence walked out of the bathroom.

'There he is,' I said.

'No, not him...'

The big bloke!

I ran back out of the pub, and Lawrence did too. We called out to the big fella who was ambling his way down the street.

He turned, and I could see him putting two and two together. He ran to us with his lumbering gait, wrapped his huge arms around me and was soon crying like a man who'd nearly forgotten how.

'Butter Boy! My little brother, little Archie.'

My brother Johnny, known to most as Horse, was laughing and crying at the same time as we went to the bar and ordered beers. With jugs in our hands, we sat down to talk. Things were different with Horse – he was quiet to a fault – but there was no doubt that the feeling was the same. Reuniting with a family member is the purest form of happiness.

I wanted to know where he'd been and what he'd been up to. I had no memory of Horse, but I knew he was the eldest of us siblings. Maybe he'd been old enough to remember a bit about what had happened on the mission when we were taken. He couldn't, though, not really. Horse had left home as a teenager.

Eventually, we decided to go back to where Lawrence was living. I hadn't seen Lawrence for a while and was surprised to find he was now living in an empty. I asked where Sally and the children were. They'd gone – Sally had taken off back to Sydney. The words landed heavily on me.

Thoughts of Ruby spun in my head, along with thoughts of Alma's children, and Lawrence's children, and then Ruby again, and then just Ruby. I wanted to kill that vertigo. I had to. We drank from one piggy at first, and then another. The more I drank, the fewer the visions that danced in my head.

We did get a little bit more out of Horse. He'd always been a wanderer. He'd lived here and there since he was a teenager, sometimes coming back to family, but only for a short while. He'd worked all kinds of jobs, from bouncing and boxing to picking and shearing. He'd been in Victoria and Queensland and had gone all the way to Western Australia. Then, in Perth, Horse got into a fight. It didn't end well, and he went on to do time in Fremantle Prison.

The air was thick, and nothing was said for a while. Lawrence was silent; maybe he was thinking about Sally and the children in Sydney. Horse was silent; maybe he was thinking about the man who had died in the fight and the years he'd lost. I was silent; I was thinking about Ruby. She was going to be a mum. I was going to be a dad.

My drunken mind told me she'd be right with Ronnie. She'd be right.

'I heard you can sing a song,' Horse said to me.

'I know a few songs.

'Reckon you could sing me one?' Horse rarely asked for anything, but he asked for that.

Lawrence went and got his guitar, and I sang for my brothers. I got lost in those old country songs, and I could see my brothers did too. As I watched the pain lift from Lawrence's and Horse's faces, I wondered to myself whether music might be more powerful than the drink.

We fell asleep in the empty, woke up late and went straight back to the pub. It took a few drinks to get our heads straight, but when they were, Lawrence decided he had something to say to me.

'Where's your little woman, Archie?'

'Ruby's in Geelong. She's right.'

'She know you're here?'

'No, but she's with Ronnie. She's okay.'

'I reckon you should go back. Go back to Geelong, see Ruby, tell your boss you were sick. I reckon you should go now. You don't want to be like us, Archie.'

Horse was nodding as Lawrence spoke.

'What are you talking about? Horse just got here, and I want to catch up with him,' I said.

'All we do is drink and sing and talk about all the shit in our lives, then we do it all over again. It works for that one day, but when you realise you've been doing it for weeks and months and years…' Lawrence was only in his mid-twenties, but I saw in him an age well past his years. 'You see your kids go away…Archie, you don't want all that. You should go back to Geelong and live a different life.'

It pained me to hear Lawrence talk like that. The self-doubt in his words was the same self-doubt that rolled around in my head, but it was strange to hear him voice it. It was almost as though he was speaking against the family, the bond that we had only recently formed. All we had was family, and now that Horse was here, the final piece of the puzzle had been found.

I told Lawrence that I'd only just met Horse. I wanted to know more about him. I wanted to stay.

'Tell me about this little woman of yours,' Horse said, surprising me.

I told him about her – she wasn't tall but had flowing dark hair, and big cheeks that matched the deepest brown eyes you'd ever seen. I told Horse she was the most beautiful girl.

'Is that her behind you?' he asked.

I turned. It was. She had her hands on her hips. It wasn't good.

If looks could kill, I'd be a dead man.

'Where the hell have you been, Archie Roach?'

I was shocked, half-expecting her to hit me.

I introduced Ruby to Horse and told her I wanted to stay around my family, especially now that Horse was back. I also wanted to be around community when the baby was born. Ruby wanted that too, with her sister and cousins around, and her younger brother, Robert, having recently arrived.

We had a good thing going on in Geelong with Ronnie, but we decided to return to Melbourne and get our own place. We could keep the rhythm we'd started in

Geelong right there in Melbourne. The drinking could be curbed; I'd get a job.

When we went to get our stuff, Ronnie implored us to stay. We told him we really missed our families and he understood. He reckoned that's what his girl had done too. We wished him well and thanked him. He said anytime we needed a place to stay, his door was always open. There was kindness in Geelong also.

Ruby and I went to the Nicholson Street boarding house, overlooking the gardens in Fitzroy, and Ruby got bigger and bigger. As she did, the dark voices in my head got louder and louder. When those voices were at their worst, I drank. I'm not proud of it, and I'm not excusing anything, but that's just how it went.

After our experience of losing our first baby, Ruby was careful to follow the doctor's orders. One day, when she was heavily pregnant, she visited the clinic. They suggested she go into the hospital for some tests.

It was early that afternoon when Ruby's brother Robert, finding me well and truly charged up at the pub, told me that Ruby was going into the hospital. He said he was going to see her, so I finished my drink and went with him.

We were walking across the park on the way to the hospital when I started to sway. A bit of left and right, a bit of forwards and backwards. Robert asked if I was okay, and I told him I was – I just needed a quick kip.

'I'm going to lie down for a little bit,' I said as I got into some bushes.

I woke in the dark with Wally, one of my cousins, standing over me.

'You all right, bud?'

I was all right, but there was something in my head, something I was doing, something I had to remember.

Then I remembered Ruby and jumped up. 'Wally, I gotta go to the hospital.'

'I reckon visiting hours are over, mate.'

He was right, and I was rotten. Rotten in my head – I'd slept through the day – and rotten in the guts with a lack of drink.

'You don't look great, Archie. Let me buy you a drink.'

I reluctantly went along.

When I got to the Builders, Wally got me a beer then Malcolm, my cousin's man, brought over a jug for me. And then another.

'You hit on the horses or something today, Malcolm?' I asked.

My eyes well up, remembering what Malcolm said next. I look forward now in life and recognise that the past is carved in stone. But thinking about Malcolm with a jug of beer in his hand, telling me words that I'll never forget, I can't help but think about how much I threw away. I can't help but think about the hurt that I'd carelessly inflicted before then, and the hurt that was yet to come. I think about what Ruby went through while I was unconscious or drunk. It's impossible not to want to go back and wish things could have been different.

Malcolm had a huge grin on his face, maybe about the happy occasion, maybe laughing at the fool who was drinking while his life changed.

'You don't know, Archie? No one told you? You're a dad.'

Me holding baby Amos, my firstborn.

Me and two of my sons, Amos (left) and Eban (right). There's enough hair here for all of us, including me.

CHAPTER 9

TAKE YOUR TIME

Oh I have known you all of your life
Yeah I have watched you grow
Now here you stand, not children but men
And I love you now, like I loved you then.

Oh yeah I know, I haven't always been there
But I need youse to know that I've always cared
And if you believe that my loving ain't real
Go ahead and feel go ahead and feel

But just slow down and ease your mind
But just slow down and take your time
Cause you got plenty of time to grow old

Yeah we have lied we have gone astray
But I know that we've cried when we fall by the way
But I beg of you don't let your life become ruined
If you grow up too fast might die too soon
Yeah if you grow up too fast might die too soon

Just slow down, ease your mind
Just slow down take your time
Cause you got plenty of time to be a child

Plenty of time, don't be beguiled
Plenty of time to be a child, stay a child

Plenty of time, to be a child
Plenty of time, don't be beguiled
Plenty of time to be a child
Plenty of time
Plenty of time
Plenty of time

I first saw my son Amos through glass at the hospital – this tiny little thing of beauty lying next to a sign that said 'Roach Baby'. Of course I felt unsure and a bit terrified, but also happy. There are some things in this world that are just good – nothing but good – and a baby is one of those things.

Ruby was still recovering when I saw her, but she looked so incredibly beautiful. She hadn't been drinking for a while and her face looked clear and pure, and when our hands touched a little magic surged from her skin to mine. It felt like a healing kind of magic, and I think some of the pain of losing our first baby eased, replaced with a bit of strength.

With a baby in tow, it wasn't right to live in the small room on Nicholson Street anymore, so we moved in with my cousin Melly and her children, Arthur and Krissy, in a place in North Melbourne that was much nicer, newer and cleaner.

Things might be able to change with me in North Melbourne, I thought. Maybe I can just stay home with Ruby and Amos, get a job, slow down my drinking.

It even worked out like that, but only for a while.

I knew I'd miss the community over at Fitzroy, so I brought some of that community home, getting my brothers and sisters to come over regularly for a drink and a singalong in the kitchen. Somehow Amos's birth lit a musical fire in me, and I wanted to play more and more.

I'd look for new songs and new artists. I started listening to folk music, and songs of protest, like those by Bob Dylan and Joan Baez. Their songs spoke of a time when the spirit of hope would triumph over repression, trauma and greed. Songs I could relate to. Most of my friends and family liked the old country songs, and any time I'd play Dylan, people would look at me funny and ask for some Charley Pride, something they could all sing along to.

This homebody period didn't last very long, though. After a bit of a charge in the kitchen, somebody would have someone that they wanted to see in Fitzroy. They'd ask me to come with them, and I could only say no so many times.

When I used to come back from Fitzroy, I'd be so drunk that I couldn't touch my little baby. Ruby would change his nappies and feed him; I'd just watch.

In the quiet times, I'd sometimes talk to Lawrence and Horse about changing things. I loved Fitzroy, but it was perhaps too much of a good thing. Maybe we had too many people to drink with. Maybe we should stop going there so much.

One hot summer's day my brothers and I decided to go down to St Kilda for a swim, and after a dip in the bay and a charge at the George Hotel, Lawrence and Horse decided that they were going to live in St Kilda for a while.

Horse was the quiet big fella, but he was the leader of our family – whatever Horse said went. A few words here or there from Horse would mean a lot, and he reckoned St Kilda could be the perfect middle ground between North Melbourne and Fitzroy for me and Ruby.

I spoke to Ruby about it and we agreed that if there was an opportunity for us to get our own place in St Kilda, then we should do it. When Lawrence heard that, he moved in with Horse and Horse's partner, Marlene, a woman from Perth, giving us his flat. Soon, all of us were living in one apartment block on Charnwood Road just off St Kilda Road.

Alma got a place across the road and, when Ruby's sister Iris split with her man, she came and lived with us. Myrtle also moved nearby with her family, and even Diana returned to Melbourne, joining us in St Kilda.

Things seemed to be good for a while. The people I cared about were all around me, Ruby and my bub, and my brothers and sisters. We were very different – Lawrence, Horse and me – which was to be expected considering our experiences before we were reunited. I'd think about Noel and Les sometimes, and how they'd drifted away and become strangers, and I wanted to make sure that never happened with me and my brothers.

It's a pity that drinking confused everything, taking its toll on all of us.

I kept having seizures, then Lawrence started having them too. We seemed to be able to deal with them, though. It never stopped us from drinking – maybe it was just the price you pay – until one day Lawrence arrived at my apartment with tears in his eyes.

'Jack…'

'What about Jack?'

We'd seen Jack the day before at the George Hotel. We'd been drinking with him only a dozen hours or so ago.

'He's dead.'

Jack had been seedy the day before, but we were all

seedy, all the time, so we didn't pay attention to it. Jack wasn't much older than me, not much younger than Lawrence. It hit me hard, Jack's death. I'd thought we had time to sort ourselves out, get straight and get our lives together. I wondered if Jack thought that too, and now he was dead.

Jack hadn't been having seizures. Doctors had told me that there was a danger I was drinking myself to death, but I never took much notice – until now. I had a baby; I had Ruby. I couldn't bear the thought of leaving them in the lurch.

If slowing down my drinking was the only option for quieting those doubts, fears and insecurities, I reckon that's what I would've done. But there was one other option: I drank more. Sobriety wasn't an option. I hated to be sober.

I hit the bottle harder, but the one who got sick was Ruby. She went into hospital to find that she was pregnant again, and quite a long way along the path.

With Ruby in hospital, Horse's missus Marlene took primary care of Amos and did a wonderful job. The little fella really loved Marlene, and she him. It would always amuse me to see him running after her.

My tiny, beautiful and very premature second son, Eban, was born while I was drinking. I was, once again, told by others that Ruby had given birth.

Eban had to stay in hospital for some time, but I managed to visit every day, often wearing a red headband, a look I'd adopted from a tribal fella. One day, when I arrived at the hospital, I found that one of the nurses had tied a tiny red headband around Eban's head, too. I thought that was funny and told the tribal fella, but he gently scolded me.

'That headband means you've gone through initiation and that you're a man. Truth is, you shouldn't be wearing it, either.'

I stopped with the headbands after that and started wearing bandanas instead.

After Ruby got out of hospital we arranged to move into a bigger council flat in Reservoir on the northern fringe of the city. Melly, Arthur and Krissy moved in with us.

Eban was in and out of hospital in the first year of his life, but the doctors were always confident he'd make it, and they were right. My sister Diana was an incredible help to Ruby in that period. I had a glimpse of what a normal life looked like, but I couldn't think too long about that because I'd start remembering how far away my booze habit and I were from what was normal and right.

As had been the case with the birth of Amos, I felt a renewed feeling of closeness between Ruby and me.

I loved seeing my brothers and sisters hold my children, especially the way that little Eban disappeared into Horse's huge hands.

In the wake of that feeling of hope I reckoned change was possible, and then change came.

Wally, Ruby's big brother, wanted to meet his nephews, so he asked their sister Iris to bring the boys over for a bit. When she came back with the boys, she asked Ruby and me if we might like living with Wally and his wife, Rosslyn, in Murray Bridge in South Australia.

It didn't occur to me then but Wally, a sober, responsible man, was concerned about his sister and his nephews.

Ruby was keen to go back. She'd been in Victoria for a while, but she was a woman of the river. We'd spent a lot of time with my family, and she wanted to spend some time with hers. I understood that. The only reasons to stay were because of my family and my drinking, and I reckoned those weren't good enough reasons.

Murray Bridge was a town about an hour from Adelaide, where I could get a train back to my family if they needed me.

Almost as soon as I got to Murray Bridge, I became friends with a group of drinkers in town and spent quite a bit of time with them in the park or a disused block of land called the Cutting. With them I drank mostly wine. I didn't really drink at Wally's, as per our tacit agreement that I wouldn't drink the hard stuff at home. Beer didn't get it done for me, so I started skulking off on my own to get into some fortified wine.

I'd always try to make it back home to spend time with Ruby and the boys.

Wally didn't appreciate me coming back with a belly full of muscat, though. He'd always know.

I took up work shortly after arriving in Murray Bridge, first getting a job at a local abattoir. My task was to push sheep up a kill run so they could be slaughtered, and then I would hose the blood away.

It was a tough job, especially for someone who woke up seedy every day. The smell of death used to turn my guts, but the hardest part of the job was seeing the thousands of pairs of eyes on me, sometimes cautious, sometimes trusting, as I led these animals to their deaths.

I asked my boss if I could be reassigned, telling him why.

'Aren't you Aboriginal, Archie?' he said. 'Aren't you blokes used to killing for food?'

I told him I was from Melbourne and got all my meat at the supermarket. I went deep-freeze fishing. It did make me wonder, though, how the traditional men treated animals from a hunt. I very much doubted they'd kill them as thoughtlessly as we did at the abattoir.

When I started getting pay cheques Ruby and I got our own place, and around that time I began teaching her how to play guitar. She took to it very quickly, and the thing that really surprised me was the sweetness of her voice. I'd heard Ruby sing before, in a group as we all made our way through a Charley Pride song or two, but on her own I heard in her voice all of the personality and soul that I'd fallen in love with.

I left the abattoir after I developed an illness from a parasite. I took work at a salt lake after a spell, forking the salt into giant bins. It was a tough, stinky job that would make your jeans literally stand up on their own, but the hot, physical exertion seemed to dull my thirst, so I didn't mind.

When we'd taken all the salt off the lake, I started picking grapes again, at a vineyard at Langhorne Creek.

I began listening to a lot of Woody Guthrie around then. He had a beautiful turn of phrase and brought dignity to experiences I felt I'd had in my own life – an affinity with the workers, itinerants and heroic downtrodden in his songs.

There was a Guthrie song I'd play that still chills me to the bone called 'Deportee'. It spoke about how identity, language, family and dignity can be stripped from a Hispanic rural worker when they cross the border in search of work. And should that worker die before they return to their home, they will forever be stuck a deportee.

We usually slept soundly in Murray Bridge, Ruby and me, except one night when she woke with the horrors. I asked her what was wrong, and she said someone was in the room with us, staring.

'He's pointing, Archie!'

There was no one there, and I told her so after turning the lights on and inspecting the room. We went back to bed and didn't think much of it in the morning, until a telegram arrived.

Dear Archie, your brother Johnny passed away last night…

I couldn't speak. My mind and body didn't work, either. It took a long time for me to be able to read the rest of the telegram and then for me to tell Ruby that Horse had died of heart failure, quickly and without warning. The telegram didn't say it was the drink that had killed him, but I knew it had. Drink had taken another one of us, and this time it was a dear brother, who I wish I'd got to know better and now never would.

Grief-stricken, I arranged to return to Melbourne immediately.

Before I left, Ruby stopped me and told me to slow down.

'I'm worried about ya, Archie. I reckon it was Horse in our room last night, and he's worried about you. I reckon he visited me. To tell me to look after you.'

I told Ruby I'd be right. I would see Horse off, see the family, and I'd come straight back.

Horse's funeral was at a cemetery near Flemington, and my sadness turned into anger when I saw him in the casket. He was a lovely man, Horse. He'd deserved a better life than prison, drink and being separated from his family.

Family separation and prison had been in my history, too, and drink was in my present, and I couldn't see it stopping. I screamed and swore as they lowered my brother into the ground. I didn't want to ask any questions, I just wanted to shout and break things. Lawrence held me back.

'No, Butter Boy. There's no point,' he said. 'Just be calm.'

I was, eventually. Before we left I poured a little of the port I'd brought with me into Horse's grave, like Albert had taught me on that first morning in Sydney when I started with the bottle.

Horse's story was set. He'd lived a drinker and he'd died a drinker, and this was a drinker's salute.

That night, a lot of the family and I went and drank at the Royal. Lawrence and I started with four whiskey shots each and beer chasers, and then four more whiskey shots and beer chasers. After that, we moved to Alma's place where Uncle Stan brought us beer.

It was rare for Uncle Stan to buy us drinks. Uncle Stan was one of the men who saw how drinking was ravaging our community, and he rallied against the bottle. Not that day, though. That day we were putting our brother into the ground, so I guess he figured we may as well drink where he could watch over us.

I stayed in Fitzroy for a few days with my cousin Melly and her children, drinking all the while. Then I went home to my family, not wanting to go like Horse had.

Back in Murray Bridge, I asked at the Nunga Aboriginal Centre about any new work I could take, and they helped me get a job at Schubert's Farm, a tourist attraction that functioned as farms did back in the 1920s, without any of the modern machinery or processes.

With my experience in the foundries, I took on the role of blacksmith and quickly learnt how to smelt and set metal using fire, wind and water. I made horseshoes and tools, as they had a hundred years ago, and I liked that work a lot. As always, though, drinking kept me from being the employee I'd wanted to be.

Some days I drank before work, just to knock the edge off my hangover. One morning I took it a bit too far and turned up drunk.

'Archie, look at you, mate,' my boss said. 'I can't have you around hot metal and kids today. Go home.'

I felt shame as I headed home, and that shame drove me into one hell of a bender. I didn't go in the next day, or the day after, but eventually my boss found me and told me to come back to work. I told him he didn't need me. I was no good.

'Shit happens, Archie. Sometimes people drink too much. Just come back. You're a good worker and we love having you on the farm.'

I did go back and kept working until there was another morning where I didn't just dampen my hangover but flooded it. I blew work off and went into town to meet my drinking mates.

Late in the afternoon I had the worst fit I'd experienced yet.

I didn't come to until I was already in hospital. The doctor told me that my blood pressure was very high and that, after being unconscious for so long, he wanted to keep me in for a few days. I didn't have any interest in that. I was ready to leave that minute. The doctor told me he couldn't hold me, but if I wanted to go, I had to sign a release saying they weren't liable for what might happen next. I asked him what that might be.

'Maybe nothing, maybe death. We don't know. That's why we want to keep you here.'

I couldn't bear to be in hospital. It was like prison for me; a place where I was bound. I couldn't force myself to stay so I signed the release and walked out, wondering if this was how I would die.

When I got home and saw Ruby and the children, I was filled with shame. Tears came, and Ruby asked what was wrong.

'I'm no good,' I told her. 'I can't do anything right. I can't keep a job and I can't slow down with the drink.'

Ruby put her arms around me. We'd blue, Ruby and I, and we didn't always agree, but we were always there for each other when it came to the crunch.

'I don't know what to do,' I said. It wasn't much like me to ask for help, but I was desperate.

'Why don't you go to the Nunga Farm?' she suggested.

Nunga Farm was a facility where some of our friends had gone to dry out; a place where Aboriginal people could get away from the pubs and parks and get counselling. The thing is, I never thought I needed to go to a place like that. I didn't see myself as badly off as those who went to the farm. I still didn't see myself the way I should have, but Ruby seemed to want me to go – so I did.

When I got to the farm, I loved it. The place was full of Aboriginal people, only none of them were drinking. Almost all had been drinkers, and most as bad as I was, but some were a week sober, some months, some years.

We worked hard on the farm, but we'd also stop and slow down for long meetings over tea and biscuits, talking about why we drank, how it affected us and the people around us.

Some of the men told dark stories. One spoke about a night when he'd fought with his brother – he'd ended up slicing his brother's throat ear to ear with a butcher's knife. Seeing what he'd done to his own flesh and blood, the man tried to drink himself to death. When he awoke in hospital his brother was there, with bandages on his neck and words of love and forgiveness.

'Even when you think you're past redemption, there's always hope,' this fella said. 'Where there's life, there's hope.'

I stayed at the farm throughout the week, and on the weekends I'd go home, where Wally had been helping out with Ruby and the boys. He was a great help, Wal. He and I might've had our disagreements, but I knew he only ever wanted what was best for his sister and his nephews.

That all lasted for about a month or so until, one weekend, an old F Trooper from Fitzroy called Charles arrived with a piggy under his arm.

'I was moving through and thought you were round here,' Charles said. 'I asked some people and found you.'

I told Charles it was good to see him, and if he needed a place to crash he could stay with us, but I said I couldn't drink with him. I was on the wagon.

'Come on, bud, I haven't seen you in years. Just have a little charge with me.'

He wore me down, and I talked myself into it. It had been a while since I'd had a drink, and I was stinging for one. I told myself that because I hadn't drunk for a month, I'd learnt how to drink like a normal person. I told myself I could share a couple with an old mate.

Of course, I couldn't. We drank enough wine for us to think it was a good idea to bomb the rest with a bottle of gin that Charles had in his bag. We drank until Charles passed out, and then I kept drinking after that.

With every sip, the shame didn't dissipate as I'd

wanted it to. That black tar of guilt washed into my brain, eventually sticking to every thought, every memory. I was useless – a drunk and nothing more.

It hurts to say it, but my thoughts took me to the darkest place.

You're no good, Archie. You'll never be any good. You're a drain on everyone. Wally is a good man; Ruby's family are good people. The boys and Ruby will be better having them around than you. Everyone will be better off without you.

Do it. They'll be sad for a bit, but better in the long run.

Do it – just do it, you weak piece of shit.

DO IT.

I woke up strapped to a bed. I was confused, sick and angry.

'What's this bullshit?!' I yelled over and over until someone stood next to me. He was a nurse, calm as they always are.

'The restraints are for everybody's protection, Mr Roach.'

'What the hell does that mean?'

'When you came to, you were a danger to yourself and the staff. You assaulted a number of nurses.'

'I wouldn't do that.'

'You punched people; you were throwing things around.'

It took a while for me to take all that in.

'Where am I?'

'You're in a hospital in Adelaide.'

I tried to get my memories back. I remembered that I'd started drinking. I remembered the gin. I remembered the shame and wanting to die.

More shame descended, more darkness. I couldn't think of many things lower than assaulting medical staff doing their jobs. It made sense that I'd wanted to end my own life, but I couldn't believe I'd tried to hurt good people wanting to help heal others.

I asked the nurses, over and over, to take the restraints off, and each time I got the same response: 'We can't do that, Mr Roach.'

'I'm not going to hurt anybody,' I pleaded, but they said they needed a little more time to be sure.

Once, after asking and being denied, I started bucking, wild with rage. 'Take these things off me! *I'll kill all of you bastards!*'

Even I didn't know where the rage was coming from. They let me burn myself out, which took a while. I was no longer my own man. I'd never had thoughts of suicide before my attempt, and I'd never had rage like I did then.

Eventually I came to an agreement with the nurses: they would remove the constraints if I started taking some pills that would make me feel better.

I didn't feel anything after I took those pills – not happy, not sad, not anything. When they transported me from the hospital in Adelaide to Northfield Mental Hospital, I barely noticed my new surroundings.

There were a couple of things I remember vividly, though, from my time at the sanatorium. The first was the two angels, beautiful and brilliantly white, who were on my left and right shoulders whenever I left the ward to go to the bathroom. The second was Ruby visiting me, telling me what had happened that night in Murray Bridge.

But nothing she said landed in my head. I just nodded and smiled, and then I told Ruby about the angels, and how things here were great, and that I didn't need to go anywhere. Even in my cottonwool brain I could tell Ruby was worried.

'This is bullshit, Archie. I don't know what's happened to you, but this isn't right,' she said.

Ruby came back to see me again – hours later, maybe, or days or weeks, I don't know. With her was Barry, a fella I'd become quite close to back at Nunga Farm. They arrived at the end of the day, when I was waiting to be medicated again. Reality was seeping in as it always did, just before the dinner pills.

I remember seeing Ruby entertaining the staff with a tale about this or that. And Barry pulling out a large coat and a beanie from his bag.

'Put all these on, Archie.'

'I'm right, thanks. Nice and warm here in the ward,' I told him.

'Come on, brus, quickly.'

Barry was insistent, so I did what he asked. He pulled the beanie down on my head, tugged the lapels of the coat up around my neck, and grabbed me by the arm.

'We're getting out of here, bud.'

He walked me out of the ward, then down the stairs, then out the front door, and then to a parked car. He put me in the back seat and got the engine running. Suddenly Ruby bolted from the hospital, and as soon as she jumped in the driver's seat she was yelling, 'Go! Go! Go! Go!'

Barry, who was pulling the car out coolly and quietly, said, 'Nah, Ruby, that's not how you do it. That's how the bank robbers always mess up.'

He drove us back to Murray Bridge, adhering to every law of the road. When we got home, I was as sober as I'd been in some time. Barry offered to take me to the farm, but Ruby was having no part of it. She was going to look after me.

Ruby did take care of me, but shame and the bottle were like peaches and cream, and I went back to drinking quickly. Mentally, I went off the deep end. I was no one you'd recognise, meeting me now or earlier in my life. After a drink I'd rant and rave; gone was the shy boy.

One day I was walking down my own street, screaming obscenities and threats, and someone called the police. When I saw them coming I jumped onto the roof of my house, where I watched four cars arrive and eight cops try to find me.

Eventually one of them spotted me. I jumped off the roof and the chase was on. They cornered me in a neighbour's front yard. I put my fists up, ready to fight.

'Come on, ya bastards!' They didn't want to fight, they just waited. I dropped my hands and let them take me. They gave me water and fish and chips, and after a sleep I woke up with the cell door ajar.

'Hey, you left the door open,' I called over to the closest policeman.

'Yeah, you can go home when you like, Archie.'

I walked out slowly, waiting for one of them to jump me and start beating me, but they didn't.

'Just try to take it easy, mate,' one of the cops said on the way out. I headed home, wondering what had happened and why.

I went through every permutation, every possibility, until I rested on the most unlikely but seemingly truthful reason: these cops were just good fellas.

People started to avoid me on the street after that incident, and Ruby heard mutterings from people. 'Poor old Ruby, having to look after Mad Archie.'

We were isolated; pariahs in our own neighbourhood, and after the most pathetic Christmas with no tree, no presents and no good food, I asked Ruby if we could go back to Melbourne.

I was less frantic then, but shame was still consuming me like fire, and I felt as if one day it would peak and something terrible would happen. I couldn't think of anything else to do but to run home.

'It's no good here, Ruby. I don't reckon I can make it.'

She understood and reluctantly agreed to pack everything up and catch the train east. People came to the station to see us off, including Wally and Rosslyn.

'I'm not scared of you, Archie Roach,' Wally said, charging up to me and poking his finger into my chest.

'I'm not scared of you, Archie, and I reckon I want to fight you.'

I had no interest in fighting Wally; he was a good man who'd done the right things for us. He was the first one taken away from Ruby's family. Bringing all of his mob back together meant the world to him. It made me sad that my behaviour had made him so angry, and I told him I was sorry that it had come to this.

Rosslyn stepped in. The boys were mine and Ruby's, Rosslyn reasoned, and if we wanted to go somewhere else then we should be able to go. I asked Wally to shake my hand, which he did, reluctantly.

As we pulled out of the station I had a moment of clarity. Wally was worried about allowing his family to go away with me. He saw me as a mad bastard and a drunk – and he knew me well. Did he see me as anything else? Was I even anything else?

I'd left a happy home as a boy to find myself and my people nearly fifteen years before. Now I was pushing thirty, and what had I found? What did I have to show for myself? I looked across the train carriage and saw Ruby taking care of our boys. I had them. I had Ruby; I had the boys. I hadn't lost everything yet.

As the old fella at Nunga Farm had said: *Where there is life, there is hope.*

The Adelaide outskirts thinned and then completely gave way to brown earth and South Australian flowers and trees; the land as it would've been if none of us had come and bothered it.

There was still hope. I felt it. It was faint, like weak sunlight on the coldest winter's day, but on my skin it suggested the possibility of spring. I thought myself absurd to allow this hope, given the mad years of drinking and darkness behind me, but I also thought a better day may be coming.

I was right. The first day of spring was coming with rebirth, joy, music and even bloody fame, something I could've happily done without.

Before all that, though, I would have to suffer through a new low. Ruby, too. This would be a place I would later know, after joining the program, as 'rock bottom'.

This would be a place where life would either restart or end.

The healing power of music. Photo by Maree Clarke.

CHAPTER 10

I'VE LIED

Sitting here in a lonely old guest house
I'm sure that my life is all through
Scratching fleas and watching a grey mouse
I'm making love to the memory of you

For without you I'm weak and uncertain
And I feel so naked and cold
Like a window without any curtains
My innermost feelings unfold

The drink I just had
It wasn't so bad as the first
But drinking won't do
When it's only for you I thirst, I thirst

For your kiss it quenches all burning
It's sweeter than sweetest of wine
Now you're gone I find myself yearning
For the love that I left behind

Nobody can heal the pain
That I feel inside
And if I said I'm strong and I'm never wrong
I've lied, I've lied

When we got to Fitzroy things had changed. Old Horse was gone, Lawrence was sleeping where he could, and none of my sisters had space for me, Ruby and the boys. Eventually we ended up landing with Melly and her children at the council flats.

We were sleeping in the lounge and I was drinking with whoever was around – in the park or Charcoal Lane, the Hole in the Wall, wherever. I didn't take any work and put in for benefits, most of which went to the pub, or the bottle shop, or to ciggies. We'd usually make sure that the boys were fed, but the food that would fill Ruby and my bellies was often from the soup van that would pull up at the bottom of the building and give out soup and sandwiches, and sometimes pies and sausage rolls.

Sometimes that van fed our children, too.

That was Ruby's tipping point.

Ruby took the boys down there once, and after they came back, she told me she'd had enough.

'We've come here to start life again, and again it hasn't got any better, Archie,' she told me. I could tell something had changed in her because while she had her hands on her hips, she looked forlorn, defeated.

'Things will get better,' I told her. 'I just need to get on my feet and get some work.'

'It's been weeks... months, maybe.'

Had it? I couldn't tell if she was right, but she probably was.

'Look, Archie, I love you, but Fitzroy, St Kilda, Reservoir, Murray Bridge, back here... Things never seem to get any better.'

'We'll be right, Ruby. We'll be right.'

She usually believed that. That day she didn't.

'There has to be a better life than this. For the boys. They deserve a better life than this.'

It hurt in the way that only the truth can.

'I reckon I'm going, Archie,' she said. I could tell this was hurting her even more than me.

'Where you going? Where? *Where?*' I started cool, but the anger got in me.

Ruby was packing clothes and things for her and our sons. 'I've got a place to stay. Don't worry,' she said.

'Where the hell do you think you're taking my boys?'

I was already charged up so Ruby let me rage myself out, quietly gathering what she needed. Eventually I told her to piss off and that things were going to be better without her anyway, without her and the boys. There'd be more for me – more grog, more smokes, more time, more everything.

'Good, see ya then,' I mumbled as she went for the door with a son of mine in each hand. 'Come here, boys, give me a kiss and a hug.'

'Say goodbye to Dad,' she said as I held them.

The boys said their goodbyes, went back to their mum and then the door closed. I was alone.

The flat was quiet and my thoughts were loud. The rage came back and I yelled and broke things. I wanted to be numb, unconscious, dead. It was all the same to me. I drank everything I could get my hands on before moving to the pub, and then the park.

This was my last bender, starting in Melly's flat and ending in hospital. I have little memory of what happened in between.

I woke up intubated, restrained and sedated. It took a while until I could breathe on my own, but I can't tell you how long. It took a while until I could talk again, but I can't tell you how long. I can't tell you how long it took for me to be able to speak properly with a doctor, but I can tell you what he said.

'You've had a grand mal seizure, Mr Roach, one of the most debilitating I've ever seen.'

There was no question of me just jumping out of the hospital bed this time.

On the second day in hospital I had a visitor; a very well-dressed Aboriginal man I'd known as a drinker back in the day, but whose clear complexion and clear eyes said his drinking days were behind him.

'Lester?' I croaked.

'G'day, Archie.'

He asked how I was and I told him about the seizures and my other injuries, and then I told him about Ruby and the boys.

'Do you reckon it might be time to clean up?' he asked.

And, finally and mercifully, it was.

I went from hospital to a rehabilitation centre called Galiamble down in St Kilda, which was run by Lester. He'd cleaned up on his own sometime before, using the principles of Alcoholics Anonymous, and had envisioned a residential place where Aboriginal men like him could recover using the same principles that had helped him. That dream became Galiamble, a two-dorm, sixteen-bed facility.

'You reckon this will work?' I asked Lester.

'That's up to you, bud,' he replied.

They got me a bed straight away. Two days sober, I was still very seedy. After a short while my bed was drenched in sweat. One of the fellas came to change my sheets, and one of the other workers wanted to know if I'd been through detox yet. I told him I hadn't.

They asked if I wanted to go to a clinic before I started

the formal program at Galiamble and go through a full medical detox. This was normally the way things went.

I knew the clinic they wanted to take me to. It was in Fitzroy, in a building we could see from the Hole in the Wall drinking spot. Sometimes the fellas in the clinic would come down, and we'd bum smokes off them. A few would even get charged up with us too. I didn't want to go to that clinic. I could've asked to go to another, where they'd give me drugs and an IV to make things easier, but the truth was I didn't want to go to any clinic. I wanted to tough it out and go cold turkey.

I'd gone sober a few days here and there, and there seemed to be a truth to the pain. Each hour sober had felt like an investment. I told the counsellor I wanted to do it dry.

I tell you, that was a tough old week.

My hands trembled, my mouth was mealy, my guts churned and I sweated so much my sheets had to be changed twice a day. I couldn't keep anything down except cups of tea, and I couldn't make those without bouncing sugar and hot water all over the kitchen.

People were there for me at Galiamble, though. I'd apologise when my sweat-stained sheets needed changing, but it was no worry for the staff. People started bringing me cups of tea too, sweet, how I liked it. The other patients would come to me with affirmations as well.

'Stick with it, brus.'

'You're getting better already.'

'I reckon you're only a couple of days away, bud. You'll feel right as rain,' one fella said to me.

Turned out he was right; I did start to feel good after a week. Better than I'd felt in years. I began to value that feeling and wanted to keep it going. I made it to a week, and then two, and then three.

I went to meetings, first with the fellas at Galiamble and then with some other brothers from around the neighbourhood who were several years along. I couldn't believe these men; many were doing well for themselves, well dressed and holding down jobs. I couldn't believe they were drunks once like me.

When I started going to those meetings I found out that I actually wasn't a drunk, I was an alcoholic. There was an important distinction. As a drunk, I was defined by something I was doing: drinking. As an alcoholic, I was defined by a disease: alcoholism.

It's a real disease too, with specific pathology and symptoms. I'd never thought about my drinking in those terms before. I just thought I was a weak bastard who liked the sauce too much.

After a while at Galiamble I became part of the group

that would go further afield for meetings, in the city's north or south. There we'd tell our stories to a room full of whitefellas and in return we'd hear stories from all kinds of people – doctors, lawyers, executives.

I was amazed to hear that their stories were often the same as ours. In fact, sometimes their stories were worse. These fellas would describe the exact same spirals that I'd fallen into, the same hopeless predictability of ruin, the same thoughtlessness and yearning for the numbness of liquor. Sometimes they'd talk about trauma, too, often from their childhood.

I thought there was something in that. I started to wonder if it wasn't our blackness that got us drinking, but our trauma.

Lester asked me once why I wanted to clean up, and I told him I was doing it to get my woman and boys back, and then be a good father for them. Lester told me that they couldn't be my reasons to get clean. If I became a great dad for those boys and a great partner for Ruby then that would be a wonderful result of cleaning up, but I had to clean up for me.

He said I had to have a reason for me, one that didn't have anything to do with other people or other circumstances. You had to believe that your life was worth not just something, but a lot.

I didn't really understand what he was talking about until, at meetings, more people started talking about a higher power, something bigger than yourself, who you were happy to hand control of your life over to.

I'd felt that higher power in my life in the joyful Pentecostal Christian churches, in the spirit of the lane the land and in my people. I'd begun to hear about the Dreamtime and the old ways, and I suspected there was divinity there too. The old fellas with the red headbands, they knew a thing or two about a higher power.

At times, I'd been confused by the two very different forms of divinity I'd felt – Aboriginal spirituality and Christian theology – but at Galiamble I started to reconcile the two. I realised that if one spirituality was true, the other didn't necessarily have to be false. Both could be access points for one truth, one spirituality.

I believed in God; I believed in the old ways. I felt the spirits in the land and in my ancestors, and the shared spirituality of my brothers and sisters. I felt the divine power in all of us, and I felt the divine right to live; all of us, every colour, every shape. Coming to that belief kept me sober.

I was always only one drink away from losing that perspective, though.

The main principle of AA is not to worry about

tomorrow, or the past, but to not drink today, to be sober one moment, one day at a time.

'One drink away from a drunk,' they'd say in the program. I still remind myself of that today, when I'm sitting down on a hot afternoon and everyone else is having a cold beer.

Until then I'd always worked my way towards being able to drink one beer, one wine, like a normal person, but after Galiamble I knew I wasn't a normal person. I was an alcoholic.

I'm only one drink away from a drunk; one drink away from losing my divine perspective.

I didn't realise the importance of affirmations and mantras until I started the program, and I didn't realise that songs are affirmations until much later.

God, grant me the serenity to accept the things I cannot change, the courage to change the things I can, and the wisdom to know the difference.

That was an important affirmation for me, 'The Serenity Prayer'. I had to change my attitudes, my behaviour. And I did that every day, with help from God and man. I loved the men who were cleaning up around me, and also the counsellors like Lester, who were all former drunks and spoke to me in the way that doctors, with their clinical answers, never could.

Every day I was sober was a day they had invested in me, a day they'd put their trust in me. Each day it became more apparent that drinking would be a betrayal, not only to these men but to the divine spirit who had chosen to give me life. LIFE – the most wonderful thing in the world, and I'd been throwing it away.

Gratitude and forgiveness: these were things that also became important to me when I started the program. That didn't mean forgetting what had been done to us, me and mine, but I needed to forgive in order to heal.

It was easy to have gratitude for the love of Ruby and the boys and my brothers and sisters. Finding the gratitude and forgiveness for the police who locked me up and then gave me fish and chips was harder. But it was necessary.

I thought about how much Mum and Dad Cox had done for me. They were part of a racist and damaging system, but they were caught in the gears of that system, like I'd been; they weren't the gears themselves. Their hearts had gone out to us. Another thing I managed to do in those first moments of sobriety was to divorce what was bad about my drinking years from what was good. It would've been quite easy to throw out the baby with the bathwater and look down on my drinking mates, the parks and the pubs, but to do that would be to deny the good, of which there was plenty. I'd learnt a lot over that time. They were family; they taught me a lot about friendship. They had my back, and I had theirs.

It was magic at Galiamble, meeting with people and speaking about your feelings and experiences and emptying your lungs into a song or two. Magic. I didn't know then, but in Galiamble I was learning the lessons I would need to become a musician and a teller of stories. These lessons were just as important as learning about scales and chords.

Hope: it came into my life again at Galiamble, first as a trickle and then as a gush.

One day, the phone rang. One of the other fellas answered.

He called out my name. It was Ruby on the other end.

After leaving me, Ruby and the boys had checked into a place close to Galiamble called Winja Ulupna, a Yorta Yorta word for 'Women's haven'. It was an emergency housing shelter for Aboriginal women and their children, but also a place where women could kick their drug or alcohol habits. What I was learning at Galiamble, Ruby had been learning at Winja Ulupna.

'It's good to hear your voice,' she said.

Hearing her voice was heaven.

Galiamble and Winja Ulupna were paired organisations and Ruby had been asking about how I was going. They couldn't tell her anything specific, but one day they suggested it was time to call me.

'Maybe you'd like to come round and see me and the boys soon?' she said.

Another suggestion from the staff.

'Nothing could make me happier, Rube.'

Lester organised to drive me round to Winja Ulupna and, over cake and cups of tea, our family was reunited.

We took it slow, as Lester had recommended. Ruby and the boys stayed where they were and I stayed at Galiamble, but I became a regular visitor for tea and cake and to sing some songs.

'I've got a job,' Ruby told me. 'You can come see me perform if you like.'

Perform? I wondered exactly what kind of job Ruby had taken on here. Ruby explained that she'd met a woman from the Melbourne Workers Theatre, who'd invited her to audition. The audition had gone well, and Ruby was currently rehearsing a show that would be staged at lunchtime in factories around Melbourne, for any worker who was interested.

I didn't have much by way of nice clothes at Galiamble, but I rustled up what I could to go and see that performance. Some of the other fellas from Galiamble came along too.

When I saw Ruby on stage that first time, I saw a whole other person. I know that's what acting is, but it wasn't just that Ruby had managed to embody her character, she'd managed to expand the definition of what I thought she could be, of what we could be. People loved her. They laughed with her and felt pain with her. People roared their approval and clapped vigorously when she finished. Ruby was affecting people.

Ruby had the vision; she was always the one. She saw a better life for the four of us and here it was. Me, clear-headed and with new mates from Galiamble, who were praising me for Ruby's performance, as though I had something to do with it. Amos in school and Eban starting soon, with two parents who were both sober and loving, and Ruby…oh, Ruby, up there on stage, shimmering like a star.

I'd fallen in love with Ruby before, and would fall in love with her again, but I remember that time as something else when I watched her on stage. My gut pulsed and my mouth was fixed in a smile. There was hope in the air like the smell of eucalyptus. It was such a special day. I don't remember the where and when, but I remember the what. The what was falling in love with my wife all over again. Tears come just remembering it.

Lester helped me get my driver's licence while at Galiamble, and I started ferrying patients to hospital and clinic visits. I never thought I'd get my licence. It's a small thing to most people, but to me it meant a lot. I was trusted with a car and other people's safety. It meant that Lester didn't think I was going to relapse. It meant that I didn't think I would, either.

I transitioned from being a patient at Galiamble to being a staff member, and that work filled my heart. Seeing these lost souls come in with empty cores and helping restore their hope and pride – no pay cheque could ever compare.

Ruby and I moved back in together with the boys, to a nice little place just round the corner from Galiamble. As much as I enjoyed the part-time work there, doing a bit of driving and putting encouraging words in some ears, I reckoned I could do even more. Ruby thought the same. We'd been helped in so many ways, and our lives were starting again; we wanted to do the same for others.

I suppose all that started the day my cousin Melly came to our place in St Kilda with her children, Arthur and Krissy. Melly had done so much for us when I'd been in my bad place, and now she was asking us to look after her children, as her drinking had got a little out of control.

'Just for a bit, please, sister?' I remember Melly asking Ruby.

Of course, we'd help Melly, and of course we'd take the kids in whenever she needed us to. Arthur and Krissy, who were only slightly older than Amos and Eban, had become a brother and sister to our boys.

We started a routine of taking the children in when Melly was in a bad way and giving them back when she was right again. Sometimes, we'd talk to her about how good it was to be sober, but Ruby and I knew better than anyone that the decision to sober up can never be anyone's but your own.

She died, Melly.

She died while her children were with us. She'd been getting sicker and sicker, and then one day she was gone. She was a lovely woman and a caring mum. It was the saddest thing, and the sadness washed over all of us.

Melly's uncle came to her funeral and told us he was going to take Arthur and Krissy. We told him they could stay with us if that's what the family wanted – we loved those children. But in the end, it was decided they were going to be with their family. We were sad to see them go, but we had no right to them.

One day I shared with Lester that I thought I could do more than I'd been doing at Galiamble. He agreed that was true, but probably not at Galiamble, which was a small facility. I could likely get work at another, larger place if I wanted. I should go and have a yarn to a fella called Kevin Coombs about that.

Back then, Kevin was the head of Aboriginal Health Victoria and already a legendary blackfella. Born in country Victoria but relocated to New South Wales, Kevin was accidentally shot in the back at the age of twelve and then lost the use of his legs. He refused to let that slow him down and picked up wheelchair basketball. In 1960 he became the first Indigenous Australian to compete at the Paralympic Games. Kevin also became the first Indigenous Australian to compete at a second Games, and a third and a fourth and a fifth.

When I met him, he was in his forties but still competing and coaching whenever he wasn't doing his excellent work advocating for Aboriginal health. He was full of mental, moral and physical strength.

'You don't have a lot of experience counselling, Archie,' Kevin said when I asked him for a job.

'No, no, that's true.'

'Why do you reckon I should hire you?'

I told him why in the way I knew best, through story. I told him about my drinking years, and what I had lost in that time. I told him about what I got back when I cleaned up and how it had happened for me. I told him that without people like Lester I might have missed my window, my moment. If there were more people like Lester, maybe Melly wouldn't have missed her window.

He gave me a job as a counsellor at a place called Gresswell Drug and Alcohol Rehabilitation Centre in the north of Melbourne. My work mostly entailed helping Aboriginal patients in their programs, whether that was keeping them positive and engaged and moving towards sobriety, or keeping them generally healthy and making sure they could make their doctor's appointments.

I loved that work, but sometimes the facility didn't have any Aboriginal patients, and I'd get a bit bored.

Once, I remember having a sit and a smoke outside, and one of the white patients sat down for a talk. He was a nice man, and he wanted to tell me about how he grew up around blackfellas. He knew Lionel Rose, which led to conversations about Framlingham and boxing.

'I don't mind talking to you, Archie. Do you mind if I come by your office sometime?'

Of course, I didn't mind. When he came by, I did for

him exactly what I'd do for my Aboriginal patients. We talked about the depths I'd gone to when I was addicted, and what sobering up had done for me. We talked about how he could sober up too. We had a great yarn. I felt good after sharing, as I always did, and I think he got something out of it too.

But afterwards, one of the supervisors approached me and gently chided me, 'Archie, you're the Aboriginal counsellor, for Aboriginal patients.'

'I know that, but there aren't any Aboriginal patients here at the moment and he wanted to yarn.'

'There's plenty of other people to help him. You should've referred him to one of us.'

I didn't understand that. One thing I'd learnt since sobering up was that, while we all may have different skin, hair, eyes, noses and different circumstances, we share one soul, one higher power. Perhaps I craved the company of Aboriginal brothers and sisters and felt a truth in their stories, but that didn't mean I couldn't understand the pain and triumph of anybody else's life who wasn't Aboriginal, nor did it mean that they couldn't understand mine, either. The disease didn't distinguish.

I thought about that a lot and it was still on my mind as I took one of my patients to a nearby hospital for an appointment. While I waited for him to finish, I watched a tiny, grey-haired woman wearing a summer dress walk slowly but purposefully along the ward, followed at a distance by an orderly. She was concentrating as if remembering something.

A nurse told me she was the wife of a patient who had died about a year ago. She came to the ward to sit in the chairs her husband had sat in, or to visit the bed he spent most of his time in, as long as the patients didn't mind.

'They usually don't. She doesn't bother anyone,' he said.

When I got home I wrote a song.

It was about that floating mournful grey-haired woman and her husband, and the love between them. (That song would be called 'Summer of My Life', and it would close out my first album.)

Previously I'd written a jaunty little tune called 'Hungover' for a songwriting competition. It is quite powerful in retrospect; there is a striking contrast in the breezy way it describes my drinking and the actual damage I recognise now, but it comes from a different place to the song about the old woman.

After that moment, the songs came to me quickly, relentlessly. I'd sit in our kitchen or lounge, the kids running around and Ruby talking about this and that, and I'd strum out some chords and some lyrics, maybe

I'd put some rhyming couplets together. It was usually just parts of songs – lyrics here, chords there, things that were in my head that needed to get out – but often they became full songs, like 'Summer of My Life' – songs with structure, verses and choruses, and even titles.

If those songs were okay, I'd play them for Ruby and the boys, and if I thought they were even better than that, I'd play them for other people.

As part of the treatment at Galiamble, I had become an active member of AA. A few of the old-timers hired the top room at the local Mission to Seafarers building, located down past the bottom of Flinders Street, overlooking the freeway. They called it the 'Freeway Club', and it was a place where recovering alcoholics could socialise, have a cup of tea or coffee, have a meal, play some pool or watch videos. Some of the boys and I would occasionally head down there.

The fellas enjoyed my guitar in Galiamble – they would gather round and listen – so I'd always take the guitar with me down to the Freeway Club. I loved it there, being in the company of people who were struggling with the same thing. It was community.

One day we noticed that they were building a small stage up front at the Club and setting up speakers and microphones. One of the organisers asked us if they knew someone who could play guitar. I looked away, staring out the window.

One of my Galiamble mates said, 'Yeah, I know somebody.' I took my eyes off the view long enough to flash him a dirty look. 'And he's pretty good, too.'

I quickly said, 'I don't think so.' You don't go to AA and say, 'I'm an alcoholic...and I play guitar and sing songs.'

Eventually I did get up to play a few country classics. Then I pulled out two originals – 'Open Up Your Eyes' and another song I'd written called 'Charcoal Lane'. I was so nervous I was shaking, and my breathing was all wrong. It was the first time I'd sung in public without having had a drink.

Everyone was encouraging. Sometimes I played alone, other times I'd play guitar for others. I played guitar for one fella who loved to sing Neil Diamond's 'Morningside', and I'd sing Woody Guthrie's 'Deportee' with another fella.

Eventually the girls from Winja Ulupna would come along, and Ruby would too.

'Open Up Your Eyes' was the first song I ever penned sober. It was the late 1970s and I was about 19 or 20 years old. During whatever free time I had outside of our chores and the AA meetings, I would have a guitar with me, and a pen and a notebook. One time, as I started writing what I thought was a poem, having always loved poetry, I looked down at the words: 'At fifteen I left my home, looking for the people I call my own, but all I found was pain and strife'.

I realised then that writing and words, poetry and prose, have a rhythm to them. I picked up the guitar and started strumming and – bang – it just came, the melody and the rhythm and everything, all at once.

I sat back, shaking my head, and called out, 'Hey, Ruby, I think I've written a song.'

'Nah, ya haven't.'

'I have,' I said, and I sang it to her.

'Well... yeah, that's pretty good!'

And that was it, my first song. It was about the choices we make in life, and not always the good ones.

Common sense told me it was better not to drink. I could see alcohol killing my friends and my family, and people dying of alcohol-related illnesses. I just assumed that that was going to be my lot in life, a hopeless situation. There weren't a lot of opportunities for young black people back then, not like there are today.

Ruby and I left Galiamble not long after, and Christmas was approaching. We had to celebrate the holidays, so we had a drink – 'twas the season to be jolly, fa la la la la, la la la la. I kept the lyrics to 'Open Up Your Eyes' in my head, though.

In the seventies, each state held an Aboriginal Country Music Festival. In Victoria, there was the Victorian Aboriginal Country Music Club, run by Uncle Harry Williams, his wife Aunty Wilga and Aunty Joyce Johnson. They held their festival at Brunswick Street Oval, the old Fitzroy VFL home ground, and a talent quest was involved, with awards going to 'Best Gospel', 'Best Male Artist', 'Best Female Artist' and 'Best Songwriter'.

Ruby and I went down to check out the festival, and Aunty Joyce walked past saying, 'I've registered you, Archie Roach.'

'Nah, Aunty Joyce, nah,' I said. 'I've just come to check it out. I'm not ready today.'

'Come on, Archie, we love to hear you sing.' She was like Uncle Harry, always encouraging me.

Uncle Harry had been a mentor; he used to come and get me out of the Atherton Gardens in Fitzroy, saying, 'Put that flagon down, put a guitar in your hands and come with me.'

I'd look at the other fellas. 'Today?'

'Yes, Archie, today.'

He'd take me over to Thornbury, to where the original Aborigines Advancement League had a singalong every couple of weeks. We'd sit around and pass round the guitar, and it would be a big shame job if you didn't perform. I'd sing country songs – Merle Haggard, Woody Guthrie, Charlie Pride, and the most popular, Willie Nelson's 'Blue Eyes Crying in the Rain', which some of the fellas would change to 'Brown Eyes Crying in the Rain'. I guess people recognised there was a glimmer of talent in me, but you never wanted to big-note yourself. Playing guitar and singing was just something I loved to do, and Uncle Harry nurtured that, in his own way.

I looked at Ruby and asked how much money she had, so we could pool it together, enough to get a charge.

'I'm not getting up on stage unless I'm well and truly on the way,' I said.

It was the first stage I'd been on in front of blackfellas from all over Victoria, not just people from Melbourne, the people we knew. But I went on to come second in the 'Best Male Artist' section and then won the 'Best Songwriter' award for 'Open Up Your Eyes'.

The winners from each category were then invited to go to the National Aboriginal Country Music Festival held later that year in Adelaide.

On the day that they were to fly me over, I was really nervous. I'd never flown on a plane before, so to try to relax, I sat at the airport bar, drinking whiskey with beer chasers, trying to get the courage up. Because the festival only flew the performer over, Ruby and Amos had to take the train, so I was on my own. Suddenly I heard my name being called over the intercom to go to the gate. Some staff asked if that was me, and they said I'd better get down there now. So, reluctantly, I did.

I boarded the plane and sat down, still anxious. The safety demonstration made things worse.

'I want to get off,' I said.

'You all right, sir?' the passenger next to me asked.

'No, I need to get off.'

'First time you've flown? You'll be all right. Safest thing in the world, safer than cars.'

The plane started accelerating down the runway, and everything was a blur.

I turned and said, 'When is this thing going take off? If we keep going, we'll drive through the bloody fence.'

It was a very unsettling experience, but once we got in the air I was fine. I had a cup of tea, and before I knew it we were landing in Adelaide.

Between the tea and the drinks, I headed straight to the toilet as soon as we disembarked. Standing at the urinal, I glanced over next to me and saw this amazing pair of snakeskin boots. Above them was a nice pair of moleskins, and then a snake-print shirt. My heart started to race. Even before I looked the fella in the face, something you never really do at a urinal, I knew who it was.

'Uncle Stan!'

'My boy!'

'What are you doing here?'

'Coming to see the festival and put on some boomerang exhibitions.'

Uncle Stan had flown in from Sydney, and we got to talking. I told him that Ruby and young Amos were coming into town as well.

'Let me know what they look like and I'll pick them up,' Uncle Stan said.

While he drove to the train station, I went on to the festival, which was being held at the Taperoo, just past Port Adelaide, and registered for the talent show.

Reg Lindsay, the famous country music singer, who had his own show on television, was the MC, and he invited me up on stage, where I again sang 'Open Up Your Eyes', this time with Uncle Harry playing right next to me. I went on to win the trophy for 'National Songwriter of the Year', which made me feel pretty deadly.

Word travels quickly around Aboriginal communities, and the news that I was writing songs came to the attention of Uncle Banjo down in Framlingham.

'You should write a song about how they took the children away from here, Archie,' Uncle Banjo said to me.

I'd first met Uncle Banjo Clarke a long time ago. He told me he'd known my dad and that I should call him Uncle. I'd got to know him better during the drinking years – when things were hectic in Melbourne and I'd escape down to the mish. I learnt that Banjo had been born between the wars, and his real name was Henry; Banjo was a name given to him. Uncle Banjo wanted to fight the Nazis in the forties but wasn't accepted into the military. Instead, he became part of the Allied Works Council, where he was awarded a commendation for the work he did after the bombing of Darwin.

I also learnt that Uncle Banjo had no formal schooling – a lot of the uncles and aunties left school early to contribute to the upkeep of the family – but he was a wise man with a wealth of knowledge about the old ways.

Back in my drinking years, I didn't have the patience that men like Uncle Banjo deserved. I was distracted and while I loved those uncles and aunties and other Elders on the mission, especially an older woman called Aunty Dolly, who I had a particular friendship with, I didn't appreciate them like I should have.

When I went back to Framlingham Mission, sober,

I saw the place with different eyes. Uncle Banjo took me to the burial sites and the river, and to the forest that he was almost singlehandedly trying to preserve. I saw visions on the mission and heard voices; I heard laughter and singing. I heard Mum and Dad, and my brothers and sisters, and my uncles and aunties and cousins.

'Things were different when you kids got taken away – quiet,' Uncle Banjo said, as though our minds were one. 'On those quiet days, you could hear the echoes of you all running amok in the forest or playing games or singing.'

I didn't know what to say. I hadn't thought much about what it was like for those left behind.

'Heard you been writing songs,' Uncle Banjo said.

'A little bit. Just country songs.'

'There's nothing "just" about country songs. I reckon you should write a song about when they took you children away.'

'Nah,' I said. I didn't think much of that idea. Why would I want to go back and think about that? Besides, I told Uncle Banjo, I didn't really know that much about what had happened.

'But I do. I remember it all,' he said. 'I remember when the coppers came and your dad wanted to fight them and all the yelling and screaming. I thought about you kids all the time. No one talks about it, but I reckon they should.'

That evening, sitting in the fading light, drinking tea brewed by Uncle Banjo and eating damper, I started putting together chord progressions and lyrics. I worked on that song until I crashed out, then woke with the sun and worked on it some more. By mid-morning the song was finished.

The song had a repeating refrain: 'Took the children away', addressing what had happened in those days on the mission, and what had happened to the mothers and fathers and uncles and aunties after the children were taken. That would be my song and Lawrence's song, and Horse's and Diana's, Gladys's and Myrtle's and Alma's too. That would be Mum and Dad's song.

I wrote another song while I was at the mish that time, a companion piece, if you like. It starts:

Uncle Banjo told me before the children went away
Life was good and life was free
Not like it is today.

It's called 'Weeping in the Forest', and that song was for Uncle Banjo and Aunty Dolly and Mummy Mick and all the old people left behind. They were like trees that had been stripped of their leaves and green branches and left like husks.

I played those songs for Ruby and the boys, who hummed the melodies and asked questions about why things had happened on the mish the way they had.

'I'm not quite sure,' I'd answer. 'Maybe one day we'll know.'

Around that time, me, Rube and the boys moved back to Clingin Street in Reservoir, and not long after that Ruby became the houseparent at an Aboriginal group home in Preston. Ruby was always a wonderful mother and, now sober, she was ready to take on the role of mum – not only for our boys, but for all the other state-ward children in the home, regardless of their age. 'Mum.' That's what everyone called her. It was a name that would stick for life.

I was watching TV when we took on our fourth son. There were calls coming from outside, 'Sister girl... *Ruby... Sister girl!*' And afterwards, a knock on the door.

Ruby and I opened it together. It was a friend of ours called Cheryl, who had spent some time with Ruby at Winja Ulupna. Cheryl hadn't been as successful as Ruby in sobering up.

'Help me, sister girl, please? Just for a bit. I don't know what else to do.'

Cheryl held a bundle of blankets and, moving some of the folds, she revealed the face of a beautiful little boy.

'His name's Terrence.'

Of course, we would help our sister. Cheryl never came right, and since that day Terrence has been our son.

We had all come from dire circumstances: Ruby and me and the baby, who we called Mr T; Arthur and Krissy. We had all lost our parents, but now, in each other's company, we had a chance for happiness.

I continued working as a counsellor at Gresswell. I was getting stronger every day and soon could spend time with my drinking friends and family without having even a hint of the thirst. Songs were pouring out of me, too.

One song came to me after watching TV. On the news there was a group of people, mostly Aboriginal, running rampant through the streets of the northern NSW town of Brewarrina.

'What's got them all riled up?' I asked Ruby.

The report said the rioting started after it was discovered that a twenty-eight-year-old man named Lloyd B had been found dead in the Brewarrina lock-up. After a spate of Aboriginal deaths in police custody, our community was at their wits' end. His death would be the last straw before an inquiry by the Royal Commission was announced.

While I was enraged about the larger picture and all the politics involved, I was more concerned with Lloyd himself. I read as much about him as I could and found out he was a young man whose life was wrecked by discrimination.

His life was mine, and mine his.

I wondered how some of us get there, us fellas. We start off as boys, so young and happy. How are we taken so far from the light? This isn't what we want for our lives, for them to be cut short brutally. Why do we so often end up like that?

My early songwriting was mostly about people and their stories, about the people around me whose pain and joy I felt so deeply I had to write about them.

I think that, for most of the people around me, they were concerned with the life directly in front of them – not necessarily the larger issues that they represented. Ruby helped children and families who had been marginalised, without spending much time thinking about *why* they were marginalised, and *how*. Uncle Banjo spent a lot of time and energy trying to gain back control over the mission forest, which was set to be sold off due to industrial interests, without too much thought about the bigger question of land rights. I was writing about my experiences of being taken from my parents, and the death of a young Aboriginal man. I was not thinking about the rest of the Stolen Generations and the epidemic of deaths in custody – an epidemic that had touched my own immediate family.

Then, in 1988, things started to change for all of us.

Throughout Australia there was talk of a huge party, one marking two hundred years since the first English fleet landed in Botany Bay. Most of Australia was being encouraged to come together around one word, one affirmation: celebration. It was plastered across buses and on billboards and in television advertisements.

It didn't seem right to us Aboriginal people. For us Aboriginal people, it seemed that in 1988 we should come together, but not around the government's word, the government's affirmation. It seemed that us Aboriginal people *should* come together around another word, one that had defined us over the last two centuries.

A word that I reckon was defining me personally.

Survival.

This photo of Ruby, me and the boys at our home in Clingin Street in Reservoir was taken for *Who* magazine in 1992.

(From left) Alma, Ruby and Myrtle, about to board the bus from Melbourne to Sydney for the 1988 Bicentenary Protest. Photo courtesy Tracy Roach, Alma's daughter.

CHAPTER 11

TOO MANY BRIDGES

Well let me tell you people, I'm getting sick and tired
Of crossing those bridges, just to get to the other side
Well some people are with us
And some people just run and hide

Oh, Monday, Tuesday, Wednesday, Thursday too
Friday, Saturday, Sunday, we're always feelin' blue
'Cause you took the land, took the children away
And now you know that you've got to pay
We crossed too many bridges
Been to too many Sorry Days

Well I remember marching with the black, gold and the red
Well we marched through the cities
Where the children and the old ones led
What do we want, land rights is what we said
What do we want, what do we want today
Land rights, land rights, land rights is what we say
We'll put on our colours and do it like the good old days

Oh, Monday, Tuesday, Wednesday, Thursday too
Friday, Saturday, Sunday, we're always feeling blue
'Cause you took the land, took the children away
And now you know that you've got to pay

We crossed too many bridges
Been to too many Sorry Days
We crossed too many bridges
Been to too many Sorry Days

The year 1988 was a pivotal moment for a lot of us blackfellas. We had some sense of what had happened to ourselves, as a people, before that year. But what did I know up to that point? My lifestyle, my drinking, having been thrown into jail. I'd been taken from my parents, who, like me, had been denied access to culture, who'd been beaten by police and thrown into jail for no good reason.

We might have lived through those traumas alone, but a collective sense of injustice began to bring us together that year. We began to find a strength in our unity, and a unity in our strength.

The government had a party planned in Sydney on 26 January 1988, to celebrate the bicentenary of the arrival of the British First Fleet of convicts, soldiers and settlers into what we now recognise as Eora country. Sailing in with them were guns and disease, grog and money, and oppressive colonial practices. There was no shortage of other things that would be detrimental to our people, that would keep us sick, poor, addicted and confused about ourselves. We had suffered; we were suffering still.

The depth of the sadness we felt was not what parties are about. It didn't feel right – a lot of our misery could be traced back to that day in 1788.

I loved Australia, modern and ancient, and I was happy to celebrate our nationhood with any Australian who wanted to celebrate with me – but not on the day that my people started being killed. Not with my people still dying to this day in prisons and on the floors of pubs and in empties.

Apparently that didn't seem right to a lot of other people too. At the end of '87 and at the start of '88, I heard that Aboriginal people from all around the country were going to go to Sydney to stage their own event, their own commemoration, on 26 January. For some, it was an opportunity to protest the celebrations, for others it was an opportunity to come together as a united Aboriginal community and show the rest of the world that we are still here, that our culture is still here. For most, it was a combination of the two. What began as a whisper turned into a murmur that built to a scream.

In Melbourne, buses were arranged to leave Fitzroy and arrive in Sydney a few days shy of the 26th. There we would camp at La Perouse, a suburb at the northern edge of

Botany Bay and the only place in Sydney where Aboriginal and Torres Strait Islander people have continuously lived from before 1788 to this day. The plan was to meet every day to talk and play music and come together, until the 26th, when we would walk through the streets of Sydney, visible and audible to the three million people expected to visit the city for the bicentennial celebration.

We would come together as one people, with one desire: to show that white Australia has a black history, and that we have survived. We have survived the black stain of what befell us over the years – the blackness beyond our skin colour, the blackness of our trauma.

In the week leading up to that day, Ruby and I loaded the boys onto a bus bearing flags of red, black and yellow, representing our one Indigenous nation. Many mobs. One flag. Even as we left Melbourne, looking through the windows of the bus, we could see people reacting to us. Some would point and talk, some would wave in support, some were visibly hostile. We'd been in the news – black people coming from all around the country to ruin the party in Sydney. We weren't there to watch the fireworks, or to listen to the free concerts, or sail on the replica tall ships; we were there to whinge and be ungrateful. At least, that's what talkback radio and the tabloid newspapers were saying.

As we drove our way through the outskirts of Sydney, people's reactions became more extreme. We got middle fingers and racial epithets hurled at us by those getting ready to head down to the harbour to celebrate.

'Go home!' some of them shouted, which seemed a particularly odd insult.

But there was support in Sydney, too. We got cheers and applause from people holding up Aboriginal flags by the side of the road. These people had been waiting for us, they were supporting us. That makes a big difference when you're putting yourself out there.

From the La Perouse parkland where we pitched our tents, you could see the approach into Botany Bay. From the stage that had been set up, you could see the headlands that the First Peoples would have gathered on two hundred years before, watching warily as Arthur Phillip's fleet of tall ships got closer and closer, some with the memory of James Cook arriving eighteen years earlier. I reckoned I could feel something of what those old people felt. I also felt proud that their descendants were here today, still strong and proud.

It was incredible to be around Aboriginal people from all around the country, old and young. My ears filled with the sounds of didgeridoo and songs in language, my nose filled with the smoke of campfires. It was beautiful and more sublime because I was sharing it all with Ruby and the boys.

Things got screwed up by politics, though, which is often the way.

Everyone at the camp had managed to assemble under one flag and with one purpose, but we didn't have much of an organised structure. Whenever you get a large group of strangers together, no matter what their skin colour, there are always a few who think they should be in charge.

On 25 January vicious bickering broke out about what route we were going to take as we marched through the city the next day. Some wanted to go from Redfern Oval to Hyde Park, others wanted to march on to the Opera House. I voiced no opinion – I didn't think it really mattered what the route was, as long as we all walked together. People were getting up on stage and threatening to boycott the march if their route wasn't chosen. I, like most, was becoming increasingly frustrated with it all. I told Ruby that I couldn't stand this divisiveness, and she pointed at the stage and told me to do something about it.

I wasn't the type to speak up in front of a large group of friends and family, let alone a huge group of strangers.

'Sing one of your songs,' Ruby said. 'It'll be a lot better than all this arguing.'

She wasn't wrong. Anything would have been better than that, but there was no way I was getting up and singing…Until I was.

I don't really know what came over me, but before I knew it I had my guitar in my hand and was treading a path through the families between me and the stage.

The fella regulating the speakers motioned me straight up on stage with a weary wave, and I muttered a few words before starting the song. I have no idea what I said. Then I strummed out a few chords before launching into the first line of 'Took the Children Away'.

This story's right, this story's true
I would not tell lies to you

As soon as those lines were out, I felt no fear, no trepidation. I was alone in my thoughts. The crowd was somewhere else. My mind was on my old dad and mum, and my brothers and sisters, and Uncle Banjo.

I didn't try to sing to impress, or to educate. I sang to honour. This is something I think I learnt sobering up. Respect and truth are the cornerstones of my life now, and when I played, I played to respect the stories. I did that by playing them true.

This story's right, this story's true.

When I played, I was almost in a dissociative state, but when I finished I came back to reality. People were stunned. Women were crying. Men had their heads bowed, shoulders heaving. People from all across this Aboriginal nation came up to me at the front of the stage to tell me that my story, my family's story, was also their story. There were young people and old people and city folk like me, and old tribal people from out in the desert and up north. They came up to me afterwards.

I was shocked. I was not prepared for how my song affected them. An old fella with a headband told me he'd been taken from his home as a child and had met his sister for the first time only the year before. I was happy to have been able to connect with people, but I was truly amazed by how many people said they too had been taken away. I asked this man how old he was, and he told me he was seventy. Seventy! He must have been taken more than sixty-five years ago.

I'd thought it had just been me and my brothers and sisters who'd been taken. And then, when I met Ruby, I thought it must've happened to a small group of people in South Australia as well. Now I realised it had been happening across the country for decades.

Later that day, it was agreed that we'd all walk from Redfern Oval to Hyde Park on a route that passed

Belmore Park, where I'd had my first charge. As we marched, chanted and sang past Prince Albert Park, not far from One Toxteth Road, Glebe, I wondered where all those people I used to drink with in Sydney were. It had been seventeen years, and I figured many of them would be dead. Most of the parkies didn't get too far past fifty, and many of the fellas I'd drank with in Sydney had been in their thirties.

Life is so short, especially for us. As we marched, I couldn't help but get caught up in the sadness of that fact. I didn't stay sad, though, because I had learnt not to. You had to be strong; all of us had to be strong. I was sober and marching with thousands of my brothers and sisters. On one side of me was Ruby, and on the other, my beautiful boys, Amos and Eban, and my sisters, Alma and Myrtle.

This was no time to be sad – there was too much work to be done. Too many songs to write and too much music to play.

A few months before, some of my music had been recorded for the first time on a cassette tape, titled *Koori*. It had been recorded as part of an exhibition of artefacts detailing the history of Aboriginal people in Victoria.

The exhibition came about in 1985, when a man walked off the street in Fitzroy and into the Aboriginal Legal Service office asking for the CEO, a Gunditjmara elder and my older cousin, Jim Berg. The man handed Jim a little green axe and grinding stone and said, as the most senior Gunditjmara elder around the place, he felt Jim should have the items for safekeeping. Over the years Jim collected more Aboriginal artefacts from around the state – some ancient, some modern – and became known as a keeper of culture around Victoria.

By 1987, he'd collected enough artefacts for an exhibition and thought it would be good for there to be some music for people to listen to as they visited. He'd heard me sing my songs and asked if I'd put some down on tape for him. I recorded the tape at 3CR, a deadly community radio station in Fitzroy that has a long history of giving voice to those who usually have none.

I put mostly my own country songs on that tape, but it also included 'Took the Children Away', 'Beautiful Child', a few protest songs and a brand-new song called 'Munjana'. Munjana is an Indigenous word used by the mob near Swan Hill, on the Murray River on the Victorian border, and it means 'burdened' or 'troubled'. My song tells the story of Beverley Whyman, a woman I'd met who'd affected me deeply when we spoke.

In 1962, Beverly had a baby – a boy she named Russell. When Russell was five weeks old he was taken by the government, fostered with a white family and renamed James Savage. At seven, the family relocated overseas to Florida. Russell never really fitted in there – he wasn't accepted by African-American people; he wasn't accepted by white people. He was eventually abandoned by his parents, and by the age of fifteen he was in a reformatory school. By the age of twenty-six he was facing the death penalty, having been convicted for first-degree murder.

When I met Beverley, she was trying to get Russell off death row and extradited to an Australian prison. She didn't know her son, but he was still her baby. He'd done terrible things, but the way Bev told it, it didn't seem right for Russell to die alone in a prison in Florida.

I couldn't stop thinking of Beverley's story.

I couldn't help but think how out of my head I'd been for many years of my life. I thought about the temporary madness of my suicide attempt, the thought arriving like a rolling storm front with no warning. I didn't want that insanity – no one ever wants that. No one is born wanting to die young, and no one is born wanting to be a killer.

When I was writing the song, I thought about myself and I thought about Russell – his story was mine. We'd both been taken from our families. But mostly, I thought about Beverley. 'Munjana' is her song.

After the *Koori* tape came out, I performed some songs live on 3CR and did a short interview with Gilla McGuinness, talking about my music, performing 'Took the Children Away' and 'Beautiful Child'. After that first interview, the office phone at the George Wright Hostel, where I was working at the time, started ringing. People called in, wanting to know who I was. Later, publicans and bookers phoned, wanting me to play at venues around Melbourne. I loved playing live, and it also didn't hurt that it brought in fifty bucks here, a hundred there.

I also liked being in pubs again, but now for a very different reason. Back then, I was chasing something, thinking I could drink my way to some sort of happiness or revelation. But now I realised I'd found that happiness at the group home with the boys and Ruby. Now, when I was in a pub, the booze and the drunken conversations didn't excite me – just the opportunity to play my music.

Some days I couldn't help but look back and think about the hard times. Once, at a pub in Fitzroy, I had to stop playing my songs and chucked in a Hank Williams number. Sometimes you just want to play a song that makes you feel good and forget.

I'd usually play the pubs on my own, arriving by myself

and drinking lemonade until it was time to perform, but often Dave Arden would join me. Dave was an incredibly talented guitarist who fronted a well-known group called Koori Youth Band. The best thing about this time was that Ruby started singing with Dave and me. Other musicians would also join us on stage – Dave's brother Wally sat in on drums, Jim (aka Tippi) on vocals, and Paul Wright on bass – and we would call ourselves Altogether. The band lasted a year and a bit, and we even played at one of the Building Bridges concerts in Sydney.

After playing at La Perouse in January in 1988, I got a little bit of national media attention. In March I did a set on ABC Radio National, on Paul Petran's Music Deli program, playing all the songs I had put together. Paul also interviewed me, and I could explain where those songs had come from.

After that, in 1989, I got a call at the George Wright Hostel from the producers of an ABC TV show called *Blackout*, a new program telling Aboriginal stories and promoting our music. The producers told me to come to Sydney to perform on the show. And so I did. On the set I played 'Took the Children Away' – without any understanding of how significant that performance would be.

Steve Connolly, the guitarist for The Messengers –

the back-up band for singer-songwriter Paul Kelly – was watching the show at his house in Melbourne. A few bars in, he reached for the phone and called Paul, telling him to turn the television on. The next week I got a call at work from a booking agent. He said he was working with Paul Kelly and the Messengers and was wondering if I was available to open for them at the Melbourne Concert Hall.

I had never heard of Paul Kelly and the Messengers, and I wasn't familiar with the Concert Hall, but they were paying, and I was free, so I agreed. The booking agent said they only needed two songs from me, and they wanted one of those songs to be 'Took the Children Away'. I chose 'Beautiful Child' as the other. When I arrived at the Concert Hall, I quickly realised that this was going to be a bit different to playing at pubs and smaller acoustic venues. I was taken to my own dressing-room, with my name on the door. After I'd been there for a little while and had made some tea and picked at the biscuits left for me, a stage manager came to ask if I was ready to do my sound check.

The idea of a sound check did not fill me with confidence. I walked onto the stage and there, out in front of me, were thousands of empty seats. The thought of them being filled with people filled me with dread.

The disembodied voice at the back of the room didn't seem particularly impressed as I played, either.

'*Got it, thank you,*' the voice boomed after a few bars of each song.

When I was finished, I packed up my guitar and went for the door but was stopped by the stage manager.

'Where are you going?' she asked.

'I'm going home,' I told her.

'We'd prefer if you could stay. That's... normally how it's done.'

'My wife is making dinner.'

'We can get something sent for you if you like.'

I supposed that was okay.

I spent the next few hours outside in the car park smoking like a chimney and in my dressing-room drinking tea, and that's what I was doing when a little fella with short-cropped hair, maybe in his mid-thirties, knocked on my door.

'Archie, just wanted to say hello.'

The bloke looked like security to me – wiry and all in black, with a nose that seemed like it might've been broken at one point.

'Nice to meet you.'

'Got everything you need here?'

Someone had brought me sandwiches and I had all the

tea, milk and sugar I'd ever want. I said I had everything I needed.

'Great, great. Thanks so much for coming and have a good set tonight.'

Nice bloke, I thought. *Very friendly for a bouncer*.

When I was called on stage I was pretty nervous. This world was strange for me, a world of stage managers and sandwiches in dressing-rooms. But at least when I got on stage the spotlight obscured the sight of most of the people in their seats and I felt quite calm.

As I picked up my guitar the crowd quietened down. I looked at the side of the stage and saw the little bouncer-looking fella again. He gave me the thumbs up and I muttered out an introduction to myself and my song 'Beautiful Child' before launching in.

I sang the first verse, and just as had been the case on stage at La Perouse in January, there was nothing else that existed in that room except the song.

Oh, my beautiful child, my beautiful child
The brightest of stars couldn't match your sweet smile
But you grew up too soon, far beyond your young years
Now all that remains is your memory and tears

I thought about Lloyd B, dead too soon, and my father,

whose life also ended in a prison cell. I thought about Lloyd's people and mine, and all those left behind after losing a loved one in circumstances they will never understand.

The song finished and there was pretty much silence.

'Maybe you'll like this one,' I said, before launching straight into 'Took the Children Away'.

I sang the story right, I sang the story true. It didn't appear that the crowd were enjoying my songs, but I would still not tell lies to them.

When I was done, there was more silence. I said thanks and headed for the wing, and that's when the applause started, first quietly, then loudly, and then with real, roaring approval. I could tell people were standing up; I could hear cheers and whoops. As I walked off, the little security bloke had tears in his eyes as he shook my hand.

It was a strange night.

I went back to my dressing-room and had a cup of tea and a cigarette. Then I was ready to go home. In fact, I couldn't wait to go home. I liked the response from the crowd, and hadn't even really minded the bright lights, but this wasn't my world.

On the way out, music came to my ears, lovely and familiar. It was coming from the stage, and I was drawn to it. The band was playing 'Before Too Long', a wonderful song about the hopefulness and irresistibility of love that I'd heard on the radio and enjoyed but had never known it was a song from this Paul Kelly and the Messengers.

And I was shocked to find that singing on stage was the little security bloke with the boxer's nose, dressed all in black.

As he and the band went from one familiar song to the next, I stood there, dumbfounded. Their sound was so full; they were so talented. I felt like a bit of an idiot, having no idea who they were.

I left well before they finished, trying to avoid the awkwardness of bumping into Paul.

When I got home, Ruby was waiting for me. She heated up my dinner and I told her about the day I'd had. The next morning I went into work and life continued as usual until, maybe a week later, the phone rang.

'Archie, it's Paul Kelly,' said the voice on the line. 'I hope you don't mind me calling you at home.'

I told him I didn't, and that I was glad he'd called. I'd been thinking a lot about not knowing who he was and I wanted to apologise. He didn't care about any of that.

'I was wondering if my friend Steve and I could come round and visit you soon. There's a few things we'd like to talk to you about,' he said.

I told him that would be okay and we arranged a time.

When Paul and Steve came around, Ruby put the kettle on. I said to the fellas that I really appreciated being able to play at their gig, and how amazed I was – they were so tight on stage. They thanked me, and Paul told me he was impressed with my set, too. He said that it wasn't just him who was impressed, either – the people from his record label, who'd also seen me play that night, had liked it as well.

'It wasn't really a set, it was two songs,' I said.

'Well, they were impressed with your two songs. We've been talking, and we were wondering if you might be interested in recording an album,' Paul said.

'Have you got many other songs?' Steve asked.

I told him I had a few others. They asked if I'd like to maybe play some music together now. I thought that would be okay.

Paul and Steve went out to the car to get their guitars and I went to the bedroom for mine and, over tea and sandwiches, we got a beautiful racket going. I played a couple of my songs and that took us into a bit of a country music retrospective. We started with George Jones' 'The Window Up Above', which led us into some Merle Haggard and Hank Williams territory, but when we moved into a raucous Johnny Cash medley, I really got the measure of these men.

They were incredible musicians, with Steve one of the best country guitarists I'd ever heard. But more than that, I felt the spirit in these blokes, that divine spirit that can be found through music. They had no problem that the boys ran in and out as we played, and they understood my songs. I started to really like these two.

I didn't have much interest in doing an album, though. It felt as though I'd only recently found a life that worked for me and Ruby and the boys, and I didn't want to upend that apple cart with any complications. After we were done playing, Paul left me with his phone number and a request to take some time and think about doing an album with them. I thanked him and said I'd call to let him know about my decision.

'How about that, eh?' Ruby said when they'd gone, her eyes glinting. 'You get to make your own album!'

'Yeah, real nice of them to ask.'

'What do you mean by that?'

'Well, I don't reckon I want to.'

'Why the hell not?'

'We're right as we are, aren't we, Rube? We get to play when we want to, and we like our home and our jobs. Things are good, aren't they?'

Even if I live to be a thousand years old, I'll never forget what happened next. Ruby seemed to gather herself up taller than I'd ever seen her before, put her hands on her hips and told me: 'It's not all about you, Archie Roach. How many blackfellas you reckon get to record an album?'

She turned sharply and went about her day, leaving me with a lot to think about. I knew exactly what Ruby was saying. If I go through that door of making an album, how many more might get the opportunity to follow behind me? I thought about Uncle Doug Nicholls, a champion footballer who played through the 1930s and bore the taunts and racism and bullshit to prove to young Aboriginal children that their race was no impediment to the fulfilment of their dreams. Uncle Doug didn't stop carving a fresh path for Aboriginal people when his playing career ended, either. He became a coach and then a tireless worker around Fitzroy, helping to house the homeless and provide legal and medical aid. He was a champion for the Aborigines Advancement League and edited their magazine, Smoke Signals.

Later in life, Uncle Doug set up a series of hostels – ones that my family have benefitted from directly. Uncle Doug even became the Governor of South Australia, appointed on the nomination of Don Dunstan, the fella with the office overlooking Victoria Square in Adelaide. Where would we all be if Uncle Doug had said, 'Nah, I'm good where I am,' when the Victorian Football League came calling? Where would we be if Polly Farmer, or Lionel Rose, or Evonne Goolagong had done the same thing?

'When one of us shines, we all shine,' Ruby used to say when she'd see Aboriginal people on the telly doing deadly things. I thought about that as she came back into the room.

'Mum, I reckon I will make that album,' I said.

'I thought you might,' she said. 'You going to call him now?'

'He's probably having his tea... I'll call him later.'

I thought I'd give it a week; I didn't want to seem too keen.

In the week before I called Paul, I came home from work and was unable to find Ruby. I asked Amos where Mum was, and he said she was in our bedroom. When I walked in she leapt up in surprise, stuffing some papers under the bed.

'What have you got there, Ruby?'

She told me it was nothing, but when I had a look it was some writing.

'It's a love letter to my boyfriend,' she joked. But I could tell what it was. It was a song.

'You been writing a song? Why didn't you tell me?'

She grabbed the paper back. 'Well, I'm not going to tell the great Archie Roach that I've been writing songs too, am I?'

She never stopped mocking me about 'the great Archie Roach' after that.

I grabbed a guitar and gave it to Ruby. I asked her to play her song for me.

'Please,' I said.

She did. And the song wasn't good – it was great. It was about the experience of being on the streets, not looking from the outside in, but from the inside out.

Down city streets, I would roam
I had no bed, I had no home

The lyrics were really evocative, and the music had the very cadence and energy of homelessness – always moving, always bouncing to the next bar. The only issue was that it was all just one long verse.

I told Ruby that I loved her song but I felt it should be broken up with a chorus and refrain. I thought that the 'down city streets' bit would work best as a chorus.

She did just that and she messed around with the key. It was all but finished. She played it again for me, and chills went up my spine. I started to wonder if there would ever be a time when this woman would stop surprising me.

A couple of weeks after our first meeting, Paul and Steve came around again with their guitars. We went through a few of my songs, this time with a view to figuring out what we'd try to take into the studio. We ended up with nine good songs.

'I really think we need ten songs, Archie. Have you got anything else?' Paul said.

'Nine songs is enough, isn't it? I reckon that'll be all right.'

'Ten is better.'

Ruby started kicking my foot under the table; I had no idea what she wanted. I turned and gave her a look. *What?!*

'*Mhysng*,' she said through a nearly closed mouth.

'What's that, Ruby?'

'My. Song.'

Of course! That would be perfect. We played 'Down City Streets', and Paul and Steve agreed that would be the tenth song. We were good to go.

A couple of days later we were at the Mushroom Records offices, me with a pen in one hand and a contract in the other. I'd read the contract, but I might as well have been reading Greek. I was about to sign, when Paul stopped me so he could have a read himself.

'This is good, close…' Paul told the executives when he'd finished reading, 'but I reckon we can do a little better.'

Ever since we'd played 'Folsom Prison Blues' together I'd trusted this bloke, so I echoed his sentiment.

The next week we came back to the offices and I went over a new contract with different numbers on it. I held the pen, received a nod from Paul, and signed my first record deal. Everyone shook hands and started patting each other on the back, but I didn't feel we'd done anything yet. I just wanted to get into the studio. Paul said he and Steve were going to produce the album and that I needed to give them a few weeks to arrange a studio and some musicians to play with me, and an engineer. That all sounded good to me. I took a bit of time off work and we were away.

I thought the experience was going to be like when I'd made the *Koori* tape: we'd all go into the studio, I'd sing my songs a couple of times and that was that.

It wasn't going to be like that at all.

We recorded at the Cotton Mill studio, a two-storey warehouse in Carlton converted by Greg Ham, a very talented multi-instrumentalist in the band Men at Work. The first thing Paul and Steve wanted me to do was go upstairs into the recording booth with my guitar and record a 'guide track' for 'Took the Children Away'. I said that was no problem and went upstairs, wondering if I should have asked what a guide track was.

I was in the booth for a few minutes, waiting for instructions. None came. Then I thought I could hear something; people speaking. I tried to listen to what those voices were saying.

'Archie? Can you hear me? Please put on the headphones.'

I put the headphones on and heard Paul's voice.

'Okay, you ready?'

'Yeah, sorry mate. I'm ready.'

Before I could start singing I heard clicking in my ears.

'Excuse me, Paul, there's clicking in these headphones.'

'That's the click track, Archie. You sing along to it. It's to keep the song at a steady rhythm.'

That took a while to get used to. I kept getting confused by the clicks and could only get through the song with the clicks turned almost all the way down.

Finally, Paul said he thought we'd got it, but I reckoned I could do a better take. Steve told me that wasn't necessary because these weren't going to be the vocals on the album – this recording was just to guide the other musicians as they laid down their parts, and I would do my permanent recording once they had done theirs.

I asked Steve what he wanted me to do now, and he said I could take a break while the other musicians did their parts. I had a smoke and came back and watched the track build.

First they recorded the drums, then the keyboards, and then the rhythm guitar, then Steve did his guitar parts. Slowly but surely, it became something that was recognisable as my song.

We had arrived at the studio around ten in the morning, and I didn't get back into the booth to record my vocals until about eight in the evening. We did dozens of takes, some good, but only one good enough for Paul, Steve and me to agree that it was it. I was so happy and relieved to have a song completely finished. Only Paul and Steve said that we weren't finished – not even close. There were more instruments and pick-ups to add, and back-up vocals, too. All that would be done the next day, and the one after that.

I got home in the small hours of the morning and into a bed that Ruby had been asleep in for hours.

'How'd ya go?' she asked.

'I think I'm going to have to ask for more time off work.'

The next day Paul and Steve recorded some back-up singers to add their voices to 'Took the Children Away'. I was honoured when Tim Finn from Split Enz said he wanted to be involved, and was ecstatic when Paul and Steve suggested Ruby. She came in on day three or four of recording, and I was much more comfortable in the studio when she was there.

I started to enjoy the process and appreciate the skills of the session musicians. It was a slog, but eventually I started to feel what Paul and Steve felt. My heart melted when I heard the extraordinary sisters, Vika and Linda Bull, adding their voices, and I couldn't help but marvel at the technical prowess of George Petronas's zydeco playing. But the most impressive part of the experience was the vision Steve and Paul had for my songs.

They saw them in a way I'd never imagined, but they stayed my songs. All the way through to the mix, Paul was constantly asking if I was happy with how my voice was coming through.

'The vocals are the most important part of this particular song,' he'd say about pretty much all of them.

One day I was having a cup of tea with Paul and Steve in the studio and they asked if I had any ideas about what the album should be called. I'd never even thought about it. In the dead air I pressed my brain for an answer.

'Memory...Road,' I said.

I hated it as soon as I said it, and from the silence I could tell Paul and Steve hated it too.

'I like the idea of using one of the songs that speaks a bit about your life, your experience. Not "Took the Children Away", but your experiences as the man you are now. What about "Charcoal Lane"?' Paul said, referring to a song I'd written about my old drinking spot, which was down the road from where we were recording.

As soon as he said it, I loved it. Charcoal Lane meant a lot to me and a lot to the people in the Fitzroy community. It was a place of drinking and family, a place where I played music for community. That was what my story was all about; what my album was all about. Charcoal Lane was a meeting place for us, somewhere where our stories were collected and completed. It had been a place where Aboriginal people drank, yes, and maybe that was what people saw from the outside, but to us it was so much more than that.

I reckoned calling the album *Charcoal Lane* might sanctify that place a little, elevate it a little, but without forgetting the reality of the place and the drinking that happened there.

I'm a survivor of Charcoal Lane

That's the last line of 'Charcoal Lane', the second song on the album. That was an important sentiment for me. It's only that which we love that can hurt us. I loved Charcoal Lane, but it did try to kill me. I will forever be a survivor of Charcoal Lane.

'Sounds all right to me,' I said to Paul and Steve, before taking a sip of tea.

Paul Kelly (left), me and Steve Connolly recording my debut album Charcoal Lane at Greg Ham's Cotton Mill Studio in Carlton.

Original sketch by Pierre Baroni for *Charcoal Lane.*

CHAPTER 12

CHARCOAL LANE

Side by side we'd walk along
To the end of Gertrude Street
And we'd tarpaulin muster for a quart of wine
Thick or thin, right or wrong
In the cold and in the heat
We'd cross over Smith Street
To the end of a line

Then we'd laugh and sing do anything
To take away the pain
Try to keep it down
As it first went down
In Charcoal Lane
Spinning yarns and telling jokes
Now the wine is tasting good
Cause it's getting closer and closer
To its end
Have a sip and roll some smokes
We'd smoke tailormades if we could
But we just made do with some city street blend

And we'd all chuck in
And we'd start to drink
When we had enough to do it again

But if things got tight
Then we'd have to bite for
Charcoal Lane

Up Gertrude Street we'd walk once more
With just a few cents short
And we'd stop at The Builders
To see who we could see
Then we'd bite round
Until we'd score a flagon of McWilliams Port
Enough to take away our misery
Then we'd all get drunk
Oh so drunk
And maybe a little insane
And we'd stagger home, all alone
And the next day we'd do it again
Have a reviver in Charcoal Lane
I'm a survivor of Charcoal Lane

Where the hell am I?

I mean, I knew where I was physically. I was in Sydney, in Darling Harbour, inching towards the Convention Centre theatre. I was in the back of a town car. A nice car, big and new. A driver wearing a suit in front of me, a five-star hotel behind me, and Ruby sitting there by my side.

I knew where I was on a map, I just didn't know where I was spiritually. I was on my way to the 1991 ARIA

Awards, and this was meant to be the start of an enjoyable evening. I was wondering when the fun was going to start.

There was a big crowd ahead of our car, split in the middle by a red carpet. I heard a roar from the crowd and craned my head to see who'd just stepped out of the car in front of us. I saw a flush of blond coiffure.

'I think that's John Farnham,' Ruby said.

'I think you're right,' I replied.

Ruby was having fun. She could fit in anywhere if she had to, but that wasn't how I worked. I wasn't looking forward to pulling up in front of the baying crowd, nor the prospect of getting up on stage later that evening.

My debut album *Charcoal Lane* had been nominated for two ARIA Awards. The first to be announced on the night, 'Best Indigenous Release', was what people thought I had a good chance of winning. The second to be announced, 'Best New Artist', was what people thought should go to either the musical comedians the Doug Anthony All Stars or the Newcastle rock group The Screaming Jets.

'Or you, Archie,' they might say afterwards. I knew what that meant.

Our car lurched forward and it was our turn on the red carpet. There was a bit of a rumble in the crowd. Who would be next? Craig McLachlan? Michael Hutchence? Jimmy Barnes?

We opened the door and the crowd went from a rumble to dead silence. Sorry, everyone, it's just two blackfellas.

I was more than a bit relieved at the response. It meant we didn't have to stop and have photographs taken; we could just forge ahead and find where we were sitting, then we could finally chill out for a bit.

'Don't look, keep your head down, just keep walking,' Ruby said under her breath as we walked up the red carpet and into the auditorium.

The launch of *Charcoal Lane* had required 'a bit of hustle'. That's what the people at Mushroom Records had said. No one knew who I was and we had to change that. This meant I had to play every gig and do every interview, all the way from Melbourne to Sydney up to Brisbane and beyond. I didn't mind. I was full of piss and vinegar with a finally finished album in my hand. When I got the first copy I said to Ruby that I was happy now.

'This is enough for me, Mum,' I told her, holding the album. 'It's my story here, and if anyone wants to know about me, it's all here. That's enough for me.'

'Not sure I reckon the people who paid for all of this feel the same way,' Ruby said with a chuckle.

When the album came out, I started a run of gigs the

likes of which I certainly hadn't done before and I haven't done since, either. Dozens of pubs and halls all down the east coast, venues big and small. I didn't mind any of them, really. It usually meant I got to play with people like my nephew Dave from Altogether, and Steve Connolly, who toured with us occasionally. I loved that they'd taken the time out of their lives to come and play with me.

The thing I didn't like was the interviews, and it seemed that almost every gig was accompanied by a raft of them – print, radio and sometimes television.

'Do you consider yourself a crusader for Aboriginal people, Archie?' people would ask.

'Which stories on the album are true, Archie?'

'What do you hope to change in Australia with your music, Archie?'

'Are you a voice for your people, Archie?'

Am I a voice for my people? My people? Archie Roach, a voice for *my* people? Don't be silly.

What the hell could I say? I'm not a crusader. I'm just an ordinary fella, and if you listen to the music you'll know that. What I *really* wanted to say was, 'Actually, all of you, listen to the album if you want to, don't if you don't want to... Now can you please leave me alone so I can enjoy this cup of tea?'

I still say to this day that if you really want to know

me, listen to my songs, or even better, see me perform live. It seems a strange thing to tell you in my own story, but it's true.

I just wanted to play my music. Everything else around it, like the interviews and the promotional gigs, had started to take its toll on me. I longed for Ruby and the group home and the children and the George Wright Hostel. I missed them deeply when I was touring *Charcoal Lane*. I wondered why I was doing it all. I guess I was doing it to repay the people who'd invested faith and money in me. When I heard the tracks from the album, I was so impressed and thankful for what Paul and Steve had managed. When I was in the studio it sometimes felt as if they were making something simple so complex, but when I listened again I heard how expertly they'd kept the acoustic heart of my music.

Like I said, though, I got lonely, and wondered what it was all for.

While I was touring, every so often I'd get a sense of how well the album was doing, not through sales receipts or chart success – I didn't understand any of that – but from hearing my songs in the back of a taxi, or seeing my album in displays or bins out the front of record shops, or gig posters on walls. It was strange for me. I began to miss the anonymity.

The fame aspect of the whole experience didn't really mean anything at all to me then. People came to the shows, so I guess they must have known who I was or had heard my music, but I was rarely pestered. I do remember one instance, though, when I was doing my sound check at the Annandale Hotel in Sydney. I came across a woman who clearly knew who I was and knew my story.

I can see her in my mind's eye – a little bit older than me with a scowl that could curdle butter. While I strummed and sang for the benefit of the sound desk, she glared at me with her arms forcefully crossed.

'Am I supposed to sit here and feel bad?' she yelled at me during a quiet moment.

'Excuse me?' I asked.

'This is my local, this is the place I go to, and while you're playing, am I just meant to sit here and feel guilty, about whatever has happened to you?'

I had no idea what to say. I'd never thought much about how I wanted the audience to respond. I just sang the songs, and any feelings they had after that was up to them.

'My intention isn't for you to feel bad,' I said. I struggled to find anything else to say, so I finished with: 'Thank you for letting us play at your pub.'

The woman walked away, angry. Maybe she thought

I was being glib, but I wasn't. I have no idea if she came back and saw me perform. I hope she did.

Nominations for the ARIA Awards are a big deal in the music industry but having just arrived in that industry they came as a complete surprise to me. Mushroom Records had arranged everything – flights and a hotel for me and Ruby, and a car to take us to the awards.

We took our seats inside the Convention Centre as quickly as we could.

'Best Indigenous Release' was one of the early awards of the night and when they called out *Charcoal Lane* as the winner, I went up in a daze. I have no memory of what I said, but I do remember walking down from the stage carefully. I'd never seen an ARIA Award before. It's really heavy and looks like the top of a giant silver spear – and seems pretty bloody dangerous!

I spent a lot of time outside the theatre smoking after that, trying to calm my nerves. I was out on the balcony when they announced the nominees for Best New Artist. I only knew about it because a breathless record company person ran out to tell me that I had to go back into the theatre immediately.

As soon as I walked in I heard my name called and

had to double-time it to get up on stage. I do remember what I said that time, though: 'Music is a great equaliser.' It wasn't something I'd planned, but as I returned to my seat I was happy it had come to me, because it was true.

When the ceremony finished and everyone else was getting ready for the after party, Ruby and I just wanted to escape. Before we could get away, we were stopped by journalists who wanted quotes and photographers who wanted pictures. John Farnham even sought me out to congratulate me and tell me how much he liked my album.

'Okay, that's enough, everybody. This way, Archie,' some fella said, pointing to the corner of the foyer.

As Ruby and I were led away, I got in this fella's ear and asked who he was.

'I'm your publicist,' he said.

Righto, good to know. He led me through the crowd to where another man was waiting. I was sure this was the American comedian Steven Wright.

'Congratulations to you, Archie, big night,' he said, shaking my hand forcefully.

'Thank you very much.'

'Now…' he said, pointing at me. 'Now is when you start work. You ready?'

This was Michael Gudinski, the founder and owner

of Mushroom Records. I'd never met him before. I told him I was ready, even though I didn't really understand what he was saying. I thought I'd been working quite hard since the album's release. He seemed happy enough with my response and then turned and disappeared into the crowd.

Did he want me to work harder? Did he want me to do more interviews? It was all a bit concerning.

'Let's go,' Ruby said. That sounded good to me.

Life become different after the ARIAs. I was fearful it would speed up, but it actually slowed down, which was nice. We did fewer gigs but with more money. I was slowly improving on stage as a live performer, but Ruby was taking leaps and bounds.

While I was comfortable as a storyteller, Ruby was comfortable as a performer. She'd light up on stage with funny little quips. Audiences gravitated to her, and it warmed my heart for them to see a bit of the magic that I saw.

Soon Ruby was performing 'Down City Streets', and not just that – other songs she'd been writing, too. I'd watch her play those new songs and sometimes I'd forget to play along because I couldn't believe that this was the same woman I'd been showing chords to only a few years earlier.

I thought I was balancing music and work pretty well. Turns out, I wasn't.

One day I got a message telling me to go and meet with Keith, my boss from Aboriginal Hostels, which the George Wright Hostel came under.

'We're really proud of your music, Archie, and we'd love for you to make more, but if you want to do that you probably have to stop working with us,' Keith said. 'You're one of our best workers and we'd want you to stay on at the hostel, but you know continuity is key with these jobs, and you have so many other obligations. I know you love working for us, Archie, and I know you love making your music, but I guess you just have to think about what you love doing best.'

Keith told me to take some time to think about it. There was likely no wrong decision, but he said he wanted what was best for me.

What did I love doing best? I loved both music and my work. Which one was best right now? I racked my brain and couldn't make a decision either way.

I took the family out to Framlingham to muse on it. As I'd grown older I'd been drawn to the place more – not just for the quiet and the company and the natural beauty, but I was aware of the spirits that Uncle Banjo used to talk about. There were ghosts in the forest and in the river, but they weren't anything to be scared of if you treated them with respect. In fact, they were there to enrich and enlighten.

I felt I would come back from Framlingham with an answer to whether I should quit music or not.

When I finally decided, I was sitting with my cousin Violet, having some tea, and she was asking about the ins and outs of being a musician. She thought it all sounded pretty good, but I told her about the parts that weren't.

'I think I actually might give it all away,' I told her.

She looked not just shocked but angry. She asked me why the hell I would do something like that.

I told her about the interviews and being on the road and how much I liked working at George Wright. I realised she wasn't really concerned with any of that.

'If you stop, what are we going to listen to?'

Violet loved me and I loved her, but her major concern was that there wouldn't be more albums for her to listen to if I quit music. She said it wasn't just her – all the brothers and sisters round those parts listened to *Charcoal Lane* all the time. They spent a lot of time anticipating what I'd do next.

'There'll be something else to listen to,' I told her.

She looked at me as if I was out of my mind. I guess I hadn't really thought about how impactful my music was to Aboriginal people, and specifically Aboriginal people at the mish. My music did benefit others; I just hadn't really noticed.

It was then and there that I decided I would continue with my musical career and promised Violet I would start working on a second album soon.

When I got home I went and saw Keith and told him I was going to be a full-time musician. He shook my hand and told me he was looking forward to hearing my new songs.

After that, the idea of doing another album became real, and that was exciting.

I'd hang on Ruby's every word when she'd tell stories about the Coorong and the old Pitjantjatjara mob who would visit her grandfather, and the connection to the land and the plants and the animals. Ruby used to explain that in her most still moments, out in the bush or next to a river, she'd remember everything in her life, even when she was a baby, and sometimes she'd remember even back before that too – back when she was a pelican, way back, even to the Dreaming.

Things came to Ruby, thoughts and feelings. They came from somewhere deep, an ancient memory.

That's what I wanted to write about.

I loved Ruby and was fascinated by that love. It was real, I knew that, but it wasn't something that could be measured in a cup or on a scale. What was that love – love that was real but immeasurable?

That's what I wanted to write about.

I needed to explain that to Ruby before I started writing, because it seemed I wasn't the only one who'd recognised how interesting she was. Mushroom Records were interested in Ruby and those songs she'd been writing and had been having conversations with her about becoming a recording artist in her own right.

'What would you reckon about that, Dad? If I ended up being a singer like you?' she said once, when we were eating dinner.

It was a rhetorical question. She knew how I felt about that: it would be great. The only issue was that I knew the songs Ruby would be writing would be like the ones on *Charcoal Lane* – deeply autobiographical and personal. Was it a problem that I was writing about Ruby too? I didn't have a right to Ruby's stories, not if she wanted to tell them herself.

I told her that and she laughed the suggestion off.

'Archie, you're not writing songs about me, you're writing songs about how you feel about me. That's not the same thing.'

She was right.

Before Ruby would go into the studio the first time, I would go in for my second album, and I was starting to get a more complete idea in my mind of what I was going to do. My first album had been centred around the acoustic guitar – it was all I knew then. But for the second album I wanted a different sound and a different feel, more of a band sound.

The ideas really started to coalesce when Ruby and I were invited to tour remote Aboriginal communities in the Northern Territory.

It was a bit different up there compared to the gigs we'd played in the southern cities. If they didn't like us, we knew about it. I remember one gig we did where the audience response was more varied. After each song people were yelling, 'Play some rock and roll!'

'I don't really play that kind of music…' I said.

I think we won them over eventually.

I remember in Kuranda, in far north Queensland, after a gig a woman came up to me and asked if Ruby and

I would come round to her place for a cup of tea. Once we got there, we were greeted by an old man with a mass of white hair and a grey beard.

'You that fella from Victoria? The one who sings those songs?' he asked.

I told him I was, and he said he wanted to have a private word with me on the veranda. He pointed to a tree in front of us and explained that it was native to where his people were originally from, further north. He told me about all the things the tree could be used for – medicine, food, basketry. He pointed to a bird in the tree and explained that his people called it a rain bird, because that bird would always sing before the rain came. He told me stories about all the things around us, and stories about the river and the fish and the history of his people.

He talked for a good two hours while I listened, and when he finished, I thanked him. He laughed and said that he wanted to thank me. I didn't understand that.

He said, 'I came here to give you these stories and for you to take them, so thank you. We owe you a big debt of gratitude, you southern people. You took the brunt.'

'The brunt?'

'You took the brunt of the invasion. They only wanted the green country for their sheep and cows. They didn't want this kind of country for a while. We got to preserve our old ways. You mob never lost your spears, though, you just put them down,' he said.

I'll never forget that.

Travelling in the north all the yarns I heard about the old ways excited me to write and record again with a new perspective. I didn't want to tell the old stories on my new album; I didn't really think they were mine to tell, but I wanted to bring the spirit of them to my songs. I wanted to hear the old voices and try to sing them in that timbre, with that soul.

The old men I'd met had told me it was easy to listen to the old voices. I just had to listen. So when I went into the studio to record my second album I resolved to do just that.

David Bridie, a very talented musician, founding member of Not Drowning, Waving and a well-known producer, put his hand up, and as soon as we got into the studio together I told him about my ambitions. He said to put away the songs I had in my back pocket for a second so that we could perform an exercise. Before we attempted any of the songs I'd already written, we were going to try to write a song right then and there in the studio, off the cuff and in the moment. David invited

John Phillips in to help create the song.

I told David I didn't reckon I'd be able to do that. I'd heard of musicians who could improvise, but I didn't see myself as one of them. He asked me to at least try and told me he'd help me start. He pressed his finger down on a key on the keyboard and kept it there. I can't remember what note it was, but I do remember that nothing came. Then he pressed a different note and asked me to get into the note, to feel the note.

I didn't know what he meant, but I tried anyway. I tried to be quiet, I tried to hear the old voices.

Nothing.

Nothing.

Nothing.

Then it came.

First I heard music, but also birdsong and other animal sounds. I heard the didgeridoo and clap sticks and a little girl laughing. The melody came and then a refrain. Lyrics, words, old voices...

Jamu dreaming
Jamu dreaming

'Jamu' is the Pitjanjatjara word for grandfather or old one. What had come to me was grandfather's dreaming, specifically the dreaming of Ruby's grandfather – the old fella who sometimes had business with the red-headband mob up over the Flinders Ranges.

It was different, writing that song. It had come from a different place, a deeper place. It was a bit like writing music, but also a bit like praying. I'd been transported somewhere, and I went to that place again as I wrote the rest of those lyrics for 'Jamu Dreaming'.

Uncle Banjo's song 'Weeping in the Forest' was on that second album too, an album I called *Jamu Dreaming*. It came from the conversations I'd had with Uncle Banjo, about hearing the laughter of the children in the forest one day, and then the silence that followed when the children were taken.

On my album I had a violin player named Jen Anderson, who Ruby took a real shine to, and when it was time for Ruby to record her album she wanted Jen to produce and engineer it. Jen told Ruby that she didn't really have any experience behind the desk, but Ruby was adamant. She wanted this album to crackle with female energy and she felt that energy in Jen. They did a deadly job together. The album is all Ruby. She called it *Thoughts Within*, as suggested by her brother Jeffrey.

My favourite song on Ruby's album is 'Sister Yappa'. When I play that song now, I'm transported back to our old place on Clingin Street in Reservoir, with me and Ruby dancing and pirouetting like mad people while the boys laughed at us.

She was so proud; I was so proud. We were so happy. When we danced around, playing that song, it felt like there was no one else in the world, no problems in the world, and maybe, at least for just the violin solo, there wasn't.

Photo by Pierre Baroni from the front cover of the *Jamu Dreaming* album.

Photo from the front cover of Ruby Hunter's 2000 album *Feeling Good*.

CHAPTER 13

MULYAWONGK

Standing on this mountain, see how far we've come
I see my brothers and sisters, still falling down
Looked across this river, this is where we want to be
Cried all our salty, salty tears into the sea

And the voice of the Mulyawongk, is calling
Yeah the voice of the Mulyawongk, is calling

Ruby left the river, cried so bitterly
She was born by the water's edge, underneath this tree
She come back to the river, cried so happily
Cause she no longer a stranger, in her own country

And the voice of the Mulyawongk, is calling
Yeah the voice of the Mulyawongk, is calling, is calling to you

She was a little girl, she never stood a chance
But she grew up and rose above her circumstance
She picked up her family, helped them to do well
She picked up her husband, saved him from his hell
And the voice of the Mulyawongk, is calling
Yeah the voice of the Mulyawongk, is calling

And we're living in the sunshine, there's rainbows in the sky
Oh we've gotta be happy now, no need to cry
And Ruby of the river, fulfils her destiny
This woman is a keeper, yeah she holds the key

And the voice of the Mulyawongk, is calling
Yeah the voice of the Mulyawongk, is calling, it's calling you.

The gig was at the Esplanade Hotel down in St Kilda, arranged for the release of Jamu Dreaming. That's where I saw her. She wasn't young – maybe in her fifties. She had white hair and looked quite serious. I recognised her as someone I knew, but I couldn't place exactly from where.

I ploughed on with my gig. I sang and told stories, about the old people up north and about the Stolen Generations, and I spoke about the Scotsman and his wife who took me on as their child. The gig was going well, and I tried to keep my eyes from this woman.

I finished a song and had maybe one or two to go. The woman walked closer to the stage and locked her eyes on mine. I couldn't help but meet her gaze. And that's when I recognised her, tears coming to my eyes.

I rushed straight down, and we hugged in the crowd. Then I brought her up onstage.

'Everybody, this is my sister. You remember the old

Scotsman? This is his daughter,' I said. Everyone cheered and clapped. 'This is the woman who taught me how to play music.'

Mary Hocking nee Cox seemed embarrassed by the applause and gave a little nod.

Afterwards we had a cup of tea and she handed me a big envelope. Inside were pictures from when we were kids – photos of me with Dad and Mum Cox, and Mary and Noel. I asked her where everybody was now. She told me that Mum Dulcie had passed away some years earlier from a diabetes-related illness. Dad Alex was still alive. He had dementia and was living in a home for the elderly, but he was holding on.

I asked about Noel. Mary got sad and said that no one from the family had seen him since he'd left.

'I wanted to explain, Archie...I wanted to apologise,' she said.

'Apologise for what?'

'We didn't know, Archie...We thought we were doing the right thing.'

I was immediately transported to an incident a couple of weeks prior when a big old fella came up to me after a show and started talking. He had the particular demeanour and sound to his voice that all cops seem to have, but his voice began to break as he explained how he used to take Aboriginal children off missions, ripping them from their mothers' arms. Then he broke down. The guilt and the years had obviously softened him. He wanted to tell me that he didn't know what he was doing until it was too late.

Mary said the same thing.

I held Mary as she started to fall apart, this woman who had borne guilt for something she hadn't done.

'We didn't know…' she said again.

'You didn't do anything wrong, Mary. It wasn't you or Mum and Dad. I have only respect and love for all of you, for treating me the way you did.'

We had a good catch-up and promised to stay in touch. She looked after Amos a few times and once she even took him to the nursing home where Dad Alex was living.

Mary told me it was rare to get any reaction from Dad Alex, but when the old man saw Amos he tried to bound out of bed.

'It's my boy! It's Archie!' he said.

Mary went to explain, but the old fella was so happy to see my son, who reminded him of me.

'He's come back! My boy, my boy!' he said.

I thought a lot about Dad Alex after that, and I planned to see him one last time, but I didn't – I just wanted to remember him the way he was. Eventually,

Mary let me know that he had passed. I still think about Dad Alex to this day when I see a crisp tartan or hear the wail of a bagpipe.

On 13 February 2008, Ruby and I were invited to perform at Federation Square in Melbourne.

Screens everywhere were filled with the face of then Prime Minister Kevin Rudd as he delivered an official apology to Indigenous Australians, to the Stolen Generations, for the pain, suffering and hurt caused by our removal from our families, communities, culture and country.

'The time has now come for the nation to turn a new page in Australia's history by righting the wrongs of the past...We apologise for the laws and policies of successive parliaments and governments that have inflicted profound grief, suffering and loss on these, our fellow Australians...We apologise especially for the removal of Aboriginal and Torres Strait Islander children from their families...'

As I heard these words, tears streamed down my face and my chest heaved. Sometimes I didn't care what politicians said – it was about what they did. As I watched the Australian Prime Minister delivering what felt like a sincere apology – an apology to me and to Ruby and to our families, and all of my people who were taken from their parents and their culture – I thought about my mother, Nellie, and father, Archie. This apology was for them too.

This gesture meant something. It wasn't final justice and it didn't bring ultimate comfort, but it was a small step towards both.

Federation Square was packed, and in the audience were many blackfellas who I knew had been taken themselves and had gone on their own long journey back to family and back to country.

I cried as I played and, midway through 'Took the Children Away', I just couldn't go on. I'd managed to get up there onstage in front of my people; I was reconnected to my mother's country; I was sober and I'd survived long enough to witness a prime minister say out loud that what had happened to me and my people wouldn't happen again. But it was bittersweet – I was sad that so many had never got to witness this apology.

Most of my siblings hadn't made it – Alma, Gladys, Lawrence and Horse – and a lot of white people too. The apology was also for Mum and Dad Cox, both now dead.

I only managed to finish the song after Ruby came and wrapped her arms around me.

Our health was up and down in these years. We kept going, touring, and moving eventually to south-west Victoria. Our children were grown. Ruby was slowing down; I was slowing down. The worst was when Ruby was hospitalised in England when we were on tour.

When we arrived back in Australia, Kutcha Edwards was at Melbourne Airport to meet us, and it was so good to see a familiar face. Kutcha has forever been a great support to me and Ruby and my family. He is a very spiritual and cultural man who is always there for his community. From the airport, Ruby was taken by ambulance to hospital, where she would stay for a couple of days under observation.

All Ruby and I wanted to do was go back to our home on Gundjitmara country, and eventually, that's exactly what we did.

We rested at home for a few months, occasionally leaving south-west Victoria to perform. We had a gig in January the following year, and we were planning on going to a First Nations festival in Tasmania. Ruby's health remained up and down. She pretended that she was okay, but she wasn't. We were in Melbourne, getting ready to fly to Hobart, when Jill asked Ruby if she was feeling all right, insisting that she get herself checked out before we headed to Tasmania. Ruby agreed, spending almost a full day at the Aboriginal Health Service in Fitzroy.

She was administered oxygen and had all sorts of tests done to see if she was fit to fly. At the end of a long day, she emerged from the doctor's rooms with her arms raised in the air, as though she'd just laid out the heavyweight champion of the world, yelling, 'I can fly! I can fly!'

After returning from Tasmania, we were approached by Bernadette Walters, who ran a small publishing company called One Day Hill. Bernadette was passionate about turning three iconic Australian songs – Shane Howard's 'Solid Rock', Neil Murray's 'My Island Home', and my 'Took the Children Away' – into three illustrated books. Jill thought it would be a great idea for Ruby to paint pictures that would accompany the lyrics, as my story mirrored her own. It was also a good way to keep Ruby at home, given her health and everything she'd recently gone through. Ruby was really excited to paint my story. She never stopped surprising me – never.

I was in the lounge room watching television and Ruby was in the kitchen, painting and playing Nintendo Wii tennis with two of our grannies. As she finished each picture – vivid, colourful, wonderful, each one a pleasant surprise – she'd run to show me.

'What do you think of this, Dad?'

'I think it's deadly, Mum. I didn't know you could paint.'

'There's a lot of things about me you don't know, Archie Roach.'

And that's what she was doing when it happened – painting and playing with her grannies. There was the sound of competitive banter and silliness and fun, and then there was a loud thump, and then there was nothing.

I ran into the kitchen. My ears were filled with screaming, and my eyes filled with the absurdity of seeing something on the floor that looked like Ruby.

I heard the crying, I saw the panic in my grannies' eyes. I dropped to the floor and held Ruby. Everything was surreal. I remember ambulance officers, frantic then solemn. And a little later, an undertaker.

Ruby was dead.

When they took Ruby away that night the house was the same structurally, but inside it felt like time itself had stopped. The stains on Ruby's teacup that she would never drink from again; her unwashed, crumpled clothes that she would never wear again. The pictures she'd been painting that night still on the table.

This strange, quiet house was full of familiar objects that had lost their spirit.

The house filled with my sons and daughter, their partners, my grannies, my sisters, nephews and nieces, Ruby's family and others who travelled the distance to Killarney, to pay their respects. In my mind they'd come and go like passing trains on a platform, breaking the silence but not taking me anywhere.

It could've been days, it could've been a week, until I looked at myself in the bathroom mirror. I looked like shit; Ruby told me so.

'Look at yourself, Archie Roach,' I heard. 'What do you see?'

I stared at the mirror and all I saw was an old, dishevelled man at the very end of his tether.

Not good, Mum. I don't look good, I said in my head.

'You have to pull yourself together, Archie Roach, one last time. Get off your moom and clean yourself up. There are important things for you to do.'

I heard it, Ruby talking to me. Clear as a bell.

'Even when you were drinking you didn't look this bad. You want to pull yourself together, please,' she said before going silent.

Of course, Mum. If that's what you want, I'll do that.

I knew Ruby's spirit was back home on Ngarrindjeri country, back with her mob who she loved so much. I knew that, just in the same way I knew she'd spoken to me and told me to get myself together.

That's where she would want her final resting place to be, I reckoned. I felt that she wanted me to do that for her.

Glen Peters, the long-time manager of the Aboriginal Funeral Service, based at the Aborigines Advancement League in Thornbury, drove Ruby all the way back to South Australia. Glen was a deeply spiritual, compassionate man, who worked tirelessly so that our people would be buried with the dignity and respect they deserved. A lot of Aboriginal families couldn't afford proper funerals or to deliver their loved ones back to their country, but Glen made sure that happened, sometimes at his own expense. That's the sort of man he was. Glen was community.

We held Ruby's service in a huge shed used for agricultural field shows, near Barmera in regional South Australia. I remember looking around the room filled to capacity, seeing the faces of family and friends from all over Australia.

It was a loving celebration of her inspiring life, full of song and kind words.

People had come from far and wide to show their love. I was not surprised. It was easy to love Ruby.

I'm not sure how I did it, but I got up and sang 'The River Song', a song I'd written about Ruby many years earlier when we were camping on the banks of the Murray River near Berri. It's about what I saw reflected in the river that day, and one of those reflections was Ruby – the river's daughter, which she was.

At the end of the service my sons and nephews carried her coffin outside, where a large group of people from Ngukurr, a remote Aboriginal community in Arnhem Land, on the Roper River, were waiting. They had driven nearly three thousand kilometres to honour Ruby, who had visited their community to perform over the years. They hadn't come inside, as their traditional cultural practices did not allow them to see any images of people recently passed.

They started singing and dancing, reaching out towards Ruby's coffin and to me. They were there to settle Ruby's spirit and help her cross over to the Dreaming. They cried for Ruby and they cried for me too. I could feel it. A motorcycle club of Nunga riders escorted Ruby's body from the service to Gerard Mission, her final resting place, where she would lie with so many of her family and mob around her.

As she was lowered into the ground, I couldn't help but run to her one last time. I couldn't believe she was gone. It was overwhelming. My grannies followed me, the little ones grabbing me and hugging me, and I went and sat back down with them, cradled in their warmth.

The next day we planned to travel home. My agent Jill knocked on my motel door early that morning to see how I was going and whether I was ready to head off.

She was at great pains to tell me that Ruby and I had been booked to play the Port Fairy Folk Festival that day, and went on to say that the organisers had left a place open for me to play if that's what I wanted to do.

If I'd known about this show earlier I would've cancelled, but at that moment I was thinking a little differently. I reckoned the Ngukurr people and Ruby's mob, and even Ruby's spirit, were telling me it was time to try to heal, not just me but other people too: her fans.

At every pit stop along the way it wasn't clear what I was intending to do. I was letting my spirit guide me. The energy around me and everyone travelling with me that day was charged. At the last stop, as we were closer to home, I asked Jill to let the festival organisers know I would be there.

I drove straight to the Port Fairy Folk Festival site and

was met by Derek Guille, a former ABC Radio broadcaster and musician, and an ambassador and MC for the festival. He's a great fan of Ruby and her music, and when I saw him you could feel his sadness.

'Are you sure you'll be right, Archie?' he said. I can hear the timbre of his voice now, all strung through with his own heartbreak.

'Yeah, Derek. I need to do this for Ruby,' I told him.

I gave him a hug, and he cried on my shoulder. It took everything to keep myself together and not break down, but something bigger than myself propelled me onto that stage. Amos, my beautiful son, who now played bass with me, stood by my side, along with my nephew Dave Arden on guitar and vocals. Later, we were joined by Shane Howard and Amy Saunders.

When I first stumbled onto the stage, I felt the nervous, expectant energy of the large audience in front of me. I could tell they were uncertain how to react.

'You'll have to bear me up. I can't do this without you. I need you all today, each and every one of you, more than I've ever needed you before, to help me pay tribute to a beautiful lady who has touched so many hearts, but most of all mine.'

There was a pause, and then someone yelled, 'We're with you, Archie!'

In that moment I felt a powerful surge of love from every single person in the audience enveloping me.

This is exactly where I needed to be – connected to the very people who had known both Ruby and me for years and years, through our songs and seeing us perform live together. These were the people who had laughed and cried with us as we shared our stories. They were family, too, and today we needed to grieve together.

I don't remember the details of what I sang during that performance, but we all got through it together, those of us on stage and in the audience. What I do vividly remember was feeling the healing power of being in that space. I don't think I'd ever fully understood the deep spiritual connection between an artist and their audience until that show at the Port Fairy Folk Festival.

I'd been playing music for decades, in front of big crowds and small, in parks with only a guitar, and onstage with an orchestra. But I'll never forget that gig, and I suspect the people who were in the audience won't either. I honestly don't think I could've gone on without the love and shared connection I felt that day. It's what makes us human.

Photo by Jamie James (www.jamesphoto.com.au)

CHAPTER 14

SMALL CHILD

I see the birds up in the tree
You know that I just want to be free
I see the clouds up in the sky
You know that I just want to fly high

Small child, I know where you live
And small child, I know what you give to me
When you speak you whisper
Words so soft and mild
Thank God I learned to listen
To the inner child
Hello, hello, hello

Is anybody listening to?
Is anybody listening to?
Is anybody listening to that child?

Don't outgrow the child inside
Remember all the times we've cried
Remember all the times we've laughed
When we all had children's hearts
Let your mind swim wild and free
Like the fishes in the sea
Imagine all that you can be

Now hold on to the one you love
Then you can fly above
This Earth, you and me

Small child, I know where you live
My small child, I know what you give to me
When you speak you whisper
Words so soft and mild
Thank God I learned to listen
To the inner child
Hello, hello, hello
Is anybody listening to?
Is anybody listening to?
Is anybody listening to that child?

Back at home I was struggling. The reality that Ruby was gone had started to take me to new depths of anguish. I fell back into a pattern of smoking yarndi till I was numb. I didn't want to do much of anything. I had no will to pick up my guitar. I didn't want to sing or play. I spent a lot of time on my own at home. Nothing seemed to inspire me.

I just didn't have any energy for that first step that every endeavour, big and small, starts with.

Jill Shelton was the one who got me going again. There was important, unfinished work to do to honour Ruby. There were the paintings, so colourful and bold, that she'd been working on the night she died, the ones for *Took the Children Away*, the illustrated lyric book.

There were also the songs Ruby and I had written with school children during a six-week tour of Cape York communities back in 1997. It was the first time we'd been to Cape York, and it was made all the more special as three of our sons, Amos, Eban and Terrence, were with us.

Back in Melbourne, Ruby and I had demoed the songs with Jen Anderson, who had produced Ruby's first album, *Thoughts Within*.

All those years later Jen unearthed those demos and, teaming up with Craig Pilkington, who has produced a couple of my albums (*Into the Bloodstream and Let Love Rule*), they took Ruby's vocal tracks, wrote music around them and brought in musicians and singers to layer the songs. Shane Howard and I sang, and Dave Arden and Amos came in to record too.

Ruby had also been compiling a sketchbook full of drawings for each of the songs. We hunted down all of the black-and-white sketches and reproduced the colours she used from the *Took the Children Away* illustrated book to bring them to life. We also tracked down film footage of the Cape York tour and included a DVD documentary.

The result was a songbook with Ruby's drawings and lyrics with a CD of the children's songs and a DVD documentary of that tour. This was exactly what Ruby had dreamt of doing, exactly the way she'd talked about it, the way she'd seen it in her head. It was deadly.

I remembered what we needed to call it as well.

'Butcher Paper, Texta, Blackboard and Chalk,' Ruby had said after I'd asked what the title would be.

'What?' I asked.

'You heard me,' she said.

At first I thought it was a jawbreaker. But as I let the words roll around in my head, I realised how perfect they were. That's how Ruby and I had created the songs with the children of Cape York, using butcher paper, texta, blackboard and chalk.

Honouring Ruby's legacy was just the kickstart I needed. I felt energised again.

Jen Anderson had recently moved to the Warmun Community (Turkey Creek) in the Kimberley region of Western Australia to work as a nurse. She had contacted Jill and asked if Shane and myself would come over for a week to run songwriting and music workshops with schools from the north-west Aboriginal communities.

That sounded good to me, like an on-ramp into some more work and some more touring.

Shane and I travelled up to Warmun and were greeted by elders of the Gija people, the traditional owners of the eastern Kimberley. The community is known internationally for their distinctive painting style, which I can recognise anytime I see it, at home or abroad. We had tea and shared a meal and toured the art galleries. We talked about music and songs with the children, and listened to a band of young fellas, who were already well on their way.

I went to sleep that first night, looking forward to the next day, and more workshops with the children.

I remember getting out of bed and falling straight to the floor. I tried to push myself upright; my right arm felt dead, as though I'd slept on it. I soon realised my right leg didn't work either and I couldn't see out of my right eye.

Something was definitely wrong. I was frightened and called out to Shane.

He appeared at my door and was panicked to see me on the floor. There was no doctor in the community so Jen called an ambulance, which was an hour away. I was driven north to Kununurra, about two and a half hours away, where doctors started to build a diagnosis. Their overwhelming suspicion was that I'd had a stroke.

I spent the night in Kununurra and then I was off to Broome, courtesy of a Royal Flying Doctor Service plane.

When I got to the hospital, they confirmed the diagnosis: I'd suffered a stroke. They wanted to get me to Perth as soon as they could for specific treatment and testing, so I was pretty quickly off again on another plane down south.

I felt no pain throughout it all and tried to remain relatively calm.

What a year, I did think to myself, though. What a shitty, shitty year.

When I got to Perth I was admitted to the Royal Perth Hospital and ended up there for quite some time. Jill, Amos, his partner and baby had flown over to be near.

The doctors told me that the neural pathways on the right side of my brain, affected during the stroke, were dead and weren't coming back, and if I wanted to gain use of my leg or arm again, then I had to create detours in my brain.

How could I do that? Hard work, they told me. I wondered if I had the hard work in me that would be required. I wondered if I wanted to get better at all.

I was thinking about that when I left my ward and went downstairs one afternoon with a view to bumming a smoke off someone.

There was a fella in his pyjamas looking quite ill and trailing a drip, who offered me one.

‘Are you sure you should be smoking?’ I asked him. He didn’t look great, this fella.

‘Should you?’ he replied.

Of course I shouldn’t. I knew I shouldn’t. Thing is, I was a smoker and had pretty much always been a smoker.

I’d had a stroke probably because of my smoking, and continuing to smoke would only court further disaster, but like I said, I was a smoker. That’s who I was. I guess it was true of the other fella too, all drip and pyjamas. I thanked him for the offer but told him I was right.

Quitting was the easiest thing in the world, and the hardest. All I needed was a sickly fella to offer me a cigarette. All I needed was a whole life of smoking. All I needed was a stroke.

That was the turning point. With that, I wasn’t a smoker anymore – not cigarettes, not yarndi.

I was diligent with my rehab: hours and hours of trying to put beads into pots and walking on white lines. I guess I still wanted to live more life, and do more work.

I slowly recovered both in the Perth hospital and then in a rehab facility back in Melbourne.

A month on and I was finally able to go home. Jill drove me back to Killarney. I still had a trembling hand, a weak arm and a slow leg, but I could walk and I was alive. She even pushed me to drive a little bit of the way.

I didn't end up running us into a ditch, and it gave me much-needed confidence in myself.

Part of my rehab saw me pick up my guitar from time to time. That hadn't been a great success, but it hadn't been a disaster either. There were things to be thankful about, though. It was my strumming hand, rather than my chord hand, that was feeble, so I had to work my way back to being as capable a strummer as I'd once been.

We launched *Butcher Paper, Texta, Blackboard and Chalk* at the local Tarerer Festival, where I could thank everyone for supporting Ruby and myself. I thought that was a good place to start playing again – on country, in an intimate space, among family and friends.

It wasn't easy getting on and off the stage, and my guitar playing wasn't the best, but I tell you, it was great to be playing again. I got stronger after that, and pretty quickly too. My hand began to get right, and my leg, and I could move and play, so I did both.

I could tell that Jill kept worrying about me, especially when I'd cough or get puffed out after walking.

She didn't say anything, though, and one day drove down from Melbourne, picked me up and took me to see my GP in Port Fairy, telling me it was a post-stroke check-up visit.

Without my knowing, Jill had earlier confided in my

doctor her concerns about my breathing and coughing. Next minute I'm having a chest X-ray and getting blood tests done. Then a couple of days later I was at Warrnambool Hospital, where they took some more blood and did a scan. Almost as soon as I got home, my GP called and said he wanted to see me.

'We see a little bit of a shadow on your left lung here, Archie,' he said. 'It could be nothing but we'd like you to go down to Melbourne and get a biopsy and scans done.'

There was no rest in the days that followed. I went straight to Melbourne, where I was scraped, pricked, prodded and scanned. In the oncologist's room, with Jill by my side, I was told the news that the shadow on my left lung was now the size of a ten-cent piece, and that ten-cent piece was cancer.

Lung cancer. I had lung cancer.

Of course, I had lung cancer. I'd lived a rough old life and hadn't treated my body or my spirit well. Many who'd live a rough life alongside me were gone, for the most part. Why would it be any different for me?

Everything the doctor told me after that sounded like he was speaking through water. I heard that I was lucky, because of the early detection, and radiation therapy was a possibility. I heard that surgery was a possibility too; in fact, it was highly recommended. But I needed to do more tests to check that my heart was strong enough to get me through the procedure.

I nodded and tried to listen, but all the emotions of the last eighteen months were bearing down on me. It was good to have Jill there to take it all in.

I felt so very old.

I thanked the doctor. He told me to have a think about what I wanted to do, but not to leave it too long. It was a fast-growing lesion, and if I didn't do anything about it I'd be dead in six months. I'd had a great life, a long life compared to many around me.

My children were older now. I'd lived a life making music – music I was very proud of. I'd written some good songs. I'd met my soulmate, and I'd toured the world with her. I gave back what I could, to community and others. What more could a man ask for? Maybe it was time to let it go, maybe it was time to rest and see Ruby again, and Horse, Lawrence and Alma, and finally meet Mum and Dad and my older sister Gladys.

Three weeks sped by, and Jill asked me if I'd made a decision. I had.

'I don't think I'm going to do anything, Jill,' I mumbled.

A heavy silence fell between the two of us, but there was so much said within it, loud and immediate.

'I don't think I'm going to have surgery or go through with the radiation.'

'Right. That's your decision, then. Well, how do we tell your family?'

I didn't say anything. If I did let the cancer take over, people would have to look after me. There'd be pain, for me and the people around me. Maybe I could suffer the pain, but was it fair to expect my family and Jill to as well?

'So that's it – no surgery?' Jill asked again.

More silence.

'Okay, I better ring the hospital to let them know you're not coming in.'

In that very moment, something shifted. No, I didn't want my family and friends to watch me suffer before I passed on. I would have the surgery.

And that was that. Jill drove me to the Royal Melbourne Hospital, and that same day one of its most skilled surgeons removed half of my left lung. It was minimally invasive surgery, which meant there wasn't a giant wound, but I still had to reconcile, psychologically and physically, to the idea of losing half of my lung capacity. Would I have the same lung power? Could I still sing? What would my life be without singing?

'Come on, Mr Roach, time to get up and go for a walk,' the nurses would say.

'Please leave me alone,' I'd mutter under my breath.

'Mr Roach?'

'Yep, no worries. Coming.'

Professor Louis Irving, a leading respiratory physician at the Peter MacCallum Cancer Centre – and all the staff at RMH – have been on this long journey with me. I'm not personally aware of too many specialists or scientists in the medical profession who take into account a person's spirit when it comes to healing. For Lou, a big part of his philosophy and practice is about mindfulness. Healing is holistic, involving the mind, body and spirit, and you need to address all three aspects of yourself.

Lou has been a continual source of strength to me. Recently I'd started to feel unwell again, and he made it his mission to get to the bottom of what was wrong with me, performing one test after another, to pinpoint the exact cause of my suffering. Like a dog with a bone, he wouldn't let it go until he hit the diagnosis: pulmonary arterial hypertension. That's true dedication.

Lou has come to several of my concerts over the years, and in 2016 we talked as doctor and patient about my lung cancer journey at a World Indigenous Cancer Conference held in Brisbane. It was a very powerful session.

I'd moved back to Melbourne temporarily to be closer to the hospital and the rehab staff. I was continually connected to an oxygen cylinder, which I would drag around after me. Things were pretty slow for a while. I was getting used to oxygen being my constant companion. I had to walk every day, to build up my strength, and was practising mindfulness as an important healing tool.

Jill bought me the HBO television series *Treme* – a post-Hurricane Katrina drama about the devastation and triumph of the people of New Orleans – to try to get my mind off the way I was feeling about myself, how I'd slowed down, my dependence on an oxygen tank, and what this meant for my future as a recording artist and touring musician, which is all I'd ever known.

It was just what I needed. I got lost in the show's story, but particularly the soundtrack.

It came slowly at first, but I started to have ideas and began shaping stories, composing lyrics in my head. I'd go to bed and wake up excited because I'd found a chord progression or a rhyme in my sleep. My days started to fill with purpose. I had momentum. I had things to say.

With diminished lung capacity and a dodgy strumming hand, my mind was still good. Better than good, it was great, firing on all cylinders. Each day was better than the last. My body was healing, and I reckoned my soul was too.

After Ruby died, my close circle of family and friends

helped me heal, and it was the people I'd never met personally, the audience at my shows, who gave me the strength to carry on. I was never going to be the same, and life was never going to be the same, but I'd now found the will. I wasn't quite as lonely as I'd thought.

Watching *Treme* had unlocked something deep inside me. Hurricane Katrina had devastated New Orleans, but it didn't kill the music or the spirit of the people – that was still strong and alive. Now I wanted to make music again.

It wasn't long before Jill and I were sitting in the boardroom of Mushroom's offices in Albert Park, talking with Michael Gudinski, now chairman of Mushroom Group, and Warren Costello, the director and co-founder of Bloodlines Music, my label, about recording my comeback album, because that's what I felt the album would be.

Coming back from a terminal diagnosis is about as big as it gets. And the reason I'd survived lung cancer in the first place was because of Jill. It was her intuition that led to its early detection, and that saved my life. If it wasn't for Jill, I wouldn't be here, and that's the simple truth. I am deeply indebted to her.

I am also incredibly thankful to Mushroom's

continued commitment to my career. Michael gave me a chance to record my first album all those years ago and continues to look after me to this day. Warren has been a staunch supporter, and I appreciate the trust he has in me and in my music. I consider both friends.

I told them I reckoned I'd be ready to go back into the studio soon. Jill had already approached Craig Pilkington at Audrey Studios to produce, and we were away.

Very much in the spirit of *Treme's* celebratory soundtrack, combined with my love of singing hymns in church as a child, I wanted to make a gospel-inspired album.

Some of the songs I brought to Craig were fully formed and ready to be recorded, like 'Mulyawonk'. Others were less shaped, and Craig and I worked collaboratively on re-imagining these songs. My old mate Paul Kelly came into the studios to help me work on one song, and we recorded it as a duet. It's one of my favourites off the album, called 'We Won't Cry'. When you read the lyrics or listen to the song, you'll see why.

Jill had big plans for this album. She thought it could be a triumphant return for me; to bring me out of that dark night, and more: a celebration and reaffirmation of the healing power of music.

That feeling was bound up in the title of the album,

Into the Bloodstream, which talked about keeping our rivers of life clean. It was meant as a metaphor of the blood running through our veins, and what we're doing to ourselves and to Mother Earth by polluting the rivers that run through our land. It was also personal, about what I'd poisoned my own bloodstream with and the choices I'd made in my life.

I have such fond memories of recording that album. We decided to film a video clip for the first single, 'Song to Sing', down on my mother's ancestral country, in an old Irish Catholic church, St Brigid's, on top of a hill at Crossley, halfway between my house and Tower Hill (Tarerer). It was a big production. We brought together an all-Indigenous cast of singers: Lou Bennett, Emma Donovan, Shauntai Batzke, Veronica Wellings, David Leha (Radical Son), Benny Walker, John Wayne Parsons and James Henry, and the band – Craig Pilkington, Dave Folley, Stephen Hadley and Tim Neal.

The stars of the video clip were Jack Charles and young Luca.

Many would know Jack as one of our great Australian actors of stage and screen. I still remember the day we met back in Fitzroy, when I when I walked into the Builders

Arms and paid my entrance fee of a pot of beer. It was early, and there were hardly any people around.

I went into the lounge, and the only other person there was a blackfella I didn't recognise. We acknowledged each other, as we do, and I decided to sit with him at the table.

'How are you, brus?' I asked.

'Good.'

I asked his name.

'My name is Jack – Jack Charles.'

From the articulate way he spoke, I could tell he was an educated man.

'I've been here in Fitzroy for a while,' I said, 'but I've never seen you before. I know pretty much everyone here.'

'I've been away for a little while.'

'Where?' I asked.

'Aw, here and there, in jail – I just got out.'

He asked me who I was, and I replied, 'Archie.'

'Oh. Archie – I've got a brother Archie.'

'I'm Archie Roach,' I said, and I could see he recognised the name.

'Are you Lawrence's brother?'

'Yeah.'

Jack asked me what I did, and I said, 'Nothing. Just drink around.'

He was an interesting man, and after a bit I asked, 'So what do you do, besides drinking beer?'

He replied, 'I'm an interior decorator.'

I looked at him suspiciously. 'I don't think there are too many blackfellas who are interior decorators.'

'Well, I rearrange a bit of furniture and then put it back to make sure it looks all right.'

I still didn't get it, thinking he was having a lend of me, then he gave me a cheeky grin and almost whispered, saying, 'I'm actually a cat-burglar. Like Robin Hood, I steal from the rich in huge mansions in Kew and other rich suburbs and give to the poor.'

'Well,' I said, 'I suppose you're only small and can get into tight spaces.'

Jack was long cleaned up and on the straight and narrow, and full of his trademark charm, by the time he starred in the film clip for 'Song to Sing'. It was such a joy to have him with me. In each other we see our stories reflected.

Jill saw a big show, touring across the country, complete with a ten-piece all-Indigenous core choir, under the expert guidance of Lou Bennett, horn and string sections, and a full band - everything required to bring the bombast and soul from the album to the stage. And that's exactly what happened.

But the greatest thrill at each show was when the core choir was joined by another ten to fifteen choir members drawn from the local community for the last two songs. Lou Bennett must be acknowledged for the work she put in with the local communities around Australia, many of whom had never sung before in a choir, as do the contributions of Deline Briscoe, Nancy Bates, Mindy Kwanten, Kirk Page and Microwave Jenny, who were part of the ten-piece core choir.

I was a little scared of the scope of the tour, and I can still barely believe it all came together. It was the biggest tour I'd ever done as a headliner. We played to capacity crowds in grand venues, like the State Theatre in Sydney and Hamer Hall in Melbourne.

That wasn't the only thing that made the show successful, though. It was the fidelity of spirit that ended up onstage. Sometimes I needed to get a hit of oxygen before or after the show, but when it came time to dance, I could dance, and when I did I reckon I could see the colours of heaven.

In the thrall of those moments, dancing with a grinning Jack Charles next to me, singing alongside colleagues like Paul Kelly, Emma Donovan, Vika and Linda Bull, and Dan Sultan, with an all-Indigenous choir behind me raising the roof, an audience in front of me, feeding off the love and deep spiritual energy in the room, I felt the pure, uncut joy of living.

Ruby had told me to pull myself together after I'd seen myself in the mirror, dishevelled and hopeless after her death, and I believe I had.

I never heard Ruby's voice again, and I reckon that's because it was the last thing she needed to say to me.

'You'll have to bear me up.' Performing at the Port Fairy Folk Festival after Ruby's funeral, 6 March 2010. I needed to be there. Being with my audience in this time of profound grief was the connection my spirit needed. They got me through this and brought me home. Photo by Rob Gunstone.

Me looking over Tarerer (Tower Hill) on Gunditjmara country. Photo by Alexis Steere.

CHAPTER 15

PLACE OF FIRE

Oh I'm waiting here
And I long to see your face
For you are so near and dear to me
Don't you realise, that we all come from this place
Open up your eyes, look and see

It's somewhere in your dreaming
In your ancient memory
Your spirit will no longer be alone
You've got to start believing
So just let your mind be free
Oh please, will you come back home

Though the road is long
You have got to face your fears
And you must stay strong, to be free
Got to find your way, through the heartache and the tears
Oh and come what may, back to me

You know there will be singing
And dancing through the night
To have you back is all that I desire
Back to the beginning, where we're basking in the light
In the light of this place of fire

Oh I'm waiting here
Yes I'm waiting here, back home
Oh I'm waiting here
In the light, in the light of this place of fire
Oh I'm waiting here
Yes I'm waiting here, back home
Oh I'm waiting here
In the light, in the light of this place of fire.
In the light of this place of fire.

A rhythm can sometimes be transcendent, divine. Like a second heartbeat, pumping a spiritual energy through your body. A rhythm that feels like it has come from the breaking of the first dawn of time, vibrating out, all the way to the edges of the universe.

I've felt that feeling more than a few times. I've felt it in the deep, ancient sounds of the didgeridoo and clap sticks, resounding through my body, through every cell, singing the story of my family and my mob.

I've had that feeling course through me as a young man in the house of Jesus with clapping hands raised towards the Christian God above, my heart full of the Holy Spirit and the possibility of heaven.

I've also felt it when the boom of a North American First Nations drum resonated deep in my chest, first in Canada in the early 1990s when Ruby and I were welcomed on country by Elders, and then on my 'against all odds' return in 2018.

As a younger man I would try to weigh up my Christian beliefs with my search for Aboriginal spirituality, and my place of belonging in the ancient ways I was coming to know. I would struggle then with those seemingly contradictory beliefs, but I don't anymore. Now I know that at the epicentre of everything, at the heart of humanity, is love.

In 2015 I wrote a song called 'Let Love Rule', which became the title track of my new album. It had been three years since I'd released *Into the Bloodstream*. I wanted to explore the themes of love – what it is, what it means, spiritual love, romantic love, love of family, of country, of life, of culture and of people. I wanted to examine all the aspects that love encompasses: compassion, respect, inclusiveness and charity.

I particularly wanted to write about letting love be the main sentiment in our life, about a willingness to love one other and find the things common to us – our shared humanity – rather than just seeing the things that divide us.

It's sad what's happening in the world today, particularly in Australia. We are closing ourselves off and not letting people in, not only into the country, but not letting them into our hearts, into our minds. Australia was built on people coming here from other places around the world. That's what made this country what it is today. Our identity comes from many cultures and peoples.

We shot a film clip for the first single, 'It's Not Too Late', down on Gunditjmara country, my mother's country. The song is a call for understanding, a prayer for a shared humanity. It's my hope that our children and the generations of children to come will grow up in a world where peace and love reign. That was the inspiration behind the song. I really believe it's not too late for peace and love, that there's still time to save Mother Earth, and we all have the capacity to create change regardless of the actions of governments and big business.

We invited the Dhungala Children's Choir, a choral performance group for Indigenous children in Victoria, to sing on 'Let Love Rule'. They also joined members of Short Black Opera, Australia's national Indigenous opera company, to sing on the 'No More Bleeding' track. Deborah Cheetham AO, acclaimed Yorta Yorta soprano, composer, educator and artistic director, created both of these ensembles.

When the young, strong, steady voices of the children's choir joined the older voices of Short Black Opera, mixed with mine, starkly damaged, I heard something truly beautiful. I heard love. At the end of the recording session for 'No More Bleeding' I broke down crying. I could see some of the young ones were concerned about me, but I told them to not to be worried. 'I'm not upset or sad or anything. It's just that you touched me in the heart.'

Having the Dhungala Children's Choir sing on both songs was so right because it is the children who will take those songs and carry them forward – voices from the future confirming that love will rule.

I believe in redemption and I believe in forgiveness, both important aspects of love, because I've seen both. I've experienced both. I think about that a lot when I visit prisons and youth correctional facilities.

Jack Charles and I visit as often as we can through our work with the Foundation I set up in 2014. Jack is a board member and the Foundation's 'roving ambassador', as he likes to say. As Elders, we want to let these young men and women know that we care about what happens to them, that they can turn their lives around and be the best they can be. We tell them about the importance of story, their story, and how through songwriting, painting, dance, or other forms of artistic expression, they can find a way through, towards healing and a redemption of sorts.

Both Jack and I have come out of those dark places. We know first-hand the vicious cycle of addiction and where it can take you. We've both done jail time. Jack has even more of what he calls 'lived experience' than I do, with crime and courts and cops, which really resonates with the young ones inside. I've been a vagrant and a drunk, and I once thought I'd be better off dead. I've wrestled most of my life with my addictions, but music has always been my saving grace. It's where I go to heal. For Jack, it's been telling his story through acting on stage and screen.

Some of these young inmates struggle with their identity – who they are and where they fit in, if they fit in at all. For some there's a disconnect from their family, country and culture. Being Stolen Generations, both Jack and I know that disconnect. When we visit youth detention centres in Victoria, sometimes we can tell the young people who they are and where they're from just by asking them their surname. It reconnects them to us.

As Elders, our message to these young ones inside is that, regardless of whatever they've done, where there is love there is hope. We let them know we believe in them just as there were people around Jack and me all those years ago – people who believed in us and helped us believe in ourselves and change our ways.

We invited Yorta Yorta rapper Adam Briggs from A.B. Original, who wrote a deadly sequel to my song, 'Took the Children Away', called 'And the Children Came Back' and David Leha, aka Radical Son, to visit and perform at both Parkville and Malmsbury Youth Justice Centres in Victoria. David also ran songwriting sessions with the young inmates.

A couple of generations younger, Briggs and David offer something different from Jack and me. Briggs doesn't have that 'lived experience' – he's an evolution, someone who can be bold and political. His music and lyrics have earned him the respect of anyone who cares to listen to what he has to say. He's someone Jack and I probably would have liked to have been when we were younger, if we hadn't been so distracted by our addictions.

Briggs says he stands on the shoulders of old fellas like me and Jack, and I tell him we've stood on the shoulders of fellas like Uncle Jimmy Little; my cousin, Lionel Rose; Bobby McLeod; Uncle Bob Randall; and aunties like Auriel Andrew and Janice Johnson, to name just a few, whose mere presence on stage was a bold statement.

David also knows what it's like to enter these places; he, too, has spent time in jail. I admire David. He has a quiet strength about him, and it's not just his size that is impressed upon you but also his words. I have worked with him through the years and what I've noticed most is his desire to become the best he can be. He is always consulting with Elders and has a deep thirst for cultural knowledge.

One thing that spins these young ones out is learning that Jack, David and I were once addicts and prisoners. For us it's important to go back to these places, to let people know you can change for the better. Our message is that we all make mistakes, and some of us learn from those mistakes. There is hope for a better life as Jack, David and myself have found. That's why we will continue to visit, to share our stories, to hear theirs, to help them reconnect to culture and help them realise that they can choose the direction their lives take.

I was touched in the heart again in 2016 when I took the *Let Love Rule* album to Europe, with shows in France, Scotland and Monaco, touring with producer Craig Pilkington; an incredibly talented and deadly Barkindji singer-songwriter and guitarist, Nancy Bates; Pitjantjatjara didge player and friend, Russell Smith and Jill.

First stop was Brittany for Le Festival Interceltique de Lorient. The town of Lorient comes alive as some 700,000 people gather to celebrate the region's unique

Celtic tradition. Each year artists from countries outside of the Celtic heartland are invited, and in 2016, William Hutton, a Scotsman from Australia who fronts a band called Claymore, put together the Australian contingent.

William had some time off following Lorient, so after a performance in the famous Spiegeltent at the Edinburgh Festival, we all set off up north to the Scottish Highlands, to the country Dad Alex had left behind for a new life in Australia.

At Dumbarton, standing on a hill and looking across a lake towards Glasgow, where Dad Alex was born, William pointed out the River Clyde. A song that Dad Alex had taught me, and one I'd not thought of for perhaps half a century, came back to me.

I began to sing the chorus, first line to last:

Roamin' in the gloamin' by the bonnie banks o' Clyde,
Roamin' in the gloamin' wi' ma lassie by ma side…
When the sun sets in the west that's the time that I love best
Oh I love to go a'roamin the gloamin.

We knew that song, Dad Alex and me. I loved how that song would transport him. In that transformation I saw joy, but I also felt his sadness at being so far from Glasgow and his people.

Further north we stopped for lunch in a restaurant overlooking the largest freshwater loch in Scotland, the breathtakingly beautiful Loch Lomond. I remember saying to Dad Alex all those years ago that I would love to visit Scotland. And here I was standing in his country, a place he sang so passionately about, seeing the landmarks I had heard about as a boy.

I walked down a long jetty, drinking in some of the most delicious air I've known.

Another song came to me, again complete:

By yon bonnie banks and by yon bonnie braes,
Where the sun shines bright on Loch Lomond,
Where me and my true love were ever wont to gae
On the bonnie, bonnie banks o' Loch Lomond.

That moment on the jetty took me over. Standing there with the Scottish Highlands in the distance, I saw Dad Alex's face – I actually saw him, felt him.

Dad Alex never got to come home, but I was there.

We don't fully appreciate how a song sounds until it's finished, and we don't really see the scope of a journey until we reach the end of it. I felt like I'd come to the end of one journey. When I had left the Coxes as a teenager I never got to see Dad Alex again. But standing on that jetty, as an old man myself, overlooking Loch Lomond, I saw his face in the distant highlands and I felt his love.

Ruby's death crushed our children, each in their own way. When Ruby died, the balance that kept us all in each other's orbits was thrown violently off course. We went off on our own paths, trying to make sense of a world without Mum.

My children have long been adults and are on their own journeys. But I believe all have been affected by the trauma of what Ruby and I went through as Stolen Generations survivors. They call it intergenerational trauma. I grew up never knowing my mother and father. Ruby grew up never knowing her mother and father. My children grew up not knowing any of their grandmothers and grandfathers. It also affects my grandchildren. It's not just my story, it's their story too. But to all of my children and grandchildren I say this: live a good life; be the best person you can be and always let love be your guide.

While writing my life story, I recorded the *Tell Me Why* companion album with my old friend and producer Paul Grabowsky.

I reflected on how my songwriting had changed over recent years, and it feels like I have come full circle. When I first started penning songs, I wrote about what had happened to me and to my people. But then other people would come up to me, non-Indigenous people, and say, 'That's what happened to me.'

Now my songwriting feels more inclusive, more universal in its sentiments. I have come to realise that it's about all of us – you can't really write about yourself without including everyone. What affects you invariably affects others as well.

I believe that all of us living in Australia suffer, at least a little, from the dispossession and disconnection that I felt in my younger years that drove me mad and to drink.

You can stick a city anywhere and fill it with pubs, fast food outlets and department stores, and it can look like any other city in the world. But the land your city stands on was probably built on the bones and blood of other cultures. That land would have had its own spirit of place, a unique ecology honed by millions of years of evolution. You may start to wonder about your own place in this continuum, your relationship to this natural world, of hills, rivers and seas, of animals and plants, of people of all colours and creeds. The heartbeat that connects us all goes way back to the very beginning of time itself.

Now my whole outlook on life is about reminding us all of the place where we all began, where we all came from.

Most people look to Africa to trace the origins of the human race, but the latest DNA studies confirm that the most continuous ancient human civilisation can be found on Aboriginal land, in Australia, dating back over 50,000 years ago. So all of humanity is Aboriginal – meaning 'from the origin'.

We were a hunter-gatherer society that lived within our clans, gathering around the fire to commune and share stories. Over human history, some people chose to stay around that fire, while others chose to leave.

Those who left spread across the lands and seas, forming tribes and later villages, moving away from the fire. The Industrial Age further disconnected us from Mother Earth, from our origins.

But there were Aboriginal people who stayed by the fire who never left and are now calling us back, to retrace our steps back to the fire to reconnect to our origins, to a love of the earth and each other. I believe they have a story, a wisdom and a way of life that can help everyone who lives in this country.

New research on my mother's ancestral country, in Warrnambool at the mouth of the Hopkins River, has just been released, suggesting that my ancestors were living here some 120,000 years ago.

For the past ten years a team of geologists, archaeologists and palaeontologists have found evidence, although inconclusive, of a 'place of fire' at a location called Moyjil by the Gunditjmara and Point Ritchie by European settlers. There, small black stones and scattered shell middens were collected around steep cliffs, 'heated in a situation reminiscent of a hearth'.

For so long we have been divided by 'isms' – racism, sexism, fundamentalism, individualism – but when we come back to the place of fire, I believe we will discover there's far more that connects us than separates us. I believe we will be one humanity again, that we will find release, healing and true freedom.

The 'place of fire' is a place of love and connection. We'll all be there – I'll be there – to welcome you back, wrap my arms around you and say, 'I've missed you. Welcome home.'

At ABC Studios, Southbank, Melbourne, July 2019, recording the companion album *Tell Me Why*. Photos courtesy Mushroom Creative House.

Recent photo by Phil Nitchie.

CODA

LET LOVE RULE

Oh when darkness overcomes us
And we cannot find our way
And thought we keep on searching
For the light of day

Oh we hear the children crying
And we don't know what to do
Gotta' hold on to each other
And love will see us through

Let love rule, let it guide us through the night
That we may stay together and keep our spirits calm
Only fools will shun the morning light
'Cause love's the only thing that'll keep us all from harm

Oh you know I love this country, every rock and every tree
The grasslands and the desert, the rivers and the sea
Oh you know I love all people, wherever they are from
Oh yes I love the people who call this land their home

Let love rule, let it guide us through the night
That we may stay together and keep our spirits calm
Only fools will shun the morning light
'Cause love's the only thing that'll keep us all from harm

Let love rule
Let it guide us through the night
Let love rule
Let love rule
Let it bring the morning light
Let love rule

The journey that started with a letter from my loving sister Myrtle, sparked a search that has continued to this day.

I am still on that journey. Courtesy of a Freedom of Information request, made while writing *Tell Me Why*, I got my official ward file. In it were details I've spent a lifetime yearning to know. It's been a harrowing read, especially the harsh and offensive words used to justify taking Gladys, Diana and myself that dark day on Framlingham.

Other file notes acknowledge the abuse I suffered at the hands of the woman from the second foster placement, used as evidence to transfer me to my third and final foster placement with Mum Dulcie and Dad Alex Cox.

I read many handwritten letters, penned lovingly by Mum Dulcie to social workers at the Family Welfare Division of the Social Welfare Department in the early 1960s about my progress at home and school, and her hopes for my future. By the early 1970s, anguished by my disappearance, Mum Dulcie wrote to them, eager for news about my whereabouts. Reading those words made me feel sad.

My own research revealed more stories about Archie, my father. I knew a little about the time he spent with my mother's people, his tent boxing days and his tragic story on the streets of Melbourne and, finally, in a cell. A rare photo of him as a much older man, wearing a dressing-gown, found in *Dawn: A Magazine for the Aboriginal People of NSW* from March 1961 places him at the Bethesda Mission, Fitzroy.

My father died in 1962, aged fifty-one.

I have also tried, in vain, to find more photos of my mother, Nellie. The only one I have is on the back cover of this book. My mother also died young at forty-nine years old in 1969. She was living in Silvan, not far from where I lived with the Coxes.

I'd never known much about my father's family, my Bundjalung heritage. I did learn about three of my Bundjalung great-grandmothers from the small New South Wales town of Lawrence, settled near the banks of the Clarence River. An Elder told me that my old people were put on some of the larger river islands in the Clarence River estuary. Life on the island was harsh for my great-grandmothers; the overseers would torment them, chasing them on horses, whipping them for their own amusement. In desperation for a better life, they jumped into the river, swimming against the treacherous tidal current to escape to Lawrence, to freedom. It made me proud to hear their story.

It's only been in recent years that I've had a chance to visit the town where my father was born and lived until showman Jimmy Sharman came to town and took him into his employ as a tent boxer. The little tidy town of maybe 400 people has a few buildings over a couple of streets, including an old radio station, now home to the Lawrence Museum.

We'd come across Lawrence purely by chance back in 2007. We were touring the *Journey* album and had got lost trying to find our way back to the highway from Grafton on our way to Byron Bay. I was with my son Amos, Shane Howard, Dave Arden and Jill. When I saw the sign 'Lawrence', my skin prickled – that was where Dad was from. We broke schedule and drove straight there.

It was a hot day. I knelt on the banks of the Clarence River and cupped my hands, splashing my face with its cool waters, paying respect to my old people and country. Seeing my reflection in the river, I felt a deep and spiritual connection with the father I'd never met. I felt the tidal movements he would have felt and heard the noise of water rushing past my ears, as he would have. The following night at a show in Byron I was telling the audience about washing my face in the Clarence River, and someone in the audience yelled out, 'Welcome home, Brother!' I guess he realised the significance of my story.

In 2013 I was back and visited the Lawrence Museum with Jill.

When we stepped inside I couldn't believe my eyes. There was a poster-sized photo of the Roach family on the wall down the end of the passage. I was stunned and just stood there, staring. It felt very strange. The museum staff had no idea we were coming, yet here was the Roach family with a whole wall dedicated to them, in pride of place. In the photo were my father's mother, Gladys; my grandmother and her children, Uncles Stan, Rupert and Denny, and my father as a very small child kneeling in front of his mother, next to my Aunty Alma. I had never seen a photo of my father as a boy before, and I had never seen a photo of my grandmother, Gladys.

There was also a photo of my great-grandmother, Sarah, known as Granny Roach, staring down the barrel of the camera, a contraption she seemed not to completely trust. In another photo she was standing next to a simple hut on the Aboriginal reserve where my family lived.

Granny Sarah had so much character in her face; I could tell she was a strong woman.

One document uncovered by the Family Records Service at Aboriginal Affairs in NSW saddened me greatly. It was a request from a police constable based in Lawrence, appealing for two blankets to be approved for my ninety-year-old great-grandmother Granny Sarah Roach for the oncoming winter. And I also discovered an accident report from the Salvation Army Home for Girls in East Camberwell, explaining a noticeable scar across the top of my thumb that I have had since I was three years old.

I have shared a selection of what my search turned up over the following pages. While they relate to my journey, it's also the story of anyone who has been stolen from family, who has been searching all their life for their identity, their people, culture and country.

Some of these discoveries made me profoundly sad. Overcome with a deep sense of loss, some connected and completed me, others hurt and angered me – every detail, photo, welfare report and handwritten letter left me asking one question: *Why?* Do those responsible think that what we gained far outweighed the immense loss?

People ask me if I ever get sick of singing my song, 'Took the Children Away'. I tell them it's my healing song.

Through songs, I have been able to deal with the pain and trauma in a more positive way. Every time I sing it, I let a little bit of the hurt and trauma go. I tell them that one day I will be singing it and it will all go...And I will be free.

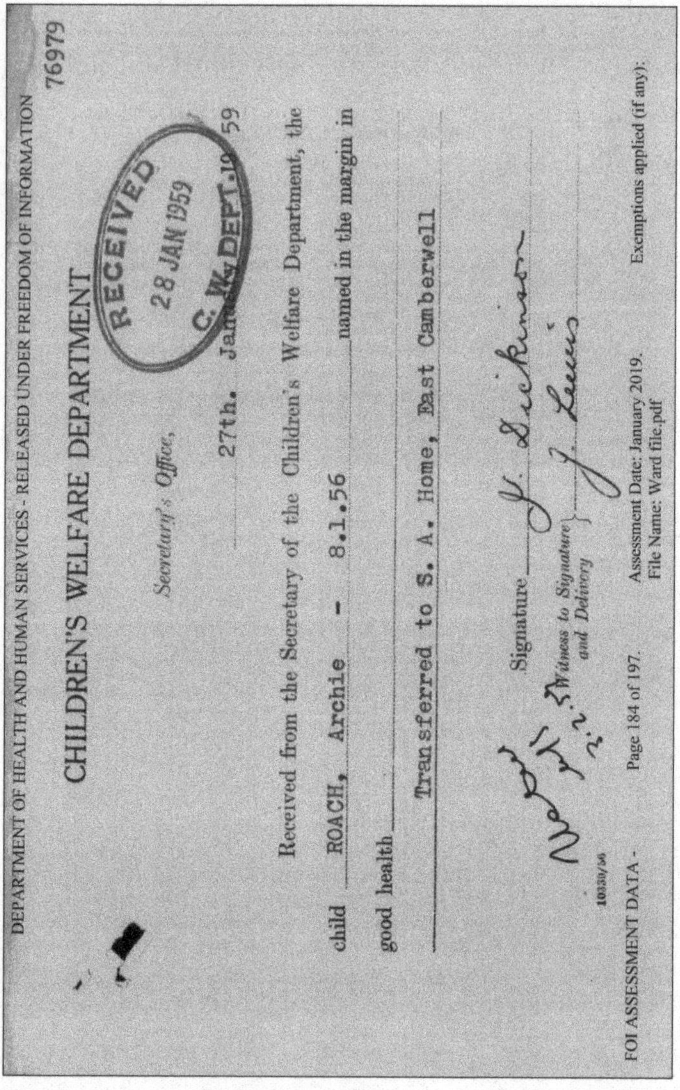

DEPARTMENT OF HEALTH AND HUMAN SERVICES - RELEASED UNDER FREEDOM OF INFORMATION

76979

CHILDREN'S WELFARE DEPARTMENT

Secretary's Office,

27th. January 1959

RECEIVED
28 JAN 1959
C. W. DEPT.

Received from the Secretary of the Children's Welfare Department, the child ROACH, Archie - 8.1.56 named in the margin in good health

Transferred to S. A. Home, East Camberwell

Signature

Witness to Signature and Delivery

10330/56

FOI ASSESSMENT DATA - Page 184 of 197. Assessment Date: January 2019. File Name: Ward file.pdf Exemptions applied (if any):

The official document detailing my transfer from the Children's Welfare Department to the Salvation Army Girls' Home in East Camberwell, dated 27th January 1959. I was just three years old.

Extension 521

ED/JS

Room 313 3

23rd April, 1959.

The Matron,
S. A. Girls' Home,
11 Brinsley Rd.,
EAST CAMBERWELL.

Dear Madam, re Archie ROACH.

As arranged in telephone conversation today, a Form of Consent to Operation &c. is forwarded herewith in respect of the abovenamed ward.

Yours faithfully,

Encl.

DIRECTOR.

15 MAY 1959

re Archie Roach

A message was received from East Camberwell Girls' Home to the effect that the abovenamed boy had cut his finger and an operation will be performed this evening to "put it on again". It was arranged to forward a form of "Consent to Operation" this evening.

23/4/59

Correspondence between the matron at the Salvation Army Girls' Home, explaining the operation on my thumb to 'put it on again'.

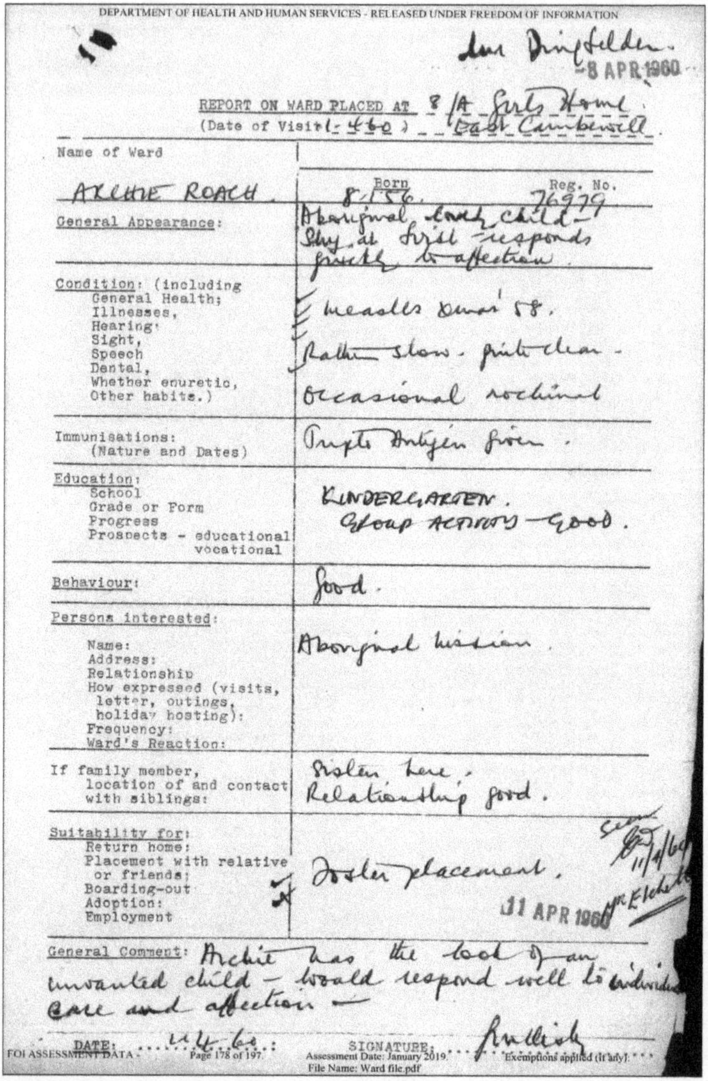

DEPARTMENT OF HEALTH AND HUMAN SERVICES - RELEASED UNDER FREEDOM OF INFORMATION

Mrs Dingfelder
-8 APR 1960

REPORT ON WARD PLACED AT S/A Girls Home
(Date of Visit 1-4-60) East Camberwell

Name of Ward ARCHIE ROACH	Born 8-1-56 Reg. No. 76979
General Appearance:	Aboriginal boy child - Shy at first - responds quickly to affection.
Condition: (including General Health; Illnesses, Hearing, Sight, Speech, Dental, Whether enuretic, Other habits.)	measles Xmas '58. Rather slow - quite clear - Occasional rocking
Immunisations: (Nature and Dates)	Triple Antigen given.
Education: School, Grade or Form, Progress, Prospects - educational, vocational	KINDERGARTEN. GROUP ACTIVITY - GOOD.
Behaviour:	Good.
Persons interested: Name: Address: Relationship, How expressed (visits, letter, outings, holiday hosting): Frequency: Ward's Reaction:	Aboriginal Mission.
If family member, location of and contact with siblings:	Sister here. Relationship good.
Suitability for: Return home: Placement with relative or friends; Boarding-out, Adoption: Employment	Foster placement. 11/4/60 11 APR 1960

General Comment: Archie has the look of an unwanted child - would respond well to individual care and affection -

DATE: 11-4-60 SIGNATURE:

FOI ASSESSMENT DATA - Page 178 of 197. Assessment Date: January 2019. Exemptions applied (If any). File Name: Ward file.pdf

Report on Ward placement of 'me' at the Salvation Army Girls' Home in April 1960. They note I have the 'look of an unwanted child – would respond well to individual care and affection'.

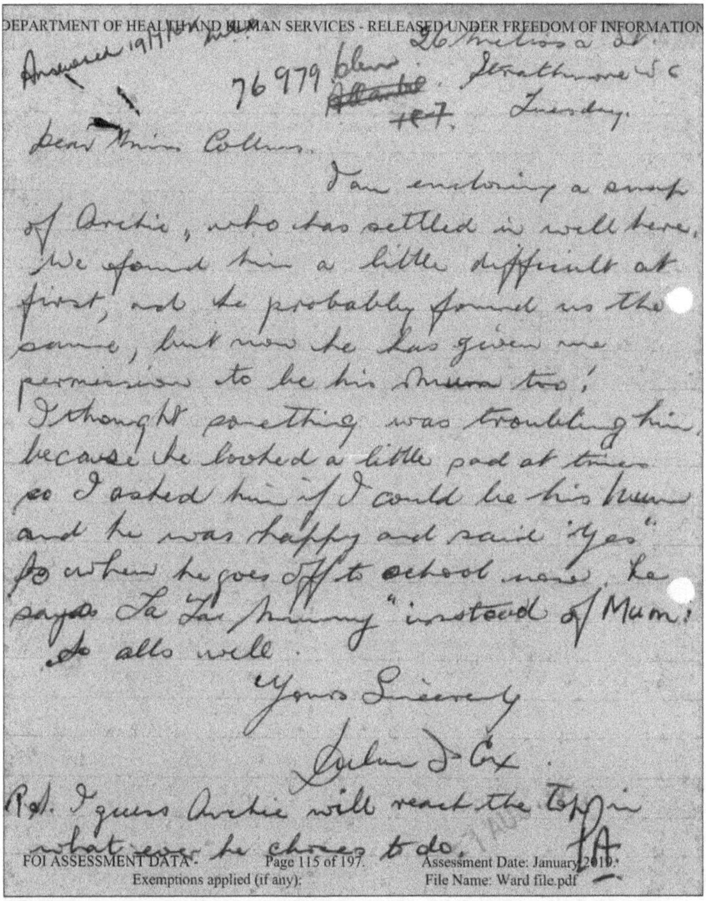
DEPARTMENT OF HEALTH AND HUMAN SERVICES - RELEASED UNDER FREEDOM OF INFORMATION

Answered 19/7/[illegible]

76979

26 [illegible] St. Strathmore W.6

Tuesday.

Dear Miss Collins.

I am enclosing a snap of Archie, who has settled in well here. We found him a little difficult at first, and he probably found us the same, but now he has given me permission to be his Mum too!

I thought something was troubling him, because he looked a little sad at times so I asked him if I could be his Mum and he was happy and said "yes". So when he goes off to school now, he says "Ta Ta Mummy" instead of Mum! So alls well.

Yours Sincerely

Dulcie J. Cox.

P.S. I guess Archie will reach the top in whatever he chooses to do.

FOI ASSESSMENT DATA - Page 115 of 197. Assessment Date: January 2019.
Exemptions applied (if any): File Name: Ward file.pdf

One of the many handwritten letters Mum Dulcie would send to my social worker at the Family Welfare Division. 'I guess Archie will reach the top in whatever he chooses to do.' Mum Dulcie wrote this letter around July 1962, not long after I arrived at the Coxes to live. Thanks, Mum Dulcie, for your faith in me.

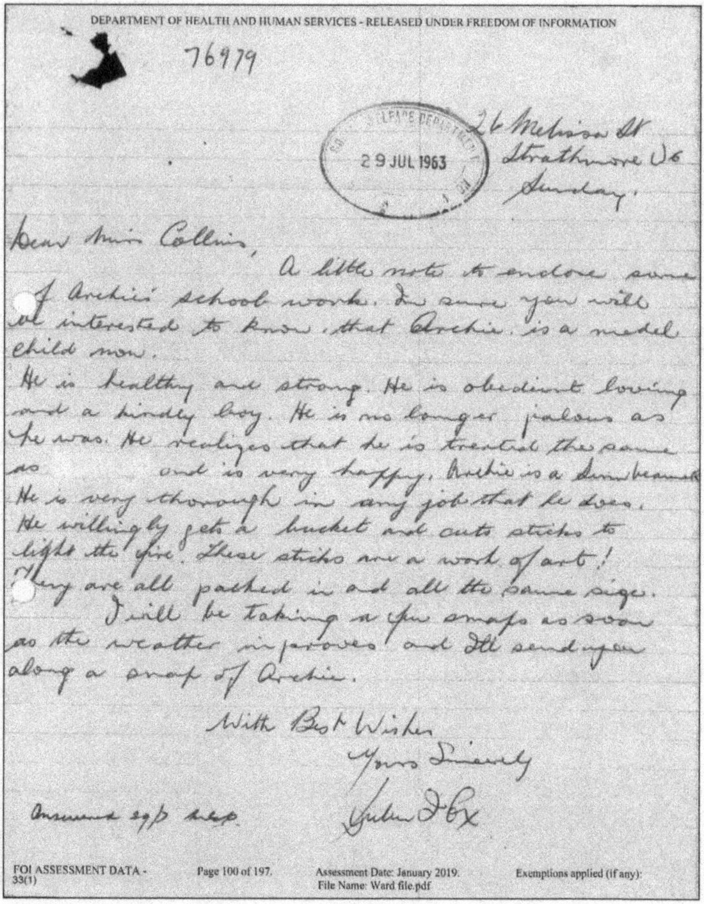

DEPARTMENT OF HEALTH AND HUMAN SERVICES - RELEASED UNDER FREEDOM OF INFORMATION

76979

29 JUL 1963

26 Melissa St
Strathmore W6
Sunday.

Dear Miss Collins,

A little note to enclose some of Archie's school work. I'm sure you will be interested to know that Archie is a model child now.

He is healthy and strong. He is obedient loving and a kindly boy. He is no longer jealous as he was. He realizes that he is treated the same as and is very happy. Archie is a Sunbeam. He is very thorough in any job that he does. He willingly gets a bucket and cuts sticks to light the fire. These sticks are a work of art! They are all packed in and all the same size.

I will be taking a few snaps as soon as the weather improves and I'll send you along a snap of Archie.

With Best Wishes
Yours Sincerely
Julia I Cox

Answered 29/7 [illegible]

FOI ASSESSMENT DATA - 33(1) Page 100 of 197. Assessment Date: January 2019. File Name: Ward file.pdf Exemptions applied (if any):

Another letter from Mum Dulcie, sent almost a year later to my social worker. 'He is very thorough in any job that he does... These sticks are a work of art!'

FAMILY WELFARE DIVISION

[redacted]

Archie ROACH b. 8.1.56 76979

(Foster/Care with Mr. and Mrs.COX, of Essendon)

18/5/67 : Home visit, Mrs. Cox, [redacted] and Archie seen.

MRS. COX 'Mrs. Cox has grey hair, is solid and slow-moving. She was very pleasant and understanding and although she is elderly she does cope well with the two younger boys.

[redacted]

ARCHIE : Archie, 11 years, said hello and then left to do a message. Mrs. Cox says he is quite intelligent and he has a talent for drawing. At present he hopes to be a Commercial Artist. He is learning to play a small organ and will commence High School next year.

Mrs. Cox does not place much value on material possessions. [redacted] The Cox's home is well furnished but not well-kept. Mrs. Cox has a particular interest in pekinese dogs and she breeds them. She does not go out very much. Social Worker was given the impression that these 3 lads are all fine boys and there are no particular problems which Mrs. Cox has not dealt with.

[redacted]

CONCLUSION :

This placement is going smoothly. The boys were rather shy, but well-mannered and happy.

L. McRae
....
Mrs. L. McRAE
Social Worker
FOSTER CARE & ADOPTION SECTION
23.5.67.

P/A

Report from a home visit by a social worker, who came to the Coxes to see me in May 1967. I was 'learning to play a small organ'.

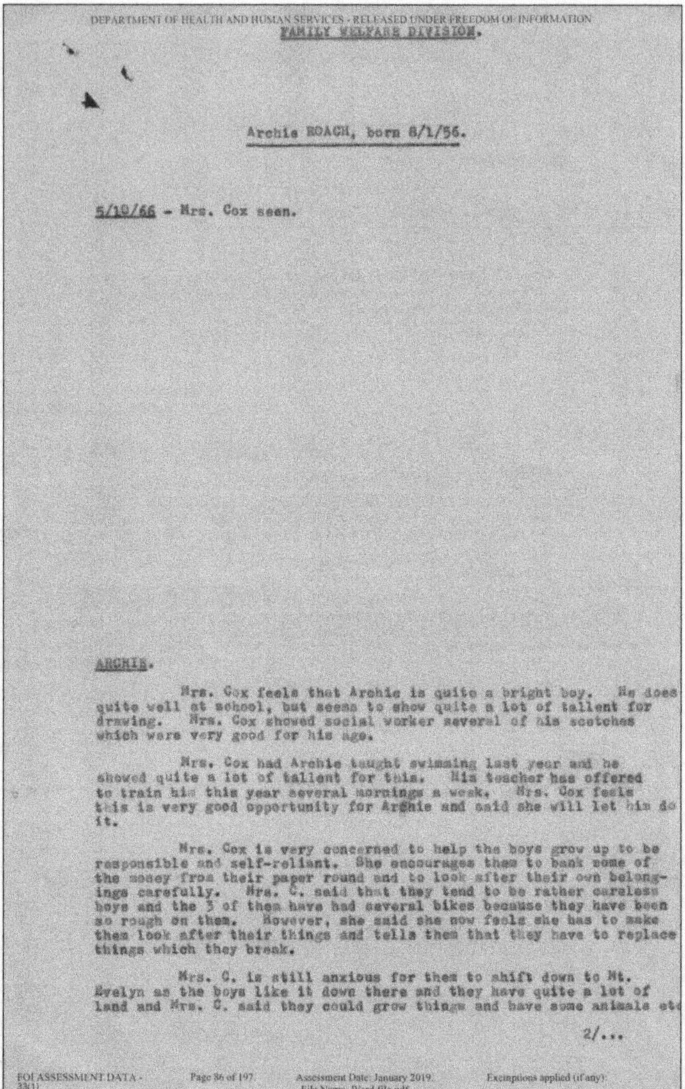

DEPARTMENT OF HEALTH AND HUMAN SERVICES - RELEASED UNDER FREEDOM OF INFORMATION

FAMILY WELFARE DIVISION.

Archie ROACH, born 8/1/56.

5/10/66 - Mrs. Cox seen.

ARCHIE.

Mrs. Cox feels that Archie is quite a bright boy. He does quite well at school, but seems to show quite a lot of tallent for drawing. Mrs. Cox showed social worker several of his scetches which were very good for his age.

Mrs. Cox had Archie taught swimming last year and he showed quite a lot of tallent for this. His teacher has offered to train him this year several mornings a week. Mrs. Cox feels this is very good opportunity for Archie and said she will let him do it.

Mrs. Cox is very concerned to help the boys grow up to be responsible and self-reliant. She encourages them to bank some of the money from their paper round and to look after their own belongings carefully. Mrs. C. said that they tend to be rather careless boys and the 3 of them have had several bikes because they have been so rough on them. However, she said she now feels she has to make them look after their things and tells them that they have to replace things which they break.

Mrs. C. is still anxious for them to shift down to Mt. Evelyn as the boys like it down there and they have quite a lot of land and Mrs. C. said they could grow things and have some animals etc

2/...

FOI ASSESSMENT DATA - 33(1) | Page 86 of 197 | Assessment Date: January 2019. File Name: Ward file.pdf | Exemptions applied (if any):

Report from a home visit by a social worker in 1967. 'Archie shows quite a lot of talent for drawing.'

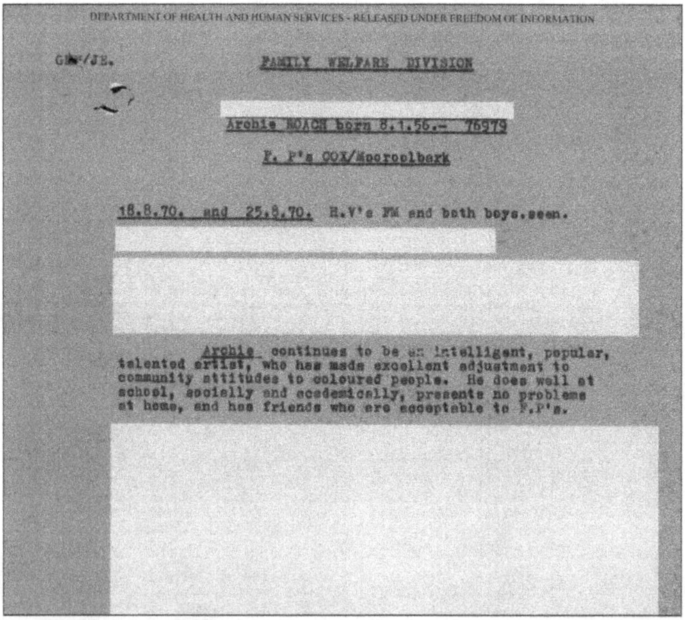
DEPARTMENT OF HEALTH AND HUMAN SERVICES - RELEASED UNDER FREEDOM OF INFORMATION

G[illegible]/JE.

FAMILY WELFARE DIVISION

[redacted]

Archie ROACH born 8.1.56.- 76979

F. P's COX/Mooroolbark

18.8.70. and 25.8.70. H.V's FM and both boys.seen.

[redacted]

Archie continues to be an intelligent, popular, talented artist, who has made excellent adjustment to community attitudes to coloured people. He does well at school, socially and academically, presents no problems at home, and has friends who are acceptable to F.P's.

[redacted]

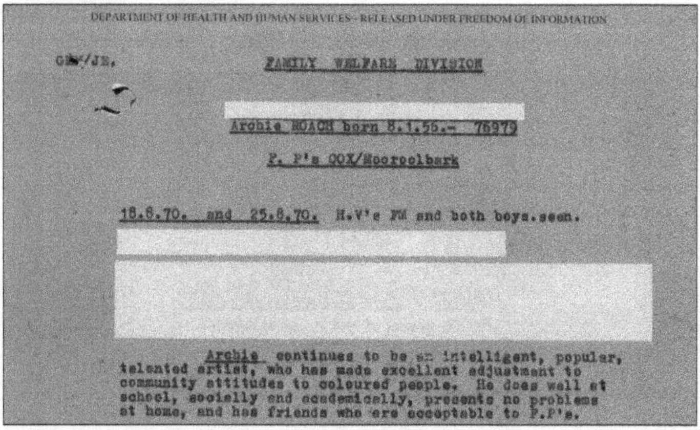
DEPARTMENT OF HEALTH AND HUMAN SERVICES - RELEASED UNDER FREEDOM OF INFORMATION

G[illegible]/JE.

FAMILY WELFARE DIVISION

[redacted]

Archie ROACH born 8.1.56.- 76979

F. P's COX/Mooroolbark

18.8.70. and 25.8.70. H.V's FM and both boys.seen.

[redacted]

Archie continues to be an intelligent, popular, talented artist, who has made excellent adjustment to community attitudes to coloured people. He does well at school, socially and academically, presents no problems at home, and has friends who are acceptable to F.P's.

Other home visit reports, noting, among other things, that the Pentecostal church I was attending was causing tension due to the fact that it 'speaks in tongues'. The report below notes that I've 'made excellent adjustment to community attitudes to coloured people'.

173.

11 MAR 1940
SYDNEY

Police Department,
Lawrence Station,
8th. March 1940.

The Chai[illegible]. Board,
Sydney.

Subject:- Issue of Blankets for winter 1940.

Reference:- Circular No. 199.

I beg to make application to be supplied with two blankets for issue to Sarah Roach of Lawrence- She is 90 years of age, a full blooded aboriginal at present having two blankets fairly well worn. She was issued with one blanket for the winter 1939.
She is now very aged and infirm and needs to be supplied with two blankets for the on-coming winter.

Edgar Keyde

Constable 1/c
No. 2091.

Archie Roach, of the Bethesda Mission, Melbourne

It broke my heart to read this letter from a constable in Lawrence in March 1940, appealing for two blankets for my great-grandmother, Sarah, for the oncoming winter. She was ninety. (Inset) Photo of my dear old dad, Archie Roach, at Bethesda Mission, Melbourne, which was featured in a Dawn magazine article, March 1961.

Old Boys help Berry St. appeal

FUND NOW $65,173

Ex-Berry St. babies and their families are helping swell the appeal to rebuild the 90-year-old home and hospital.

The home has already cared for 41,000 babies.

And the letters that come with their gifts are among the happiest received at the appeal office.

Like the round-handed note from a Reservoir boy that simply said . . .

"Thank you for my lovely sister Helen. I love her very much."

And the $10 gift from Highett that accompanied another note: "To the little babies at Berry St. from a little Berry St. 'Old Boy', Davie (aged 5) and his ever-grateful Mum and Dad."

Others tell their story in more detail. And one records the chance in life that came to several aboriginal boys through the Berry St. home.

Sending his $5 gift to the appeal, Mr A. Cox, of Mckay [illegible] St., Strathmore, recalled "one of the happiest days of my life.

HAPPINESS

"That was the day I accepted a little aboriginal baby of about 10 months from the Berry St. Home. Since that day this little boy, Noel, has brought me a great lot of happiness, as well as being very popular at school and among my own children.

"I also have this little laddie's elder brother and another little aboriginal boy, Archie, the same age as Noel 'under my wing.'

"I have enclosed a snap of Noel just taken recently on return from Sunday school. That is him with the book in his hands."

Another "old boy" of Berry St., **Mr Ray Willis**, is now superintendent of the Northern Tasmanian Home for Boys, Franklin Village, Launceston.

"I have nothing but praise for organisations like yours and the St. John's Home for Boys," he wrote.

"I educated myself by completing a two-year full time course in youth leadership. I then completed an accountancy degree," Mr Willis said.

"Best of luck for your appeal. Without the Berry St. Foundling Home the community would be a little worse off," he wrote.

The total in the Berry St. Babies Home Appeal now stands at £65,173. Gifts should be addressed to the Appeal [illegible]

NOEL and Archie Cox, both 9. A pair of ex-Berry St. boys.

Today's weather

The government advertisement Mum and Dad Cox saw in a Melbourne newspaper.

Photo by @missfarmerjojo (Jo O'Keefe)

ELDERS SPEAK, THE ARCHIE ROACH STOLEN GENERATIONS RESOURCES

Uncle Archie Roach (Gunditjmara/Bundjalung)

It's so important that we listen to the stories of our old people, us Elders who have the lived experience of the Stolen Generations, who were taken away from our families when we were just children and to reflect how hard it was for us just to survive day by day. We need to talk about the Stolen Generations and how Aboriginal and Torres Strait Islander people were treated during Settlement. Our stories will hopefully give all Australians a better understanding about the struggle that we faced and continue to face as First Nations people.

I've seen too many of my family and community not talk about what they went through. They didn't know how to process the pain. I'm lucky that I have had music to do that; it has helped me to deal with the trauma.

To this day people come up to me and ask, 'Archie, don't you ever get sick of singing "Took The Children Away?"' I tell them, 'No, it's a healing song for me. Every time I sing it, I let a little bit of the pain go. I've been singing this song for a long time and one day, I'm sure I'll be singing it and it'll all just go and I'll be free.'

Please visit the Archie Roach Stolen Generations Resources, created by Culture is Life and the Archie Roach Foundation, and hosted on the ABC Education website.

The first steps in healing include knowing the truth and understanding the intergenerational impact of Stolen Generations on the wellbeing of Aboriginal and Torres Strait Islander families and young people nationally. We are honoured to stand with Uncle Archie and his Foundation to ensure the true history of this country is told, in particular that of Stolen Generations.

In connecting with the Elders' stories, we acknowledge the Stolen Generations and their families, those who were separated and never found their way home, those who are still healing and those who continue to endure the intergenerational impact.

We acknowledge Uncle Archie for his generosity, passion and dedication to our First Peoples and Stolen Generations survivors, and for all the healing work he has done sharing his song stories and spirit with the world.

We deeply honour the strength, knowledge and wisdom of our Elders in sharing the traumas they have endured, and in telling the truths of this country in the hope that we can heal as a nation and not repeat past wrongs.

BELINDA DUARTE (Wotjobaluk/Dja Dja Wurrung) CEO, Culture is Life

Culture is Life

Aunty Lorraine (Weilwun/Gamilaroi)

I'm one of eight children, six girls and two boys. We were taken from our family. My brothers were sent to Kinchela, a boys' home in northern New South Wales, and my sisters and I went to Cootamundra Girls' Home in western New South Wales

When I heard Archie's song, 'Took The Children Away', I thought, here's a song that says lots of children were taken away and that normalised it all for me. I thought, I'm not the only one. It was that realisation that helped me heal. I don't know how many times I played that song to get me through. Two things I always said they couldn't change was the colour of my skin and my spirit. So I had those to hang on to.

Archie is a healer through music. We've got healers in our culture and we come in many forms. Archie's is music. Mine is teaching and healing spirits, which I have been doing for the last twenty years.

Aunty Iris Bysouth (Barkindji)

I'm from Wilcannia in New South Wales. I'm a Barkindji woman. I was removed from my family at eight years old and fostered in Melbourne. I found this out through my Elders, and I now work with the Stolen Generations for the Bendigo and District Aboriginal Co-op in Dja Dja Wurrung country.

I think we need to talk about the Stolen Generations. We need to talk this out and tell all our stories, because I think it's good to educate people. It's all around the education side of it now. It should never happen again. Enough's enough, you know?

Mum used to always play Archie's songs. His songs brought us together as a family. When she played 'Took The Children Away', my heart was just breaking and I said, 'See, this song brings all that back, Mum.' It's very strong and powerful. It's healed a lot of people.

Aunty Eva Jo Edwards (Boonwurrung, Mutti Mutti, Yorta Yorta)

I'm a Boonwurrung, Mutti Mutti, Yorta Yorta woman. I am a survivor of the Stolen Generations. I was removed as a child. I was five years old and was in care in Kew until I was eighteen, thinking I was the only black kid who'd been taken.

It's not something we choose as a child. It still affects us today. When I heard Archie's song, 'Took The Children Away' and his song 'Munjana', he sang my life. It still resonates, and it will forever.

I think it's really, really important that we continue to keep Stolen Generations on the table of education, because it's an important part of our history. My passion will always be talking about the Stolen Generations, making sure we are always heard. It's important for our healing.

Uncle Sydney Jackson (Wongai/raised on Noongar Country)

People don't know that I'm part of the Stolen Generations. I was taken away as a four-year-old from the Leonora area, from the Wongai tribe which I was born into. I was taken away on the back of a truck with my two sisters and lots of other kids. One of my sisters went to Marybank and the other went to another institution. I was taken further down to what was called the Roelands Native Mission and that's where I stayed until I was sixteen years old.

Now I work at the Roelands Village where I was brought up as a kid. We do lots of work out here, all sorts of programs and corporate and school visits. We turned it around to be a positive place. Talking about the past is part of who we are and our culture. I think everybody should know about it.

I found a lot of healing and support through sport and football. I didn't want to dwell on things any further. I wanted to look positive at things and do what I could to help my younger brothers and sisters come through the system, to be brave, positive and proud of themselves in their lives as they went forward.

Photo by Dale Lynch.

Uncle Jack Charles (Boonwurrung/Dja DjaWurrung)

I'm seventy-seven now and I've come a long way. I was taken from my mother at only four months and placed in the City Missions Children & Babies Home in Brunswick. When I got too old, at only two years old, I was moved to Box Hill Boys' Home, run by the Salvation Army.

In the early to mid 1950s an uncle and aunty of mine came to check in on me at the home and through this visitation I discovered that I was not an orphan. I never believed I was and here was positive proof. And just before I left the Box Hill Boys' Home a group of Aboriginal kids came into the home and one of them said he had the last name Charles and I said to him, it'd be funny if we were brothers, hey?

In telling my story I now understand the full extent of what was denied me as a young person – my lost heritage. Still to this day I'm catching up, finding so many relatives in the course of performing around the nation. People know who I am and they want to tell me things, they want to tell me more stories about my mum.

ALL OUR STORIES, SINGING THE FUTURE

It's so important that the voices of our young people are heard. Being a part of the Stolen Generations affected not just me but my children and grandchildren. The impact is intergenerational. It has become a part of their story as well. They know what I have been through and about the big role music has played in my healing journey. Young people need to find a way to process the trauma as we have. We need to hear your voices. It could be through the arts: music, dance, singing and writing. I am so proud to introduce you to the young people whose reflections you will read in the following pages.

UNCLE ARCHIE ROACH (Gunditjmara/Bundjalung)

To honour Uncle Archie's music and cultural legacy, The Archie Roach Foundation in partnership with Culture is Life and the Barpirdhilla Foundation instigated a music mentoring program for young emerging First Nations artists.

Collaborating with talented established First Nations artists, the young artists connected with Uncle Archie's story and musical journey through the powerful iconic song, 'Took The Children Away' to write and produce a song honouring Stolen Generations survivors and families.

The collaborative process, inspired by Uncle Archie's life and work, provided an opportunity for our young people to voice their own ancestral stories and experiences. My hope is that all Australians connect with and listen to the stories of our First Peoples to gain a deeper understanding of, and respect for, the true history of our cultures, country and peoples.

THARA BROWN, (Yorta Yorta) Culture is Life

MAYA HODGE

(Lardil), age 22

She lay in the hospital bed
I went over and touched her head
She lay in a state of sleep
I said to her in her trance of peace
I came back

My mother lay in bed
Next to her mother in her last moments
Holding her hand for the last time
And said to her
We came back

I am my mother.
my mother's child
She came back
We came back
I came back

LAUREN SHEREE
(Wakka Wakka), age 22

Don't know about your story
But I sure know mine
I feel it in my veins
Rediscovery over time
I heard you buried your heart
below the surface of the ground
Maybe you left it there for me
Waiting to be found

They took you away - took you away
Away from your sister and mum
when you were a little one
Took you away

A whole bloodline displaced
Tried your hardest to erase
A whole bloodline displaced
Trying my hardest to retrace

This story's right, this story's true
about our elders, ancestors and us here too

DEKLAN JOHN GARCIA
(Woolagin from Doon Doon WA), age 18

When my nana was taken away
She was taken away from her mother
Her mother cried all night
In pain all day

Why did you take her away?
You broke her mother into pieces
My nana was crying
She was a little girl who wanted her mummy

SETH WESTHEAD
(Awabakal/Wiradjuri), age 26

There is not one Aboriginal or Torres Strait Islander person that has not been impacted by what took place in this country. It deeply hurts my heart when I think of the past, but this does not define us. Today we carry inside us both the traumas of the past and the strength that pulled us through them. The wisdom, knowledge and spirit of our ancestors burns inside of us. This is what defines us. The continued culture that can never be taken away.

NEIL MORRIS
(Drmngnow, Yorta Yorta)

Uncle Archie's work to me is that of spiritual legacy. As a Yorta Yorta Yiyirr who grew up on Country, born in Shepparton and raised on the other side of the river Kaiela in Mooroopna, there is a strong direct link to Uncle Archie who was born in the Mooroopna hospital, and where my mother was also born six years later. I first heard Uncle Archie when I was about twelve or thirteen, hanging with cousins in Mooroopna as well. I was immediately amazed by the power of his work. It was like the land and ancestors were singing seamlessly through this amazing channel that was Uncle Archie. It gave music a whole new meaning for me at the time. So potent and haunting like nothing I had connected to before and to this day.

UNCLE ARCHIE'S PLAYLIST

This is a playlist I have put together for you to listen to – songs I wrote over many years that shine a light on the impact of the Stolen Generations. Writing and singing songs has been a big part of my healing.

SONGS ABOUT MY OWN STORY

Took the Children Away This song is so important to me because it's part of my healing. I wrote this song not just for the children taken away but for those we were taken from.

Old Mission Road A song about what could have been if I had been given the chance to grow up with my family and walk down the old mission road with them.

Open Up Your Eyes The first song I ever penned, written in the late 1970s while in Galiamble, a Men's Alcohol and Drug Recovery Centre in St Kilda. I was about nineteen or twenty. I started writing what I thought was a poem but I realised then that writing and words, poetry and prose, has a rhythm to it. I picked up the guitar and started strumming and – *bang* – it just came, the melody and the rhythm and everything, all at once.

Move it On A song about the place where I was born in Mooroopna, in Victoria and how my family was forced into moving from one place to another to avoid the threat of us being removed.

Tell Me Why A song asking why we were taken away and the painful consequences it caused to my mum and dad and us children.

Weeping in the Forest Inspired by my Uncle Banjo Clarke from Framlingham Aboriginal Mission who told me how he loved going to the forest and hearing the laughter of the children running and playing about until one day he went and couldn't hear the sound of children's laughter anymore as they had been taken.

Mighty Clarence River A song about three of my Bundjalung grandmothers, my great grandmother and her sisters on my father's side, from northern New South Wales, and how they escaped to freedom by swimming across the mighty Clarence River.

SONGS ABOUT RUBY'S STORY

From Paradise A song about Ruby Hunter being taken away from an idyllic life with her brother and sister on the beautiful Coorong in South Australia, which must have been a paradise where the land provided plenty.

Nopun Kurongk A song about the Coorong in South Australia where Ruby lived as a child before she was taken and about her returning to see it again many years later. The language words are from Ruby's Ngarrindjeri language.

Mulyawongk A song about Ruby Hunter's connection to the Murray River where the river guardian spirit, the Mulyawongk, lives. It's about Ruby reconnecting with her people who are from the lower Murray River and the Coorong area.

SONGS ABOUT THE IMPACT OF THE STOLEN GENERATIONS ON OTHER FIRST NATIONS PEOPLE

Munjana A song about an Aboriginal woman, Beverley Whyman, whose baby, Russell, was taken from her, adopted out and taken to America. It's also about how unwed young women having babies were punished and had their babies taken off them, resulting in another Stolen Generation of children. Munjana, meaning 'trouble' was a nickname given to Beverley when she was young.

Louis St John A song about a young Aboriginal man, originally from Alice Springs who was adopted into a non-Indigenous family from Perth, Western Australia and who was murdered by a group of white youths when he was returning home after celebrating his 19th birthday with a friend.

Lighthouse, Song for Two Mothers A song about a young Aboriginal man, who was taken from his Aboriginal family and adopted by a non-Indigenous family. He died at nineteen years old and was buried back in Alice Springs where he was born. I saw a photo, taken at his graveside, of his Aboriginal mother and his white mother holding hands. It was one of the most powerful images I have ever seen.

You've just read an abridged version of

Tell Me Why: The Story of My Life and My Music.

The full story is in the adult edition.

Winner of the 2020 Indie Book of the Year Non-Fiction

Shortlisted for the 2020 ABIA Biography Book of the Year

Shortlisted for the 2019 Victorian Premier's Literary Awards, Non-Fiction

Shortlisted for the Booksellers' Choice 2020 Book of the Year Awards, Non-Fiction

Shortlisted for the 2020 Victorian Premier's Literary Awards, Indigenous Writing